C. S. Lewis at Poets' Corner

C. S. Lewis at Poets' Corner

EDITED BY
Michael Ward
AND
Peter S. Williams

FOREWORD BY
Canon Vernon White

CASCADE Books • Eugene, Oregon

C. S. LEWIS AT POETS' CORNER

Copyright © 2016 Wipf and Stock Publishers. All rights reserved. Except for brief quotations in critical publications or reviews, no part of this book may be reproduced in any manner without prior written permission from the publisher. Write: Permissions, Wipf and Stock Publishers, 199 W. 8th Ave., Suite 3, Eugene, OR 97401.

Cascade Books
An Imprint of Wipf and Stock Publishers
199 W. 8th Ave., Suite 3
Eugene, OR 97401

www.wipfandstock.com

PAPERBACK ISBN: 978-1-4982-0258-9
HARDCOVER ISBN: 978-1-4982-0260-2

Cataloguing-in-Publication data:

C. S. Lewis at Poets' Corner / edited by Michael Ward and Peter S. Williams.

xxvi + 246 pp. ; 23 cm. Includes bibliographical references.

ISBN 978-1-4982-0258-9 (paperback) | ISBN 978-1-4982-0260-2 (hardback)

1. Lewis, C. S. (Clive Staples), 1898–1963. 2. Lewis, C. S. (Clive Staples), 1898–1963—Religion. 3. I. Ward, Michael, 1968–. II. Williams, Peter S. 1974–. III. Title.

PR6023.E926 Z945 2016

Manufactured in the U.S.A.   03/28/16

Poems by CS Lewis © copyright by CS Lewis Pte Ltd. Reproduced with permission.

Contents

Foreword—Vernon White | vii
Preface—Peter S. Williams | xi
Introduction—Michael Ward | xv

Part One—Symposium at St. Margaret's, Westminster

1. Alister McGrath—Telling the Truth through Rational Argument | 3
2. Malcolm Guite—Telling the Truth through Imaginative Fiction | 15
3. Panel Discussion—What Can Twenty-First Century Apologetics Learn from C. S. Lewis? | 25

Part Two—Memorial Service at Westminster Abbey

4. Order of Service—including the Address by Rowan Williams | 53

Part Three—Reflections on the Westminster Commemorations

5. Paul Mealor—Reflections on Composing *Love's As Warm As Tears* | 85
6. Acton Bell—Mystery Worshipper: Westminster Abbey | 89
7. Jeanette Sears—C. S. Lewis's Memorial Service | 96
8. Holly Ordway—Stonecrop: Lewis Takes His Place in Poets' Corner | 99
9. Sarah Clarkson—The Best Tale Lewis Ever Told | 102

Part Four—Cambridge Conference

10. Rowan Williams—Rhetoric, Doctrine, and the Ethics of Language: C. S. Lewis on *Paradise Lost* | 111
11. Ad Putter—C. S. Lewis on Allegory | 125
12. Helen Cooper—C. S. Lewis as Medievalist | 139
13. Malcolm Guite—*The Abolition of Man*: From Literary Criticism to Prophetic Resistance | 152
14. Stephen Logan—The Soul of C. S. Lewis | 166
15. Stephen Prickett—"It Makes No Difference": Lewis's Criticism, Fiction and Theology | 186

Part Five—Oxford Addresses

16. William Lane Craig—God and the Platonic Host | 201
17. Walter Hooper—Remembering C. S. Lewis | 217

Recommended Resources | 229
Bibliography | 235
Index | 241

Foreword

THERE WAS NEVER ANY real doubt that C. S. Lewis would be widely remembered and honoured on the fiftieth anniversary of his death. Far from indicating that his influence is waning, the passage of time has shown it to be increasing. Why is this? This collection of lectures, essays, talks, reflections, and dialogues about Lewis helps provide an answer. As a literary critic, a Christian apologist, and a creative writer, Lewis had an unerring instinct for the heart of matters that will continue to matter: the matter of language and reality; the matter of God; the matter of the meaning of life itself. Moreover, his arrows somehow hit the centre of their targets convincingly without compromising their complexity; he managed focus without being one-dimensional. His celebrated distillation of theology and religion into "mere" Christianity is characteristic. He regularly treated important and complex issues by translating them into a memorable essence, but without reductionism or crass dumbing down. This might sound like a merely rhetorical device. It was not. Lewis believed wholly and sincerely in the substance of what he was trying to communicate, not just the form of it. Small wonder his thought continues to inspire, and to be honoured. Aspects of it may date: the heart and spirit of it never will.

But was it also inevitable that Lewis should be honoured specifically in Westminster Abbey? Clearly not. All sorts of contingencies are at play here. The Abbey is a place for British national remembrance of many kinds: it honours statesmen and social reformers, monarchs and military leaders, scientists and secret service heroes, engineers and explorers, not just literary and religious figures. So there is no space for every possible candidate. Decisions will depend on a variety of judgements and priorities.

Yet in the end Lewis's place amongst all these others now seems utterly obvious, entirely right. The oft-quoted final words of one of his essays, used as the inscription on his memorial stone, are an elegant expression of why this is so: *"I believe in Christianity as I believe that the sun has risen, not only because I see it but because by it I see everything else."*[1] In other words, a robust and authentic Christian faith is not an exclusive vision. It is an all-embracing one. Lewis's vision was never narrowly ecclesiastical but of a God who is truly God precisely because God is of the whole world, not just of the church or of religion. As such he surely sits well with all that social, scientific, political, artistic effort represented in those other Abbey memorials.

To be sure, Lewis had sharp words and warnings to offer about the way in which this "worldly" human effort is sometimes interpreted in a reductionist or self-referential way (not least in his warnings about scientism). But he never retreated from full-blooded endorsement of the world *per se*, and everything in it, both natural and human. And that is because, for Lewis, its concrete reality (and value) is inseparable from the even more concrete reality of God as its ultimate source. As he wrote elsewhere: "it will be agreed that, however they came there, concrete, individual, determinate things do now exist: things like flamingos, German generals, lovers, sandwiches, pineapples, comets and kangaroos, . . . a torrent of opaque actualities . . . *God is precisely the source of this torrent.*"[2] It was a vision that Lewis pursued not only in explicit apologetic but also in his fictional narratives, which celebrated the wider world of nature; in his science fiction, which encompassed the whole cosmos; in his repeated recognition of all people of good faith and character (whether or not Christian); and in his willingness to broadcast this "mere" Christianity to the whole nation in time of war. So it is that the memorial's setting in Westminster Abbey is indeed so fitting. For the Abbey too, founded as the Monarch's church to serve nation and wider world, is bound to this vision—one that relates God to that wider world, not just to religious or ecclesiastical life.

It is also fitting because of the transcendent frame of the vision. As a full-blooded theist, and (in some respects) a Platonist, Lewis equally affirmed another world, not just this one. There is no contradiction here. The crude caricatures of both Christianity and Platonism, which chide them for downgrading this world by their belief in another, are just that— crude caricatures. It is *because* of the transcendent source and goal of this world, not in spite of it, that the world matters as much as it does. This vital

---

1. Lewis, "Is Theology Poetry?" Paper read to the Oxford Socratic Club in 1944. Reprinted in *C. S. Lewis. Essay Collection and Other Short Pieces*, ed. Lesley Walmsley.

2. Lewis, *Miracles*, 90, emphasis mine.

connection between this world and another appears throughout Lewis's writing like Blake's golden thread, woven within it all. It is the same thread that gives "joy"—as he writes about it in *Surprised by Joy* and "The Weight of Glory"—both its poignant pull and its elusiveness. It appears most memorably in *The Great Divorce* and in *The Last Battle*; it becomes gossamer thin in *A Grief Observed*; but it is never entirely broken. So too in the Abbey. There too transcendence is embodied inescapably in its Gothic architecture, and gestured daily through its liturgies; there too it can be stretched and strained by the many memorials to bitter experience; but there too, like the paschal candle in its most sombre vigils, it is never finally extinguished.

There are other places where Lewis is actively honoured. Most notably there is Oxford, the provenance of several contributions to this collection, where the University's C. S. Lewis Society has been in continuous existence since 1982.[3] There is Cambridge, where students will benefit from a scholarship supported by proceeds from the memorial service.[4] Likewise there is the work on Lewis carried out by a number of distinguished U.S. institutions.[5] So, when over six hundred people came to a day's symposium at the Abbey, and many more joined us to dedicate the memorial itself, we were adding to a worldwide tribute that already had great momentum—and all of which is similarly fitting.

None of this, of course, is to idolize either the man or his work. He was of his time and is open to critique like anyone else. But it is to show how much of his work also transcends his time and richly deserves to. Our sincere hope now is simply that this collection of essays, and the memorial itself, will help make this happen, even more.

Canon Vernon White[6]

---

3. E.g., see *C. S. Lewis and His Circle: Essays and Memoirs from the Oxford C. S. Lewis Society*, ed. Roger White, Judith Wolfe, and Brendan Wolfe.

4. Enquiries about donating to the C. S. Lewis Scholarship Fund should be sent to database@alumni.cam.ac.uk.

5. E.g., The Wade Center at Wheaton College, Illinois; The Center for the Study of C. S. Lewis and Friends at Taylor University, Indiana; The Department of Apologetics at Houston Baptist University, Texas; The C. S. Lewis Foundation, Redlands, California; The C. S. Lewis Institute, Springfield, Virginia.

6. The Revd. Professor Vernon White is Canon Theologian at Westminster Abbey and Visiting Professor of Theology at King's College London. He is the author of *Atonement and Incarnation: An Essay in Universalism and Particularity* (Cambridge University Press, 1991) and *Life Beyond Death: Threads of Hope in Faith, Life and Theology* (Darton, Longman & Todd, 2006).

Preface

LOOKING THROUGH THE CLOAKROOM window I saw, looming over the quad, Elizabeth Tower—the clock tower that houses the bell known as "Big Ben." I was privileged to be staying overnight in the guest quarters of Westminster Abbey's Deanery, having played a role earlier that day in the Abbey Institute's Symposium at St. Margaret's Church, celebrating the legacy of C. S. Lewis as a Christian apologist.

Alister McGrath and Malcolm Guite gave scintillating presentations on the intellectual and imaginative aspects of Lewis's apologetics, after which Michael Ward chaired a series of mini-presentations (from William Lane Craig, Michael Ramsden, Jeanette Sears, Judith Wolfe, and myself) and a panel discussion about what contemporary Christian apologetics can learn from Lewis.

All this was topped off by a sumptuous evening meal hosted by the Dean, Dr. John Hall. (Upon seeing the amount of chocolate involved in dessert, Michael Ramsden quipped that everyone at Westminster Abbey "must really love Jesus, because after we eat this we'll all be meeting him sooner!")

The following day, Friday 22nd November 2013, the fiftieth anniversary of Lewis's death, I sat in a choir stall of the Abbey for a service that saw the dedication of a permanent memorial to Lewis in Poets' Corner (Michael Ward gives more detail about these Westminster commemorations in his interview with Lancia Smith).

It was William Lane Craig who asked if anyone had thought about publishing a book commemorating Lewis on the fiftieth anniversary of his death? We had not, but agreement was quickly secured from various quarters that this was a good idea and I found myself appointed to try getting such a project off the ground. Michael Ward kindly volunteered to share editorial duties and we approached Wipf & Stock, who promptly said yes.

It became clear that the thing to do was to collect together a written record not only of the Abbey Institute's Symposium, but also of the memorial service, along with some personal reflections upon it from the blogosphere, and to round out the collection with the presentations made at two other events held in November 2013 in honour of C. S. Lewis, at the universities where he worked—namely Oxford and Cambridge.

On Saturday 23rd November 2013, Magdalene College Cambridge held a conference on "Lewis as Critic," marking his professional career in the field of English Literature. The complete proceedings from that conference are reproduced here, in the order that the lectures were delivered on the day.

On the evening of that same day, Magdalen College Oxford held a celebratory event and dinner. The speakers on that occasion included Rowan Williams (who had travelled across from the Cambridge conference in order to make his third presentation on Lewis in the space of thirty-six hours!) and Alister McGrath, following on from his appearance at the Abbey Symposium. Since Lord Williams and Professor McGrath are already well represented in these pages, we decided not to include their contributions to the Magdalen event. However, we are glad to include that of Walter Hooper, Lewis's editor and biographer. We also include a Lewis-tinged lecture given that same week by William Lane Craig at the Oxford University C. S. Lewis Society.

Altogether, these different contributions present a detailed picture of the way Lewis was commemorated in the United Kingdom on the fiftieth anniversary of his death. Their generic variety—interview, address, panel discussion, homily, article, lecture, personal memoir, poetry—aptly reflects the breadth of Lewis's own output. The numerous fields of expertise represented by our contributors—theology, pastoralia, apologetics, literary criticism, literary history, philosophy, psychology, biography, journalism, music, creative writing—reflects not only the broad sweep of his own interests but also the extraordinarily wide reach of his legacy. Editors of collected volumes like this one often try to impose uniformity on disparate perspectives in order to "theme-atize" their materials. We make no such attempt, but rather consider it a virtue that what follows is so very various. The diversity and colourfulness of these pages deliberately mirrors that of Lewis's own life and work, for as the inscription on his memorial bears witness, he did not just believe in "Christianity" but also in "everything else."

Michael Ward and I would like to take this opportunity to thank: all our contributors for agreeing to participate in this collection; everyone at the Westminster Abbey Institute, especially its Director Claire Foster-Gilbert and Canon Vernon White; the Dean of Westminster, the Very Revd.

Dr. John Hall, for granting permission to reproduce the Order of Service; Professor Steven A. Beebe for granting permission to reproduce the photograph of C. S. Lewis in the Order of Service; Simone Fryer-Bovair, organiser of the Cambridge Conference, for allowing us to put its proceedings in permanent published form; Essential Secretary Ltd. and Peter Byrom for help in getting a transcription of the Symposium's panel discussion; Robin Parry and his colleagues at Wipf & Stock; and everyone else who generously gave their support in various ways during the process of putting this volume together.

Peter S. Williams[1]

---

1. Peter S. Williams is Assistant Professor in Worldviews and Communication at Gimlekollen School of Journalism and Communication, NLA University, Norway. He is the author of *A Faithful Guide to Philosophy* (Paternoster, 2013) and *C. S. Lewis vs. the New Atheists* (Paternoster, 2013). He maintains a web presence at www.peterswilliams.com.

Introduction

Interview with Michael Ward[1]

Michael Ward introduces the Westminster Abbey commemorations in an interview with Lancia E. Smith, who is a long-time supporter of The C. S. Lewis Foundation, the charitable organization that owns The Kilns, Lewis's former home in Oxford.

Lancia, a professional photographer, hosts a popular blog entitled "Cultivating the Good, the True, and the Beautiful" at lanciaesmith.com. In early 2013 she interviewed Michael Ward about the forthcoming commemorative events in Westminster. The following is an edited version of their exchanges:

> 22nd November 2013 will mark the fiftieth anniversary of C. S. Lewis's death. To honour his extraordinary contribution to the world of literature, Westminster Abbey will be unveiling a permanent memorial to Lewis in Poets' Corner and hosting a Symposium in recognition of his

---

1. Dr. Michael Ward is Senior Research Fellow at Blackfriars Hall, University of Oxford, and Professor of Apologetics at Houston Baptist University, Texas. He is the author of *Planet Narnia: The Seven Heavens in the Imagination of C. S. Lewis* (Oxford University Press, 2008), co-editor of *The Cambridge Companion to C. S. Lewis* (Cambridge University Press, 2010), and presenter of the BBC television documentary, *The Narnia Code*. He maintains a web presence at www.michaelward.net.

accomplishments and his continuing influence on British national life.

It has been my privilege to interview Dr. Michael Ward, lead organizer of this fast-approaching celebration.

SMITH   Dr. Ward, what is the significance of Poets' Corner—especially from a British point of view?

WARD   Poets' Corner is perhaps the most famous part of Westminster Abbey. Over one hundred poets, novelists, dramatists, and other artists (including actors and musicians) are buried or commemorated there. The first poet to be buried in the Abbey was Geoffrey Chaucer, the "father of English poetry," in 1400. Others who have been honoured include Shakespeare, Wordsworth, the Brontë sisters, and Jane Austen.

To be memorialized in Poets' Corner means you've received national recognition for your contribution to the arts. Westminster Abbey has been at the heart of religious and civic life in England for over a thousand years and is known as "the coronation church." William the Conqueror was crowned there on Christmas Day 1066. Our present monarch, Queen Elizabeth II, was crowned there in 1953. So, for C. S. Lewis to be memorialized in the Abbey is an indication of the respect in which he is held and an acknowledgement of his enduring place in the world of English letters.

SMITH   Why is this particular event significant—globally and within the community of Lewis scholars and readers?

WARD   Globally, because Westminster Abbey is renowned worldwide and almost everything that happens there receives attention internationally.

It's significant among the community of Lewis scholars and readers because so much of that community has, hitherto, been based in America, and now things are beginning to even themselves out. In comparison to Americans, the British have been rather slow to recognize Lewis's importance. I don't say that the British have completely ignored him till now; he has always been reasonably popular here, but less so than in the United States. Part of that is simply to do with differences in national temperament: the British (and, in particular, the English) are reluctant to make an enthusiastic noise about their favourite authors because we fear being mocked for it. "Moderation in all things," tends to be the English way! Partly it's to do with a strain of Anglophilia in certain parts of American culture. And partly, perhaps, it could be to do with the fact that "a prophet is not without honour, save in his own country."

Another reason it's significant within the community of Lewis scholars is because several attempts have been made over the years from within that group to have Lewis memorialized in the Abbey, and at last the Abbey has said yes. Dr. Stan Mattson of the C. S. Lewis Foundation had suggested it on previous occasions; I myself had tried back in 1998; I think various other people had tried too—and always the Dean of the Abbey, whose sole decision it is, had declined. But now the present Dean of the Abbey, Dr. John Hall, has graciously consented to the suggestion and it's going ahead. So, I know that a lot of people within the community of Lewis scholars and readers will be pleased—delighted—and I think everyone who has petitioned the Abbey about this matter over the decades can consider themselves to have contributed to the present positive situation.

SMITH In the official press release announcing this memorial, Vernon White, Canon Theologian at Westminster Abbey, said: "C. S. Lewis was an extraordinarily imaginative and rigorous thinker and writer, who was able to convey the Christian faith in a way that made it both credible and attractive to a wide range of people. He has had an enduring and growing influence in our national life."

There is a fairly widespread belief that Lewis was less well accepted by the British after World War II and was hailed as an evangelical hero in America. Neither side of this spectrum is really accurate. Obviously, the British people were deeply influenced by Lewis through his broadcast talks and his "popular" writings. And Americans went through a period after his death of declining interest in Lewis, which was later followed by a renewal of esteem that hasn't waned. From your perspective, what is Lewis's enduring and growing influence on British national life?

WARD The most easily recognisable influence, I think, has been through the popularity of The Chronicles of Narnia. Those books, and in particular the first, *The Lion, the Witch and the Wardrobe*, are very widely known in Britain. People have grown up knowing about Narnia and it's now an established point of reference in the culture at large. Several times in recent years, I've been watching BBC comedy programmes and have observed various comedians making jokes—usually friendly sorts of jokes, I'm pleased to say—which assume knowledge of magic wardrobes or how time stands still when you're in Narnia or the danger of eating Turkish Delight. And these comedians are right: everyone in Britain, pretty much, can be expected to know about these things. The Chronicles represent that aspect of Lewis's influence which is truly national and ubiquitous, and who can say exactly what that impact has been? All I can say is, from the reading I've done and from countless conversations I have with people over the years, that it's immeasurable and very largely positive.

The other aspects of his influence—his Christian apologetics (such as *The Screwtape Letters* and *Mere Christianity*) and his academic writings (such as *The Allegory of Love* and *A Preface to Paradise Lost*)—are more confined to particular groups within the nation. And there again, it's impossible to quantify. But many, many people have been brought into a Christian faith, or strengthened within an existing faith, by his writings and by his personal example; and many scholars, both Christian and non-Christian, have been inspired by his academic output. It's really remarkable how much of an influence Lewis has had, in his imaginative writings, his apologetics, and his professional works of literary criticism. By any standards, it's an outstanding achievement and an unparalleled range of influences.

Then, of course, there's an influence that is related to Lewis, but not directly part of his own life and work, I mean the *Shadowlands* story of his marriage and bereavement. This was first of all a BBC television film, then a West End stage-play, then a feature film starring Anthony Hopkins, and finally a BBC radio-play. The writer, William Nicholson, managed to get four iterations of the drama, which is quite extraordinary! A lot of people who may know very little about Lewis will have encountered *Shadowlands*, but of course the story has been greatly simplified and dramatized and romanticized and actually bears only a fairly loose connection to reality. Still, it's part of the overall picture of Lewis's place in the British national consciousness, and worth bearing in mind. Lewis is widely thought of not just as a writer, but as a man who loved and lost, who suffered bereavement but still trusted in God. And although *Shadowlands* is very unreliable, it is at least right in those respects and has had a part to play in making Lewis known to certain people who might otherwise never have heard of him.

SMITH   How did the idea for this memorial come about?

WARD   The Abbey has an Institute for public education; it puts on lectures, debates, seminars, and other events of various kinds. One of the canons at the Abbey, Vernon White, thought that the fiftieth anniversary of Lewis's death would be a good time for the Institute to organise some sort of event focusing on Lewis's work as a Christian writer and apologist. Canon White got in touch with me to discuss ideas and, in consort with the Institute's Director, Claire Foster-Gilbert, we decided to have a one-day Symposium, featuring two lectures from leading Lewis scholars, plus a Panel Discussion in which a group of invited experts would assess Lewis's legacy for Christian apologetics in the twenty-first century. The Institute was already planning a programme of events for autumn 2013 under the title "Telling the Truth," and so we agreed to incorporate the Lewis Symposium within that larger undertaking.

And while we were talking about the Symposium, I asked whether it might not be an opportune moment to revisit the notion of a Poets' Corner memorial. Vernon indicated that the time could be ripe, and so I approached several friends and colleagues who agreed to be co-signatories to a letter that I wrote to the Dean, suggesting that very thing. The co-signatories were:

i. Helen Cooper, Professor of Medieval and Renaissance English at the University of Cambridge. She holds the professorial chair that Lewis was the first occupant of;[2]

---

2 Helen Cooper held Lewis's old Chair from 2004–14.

ii. The then President of the Oxford University Lewis Society, Ryan Pemberton;

iii. Alister McGrath, author of *C. S. Lewis, A Life*, and Professor of Theology, Ministry and Education at King's College, University of London;[3]

iv. Michael Ramsden, Director of the Oxford Centre for Christian Apologetics;

v. Dr. Judith Wolfe, Fellow of St. John's College, Oxford, and editor of *The Journal of Inklings Studies*.[4]

The Dean of the Abbey, Dr. John Hall, wrote back very positively and it was agreed that news of the memorial would be announced in November 2012, giving us a whole year to raise the money for it. The Abbey doesn't fund such memorials itself, so it is up to me, as the main initiator of the project, to find the necessary support from Lewis's readers and admirers round the world. Jason Lepojärvi, the current President of the Oxford Lewis Society, is helping oversee the finances.

Even a relatively small memorial, such as this one, costs a huge amount of money because anything that affects the fabric of the Abbey has to be of high quality, both in materials and design. Also, the Abbey requires, quite properly, an additional sum as a contribution to the ongoing maintenance of memorials. And finally, certain other incidental expenses also need to be met by supporters of the project (for instance, the cost of producing the Order of Service).

The names of contributors will be compiled into a list and deposited in the Bodleian Library in the University of Oxford, among the papers of the Oxford Lewis Society, so that future generations of scholars can see who helped this memorial to be realized. We won't mention the size of individuals' contributions, because we understand that people have all sorts of claims upon their giving and the amount you donate is not really the relevant thing. Any amount is very gratefully received, be it large, medium, or small. What we want is for

---

[3] Alister McGrath is now the Andreas Idreos Professor of Science and Religion at the University of Oxford, Director of the Ian Ramsey Centre for Science and Religion, and Fellow of Harris Manchester College.

[4] Judith Wolfe is now Lecturer in Theology and the Arts, School of Divinity, University of St Andrews.

this list to demonstrate the extent of Lewis's readership; and it will also provide an opportunity for people whose lives have been deeply impacted by Lewis's work to put that on record in a permanent form in the library of the university where Lewis spent most of his career.

SMITH   Can you tell me anything about the design of the memorial, and how it will be worded?

WARD   It will be a flag-stone kind of memorial, embedded in the pavement of Poets' Corner. The exact size and shape and location will be decided by the Abbey authorities, taking into account the existing memorials and the space available and so on. Ptolemy Dean, Surveyor of the Fabric at the Abbey, will have oversight of all the practical details relating to its design and manufacture.

Regarding the wording: obviously Lewis's name and dates are the main things. As for a possible inscription from his own writings: I took soundings among Lewis experts and among the co-signatories to the letter, and the most popular option was the closing sentence of one his most famous addresses to the Oxford Socratic Club, the university debating society of which he was President for many years:

> *I believe in Christianity*
> *as I believe that the Sun has risen,*
> *not only because I see it*
> *but because by it I see everything else.*

We put this suggestion to the Abbey and, after careful consideration by a committee that deals with these things, they approved the idea. It's an eminently suitable quotation, memorable, meaningful, not overlong, and with a beautiful balance to it. I will have a chance to explain some of the deeper thinking behind the choice in a note in the Order of Service, so that the congregation can understand the way it neatly ties together many different areas of Lewis's life and work. The fact that it comes from an address entitled "Is Theology Poetry?" makes it particularly apt for Poets' Corner, I think.

SMITH   It's been fifty years since Lewis died and in that period his reputation has been developing in various ways. How would you describe what his legacy is and is becoming?

WARD   It's too big and too varied to speak about in just a short answer. You only need to look at the huge numbers of books and articles that are published about Lewis every year to see the size of it. Some people dislike Lewis intensely. Some people simply dismiss him. But I think that the majority of those who engage with him seriously, even though they may disagree with him, find him stimulating, helpful, even inspiring in a number of different ways, as a scholar, as a thinker, and as a writer.

I think that, as time goes by, people are coming to realize that Lewis, whether you happen to agree with him or not, is a very substantial figure who needs to be reckoned with. His combination of intellect, imagination, and faith is rare. It's influential. At the very least, it's interesting. I think it's not insignificant that the publishing houses of Lewis's two universities, Oxford University Press and Cambridge University Press, have in recent years begun to publish scholarly works that address and analyse his impact. OUP has to date published three titles on Lewis's writings, and CUP has published *The Cambridge Companion to C. S. Lewis*. As time goes by and Lewis's readership shows no sign of waning—on the contrary, it only seems to be growing and deepening—he is coming to the attention of many people who wouldn't automatically regard him as worth consideration. But an enduring audience, fifty years after death, is unusual and can't be ignored for ever. And I think the fact that Lewis's great friend, Tolkien, is also showing no signs of disappearing from the cultural landscape reacts favourably on Lewis's own standing.

The two men together are now established, I think, as unavoidably major figures from the middle of the last century. If you want to understand the intellectual and imaginative history of the English-speaking world over the last sixty or seventy years, you have to take these two into account. They're becoming increasingly rooted as a pair of giants, like Wordsworth and Coleridge, for example, from the previous century.

SMITH   What do you hope will be the broader outcome of this event and the memorial?

WARD   The unveiling of the memorial is bound to receive a lot of media attention round the world, and I'm sure that that will result in people being introduced to or reminded of Lewis's works.

More generally, I hope the whole two-day memorial event will focus people's minds on carrying Lewis's legacy forward into the future and help engender ideas about how that might best be achieved. It's important in every generation for there to be talented artists, diligent scholars, and faithful apologists who are able to work both through argument and through story. By thinking about what Lewis achieved in these respects, people will be encouraged, I hope, to find ways of emulating and updating his example in the modern day.

SMITH   I would imagine that you will feel a sense of satisfaction in seeing this accomplished. With this particular milestone in the Lewis community and the wide spectrum of Lewis admirers, what are you most pleased about and proud of?

WARD   There are two things that most please me about this event. The first is that it's going to be international and will feature almost every conceivable constituency in what you might call "the Lewis world": people who knew him, people who worked with him, theologians and philosophers and poets who admire him, scholars who have studied and written about him, professors who have tutored and lectured on his works, priests and pastors and ministers who have handed on his wisdom, children who love Narnia, regular readers who just like his stories or his style, and so on and so forth. And I'm particularly pleased that it will involve people who knew him and worked with him, because their number, alas, is getting smaller every year. This is really the last chance for a gathering of this kind on such a scale.

And the other thing that especially pleases me is that this event is being organized by British people and in an Anglican context. Lewis himself was British and Anglican, and at last he is being commemorated by his countrymen in that setting, but with the whole world, as it were, welcome and involved at the same time. So many previous Lewis-related events have been principally American and Evangelical, and although those events have often been excellent and I've been proud to be associated with many of them myself, this event is different. It feels like a sort of home-coming or a long overdue recognition. It's going to be, I trust, a very happy occasion for everyone who attends, wherever they come from and whatever their particular connection with Lewis. I count myself tremendously fortunate to have a role in helping bring it about.

SMITH   What will be involved in the two days?

WARD   During the afternoon and evening of Thursday 21st November, there will be four events:

i. a lecture by Professor Alister McGrath, looking at how Lewis presented the Christian faith through rational argument;

ii. a lecture by Dr. Malcolm Guite, looking at how Lewis presented Christianity through story and poetry;

iii. a service of Choral Evensong—as happens every evening in the Abbey;

iv. a panel discussion that I will chair, featuring William Lane Craig, Michael Ramsden, Jeanette Sears, Peter S. Williams, and Judith Wolfe.

Then on Friday 22nd November, there will be a Memorial Service, at which the Lewis memorial will be formally unveiled; Walter Hooper, Lewis's editor and biographer, will lay flowers on it. The service will feature hymns, prayers, and readings both from Scripture and from Lewis's works, including an audio-recording of his own voice reading a passage from *Mere Christianity* (a passage that, by a pleasing coincidence, contains the phrase "telling the truth"). There will also be a specially commissioned choral anthem, a setting of one of Lewis's poems, composed by Paul Mealor. The address will be given by Rowan Williams, the former Archbishop of Canterbury, and now Master of Magdalene College, Cambridge (the college where, of course, Lewis finished his career).

SMITH   Where will the Symposium events take place?

WARD	The two lectures and the panel discussion will take place in St. Margaret's Church, which is right next door to the Abbey and is part of the overall Abbey foundation.
SMITH	Will there be any official gatherings before or after the conference?
WARD	Dr. John Hall will kindly be hosting a dinner for the lecturers and the panelists on the Thursday night in the Deanery. There'll also be a reception for a number of invited guests, after the Memorial Service, in the Jerusalem Chamber—a beautiful fourteenth-century room where the translators of the Authorised Version met in 1611, and where Henry IV famously died in 1413. The room can only accommodate about seventy people, so the guests will be mostly those with a particular connection to Lewis—relatives, colleagues, friends, former students, and so on.
SMITH	Are there any final details you would like to add?
WARD	I ought to add that the Westminster events will not be the only commemorations being held in England for the fiftieth anniversary of Lewis's death. There will be a day-conference at Magdalene College Cambridge, a celebratory event at Magdalen College Oxford, and the Oxford University C. S. Lewis Society will also be marking the occasion. But as regards the Westminster events specifically: one very exciting piece of news, which I alluded to earlier, is that the Director of Music at the Abbey, Professor James O'Donnell, has suggested that a special piece of music, a choral anthem, be commissioned for the Memorial Service. He asked me to propose some passages that might serve for the libretto, so I pored over Lewis's poetry, looking for poems that were short enough and lyrical enough to be viable candidates for a musical setting. There were lots of contenders, of course, but eventually I settled on three possible choices ("Love's As Warm As Tears," "The Naked Seed," and "After Prayers, Lie Cold"), which I submitted to the Abbey for their consideration. I also suggested Paul Mealor as a suitable composer, having greatly admired his motet, *Ubi caritas*, which he wrote for the 2011 Royal Wedding; and James O'Donnell instantly agreed that

Paul would be a very fine choice. Paul consented to come on board and to work on that poem which was—very happily—the first choice of both the Dean and myself, namely "Love's As Warm As Tears."

An anonymous donor has kindly come forward to fund the commission and my hope is not only that this piece of music will bring beauty and creativity to the Memorial Service, but also that it will become a standard part of the choral repertoire in this country—maybe even throughout the world—and be performed long after these commemorative events have passed into history. The poem in question is suited equally, I think, to weddings and funerals, but is also apt for any religious service or musical concert that aims to celebrate human and divine love. The way the poem talks about love as being "as warm as tears", "as fierce as fire", "as fresh as spring", and "as hard as nails", makes it applicable in all sorts of circumstances. I suspect Lewis was wanting to allude to the four elements (water, fire, air, and earth) in those four descriptions. Subtly, he's suggesting that love informs the entire cosmos, it "moves the sun and the other stars"—in Dante's immortal line.

SMITH   How can readers and Lewis admirers participate and help support this effort?

WARD   If you pray, please pray that this whole project will be edifying and successful. If you want to attend the events, please feel free to come to London in person on 21st and 22nd November. And if you don't pray or can't come, then please at least make a donation or encourage others to do so! And please also spread the word in general through social media. We still need to raise nearly £15,000. Any money raised over and above the costs of the memorial will go towards a new C. S. Lewis Scholarship at the University of Cambridge.[5]

SMITH   My thanks to Dr. Ward for his efforts to bring the Lewis Memorial to fruition and for his generous sharing in this interview.

---

5. Donations to the scholarship may still be made. Enquiries about how to contribute should be directed to database@alumni.cam.ac.uk.

PART ONE

Symposium

— 1 —

Telling the Truth through Rational Argument

C. S. Lewis on the Reasonableness of Christian Faith

Alister E. McGrath[1]

IT IS A GREAT pleasure to be able to contribute to Westminster Abbey's series of public lectures on "Telling the Truth" by exploring how C. S. Lewis used rational argument to commend and communicate the Christian faith.[2] Lewis is now firmly established as one of the greatest apologists of the twentieth century, with a continuing legacy of influence in the twenty-first. Few apologists have achieved anything approaching his impact, which transcends denominational barriers.

Lewis was British, and a layman of the Church of England. The decision to honour him here at Westminster is an important reaffirmation of his

---

1. The Revd. Dr. Alister E. McGrath is the Andreas Idreos Professor of Science and Religion at the University of Oxford, Director of the Ian Ramsey Centre for Science and Religion, and Fellow of Harris Manchester College. He is the author of numerous books, including *C. S. Lewis: A Life* (Hodder & Stoughton, 2013) and *The Intellectual World of C. S. Lewis* (Wiley-Blackwell, 2014). He maintains a web presence at www.alistermcgrath.weebly.com.

2. This article represents the full, corrected text of the lecture given at Westminster Abbey on 21 November 2013. A shorter version, rewritten for a more academic readership, was published as "An Enhanced Vision of Rationality: C. S. Lewis on the Reasonableness of Christian Faith," *Theology* 116.6 (2013) 410–17. The author and editors are grateful to the editor of *Theology* for permission to reproduce some material from this earlier article. A video of Professor McGrath's lecture is available online: https://youtube/aAJh6Z9Q3c4.

cultural and religious identity, here at the heart of the British religious and political establishment. Lewis's genius is such that he is loved and valued far beyond the confines of Great Britain and the Church of England; yet, as the recent anniversary events here in Britain have made abundantly clear—attendances have been huge!—Lewis is both remembered and admired here, in this nation and church.

Lewis also appeals to both fans and academics. If I might borrow a phrase from Gregory the Great (c. 540–604), his works are "like a river, both shallow and deep, in which a lamb may walk and an elephant swim."[3] The point that Gregory was making was that the Bible could be read and appreciated at multiple levels, popular and academic. And that is most certainly true of Lewis. Lewis is read and loved by a wide readership. Yet this anniversary year has marked an important transition, in that Lewis is now being taken with increased seriousness by academics, especially at Oxford and Cambridge. Many of you will have read Rowan Williams's brilliant engagement with Narnia.[4] It is surely significant that one of the world's greatest theologians, a former archbishop of Canterbury who is now Master of Lewis's old Cambridge college, takes such delight in Narnia, and helps us find new depths of meaning within it.

This recognition is long overdue. The foundations for this recognition were laid as long ago as 1946, when the ancient Scottish University of St. Andrews awarded Lewis the honorary degree of Doctor of Divinity. Professor Donald Baillie, Dean of the university's Faculty of Divinity, declared that Lewis had "succeeded in capturing the attention of many who will not readily listen to professional theologians," and had "arranged a new kind of marriage between theological reflection and poetic imagination." The passing of time has confirmed that Baillie was right on both counts. Perhaps, to use a musical image, Lewis is better seen as an arranger than as a composer. But some of his theological "arrangements" and "variations on themes" seem to have captured the popular imagination, where the originals did not.

So what is Lewis's approach to telling the truth, and why has it been so successful? In this lecture, I am going to explore Lewis's distinctive understanding of the rationality of faith, which emphasises the reasonableness of Christianity without imprisoning it within an impersonal and austere rationalism.

Lewis himself was an atheist as a younger man,[5] convinced of the fundamental irrationality of faith, and its incapacity to accommodate the

---

3. Gregory the Great, *Moralia*, 4; J. P. Migne, *Patrologia Latina* LXXV, 16.
4. Cf. Williams, *The Lion's World: A Journey into the Heart of Narnia*.
5. For further details, see McGrath, *C. S. Lewis—A Life*.

brutality and senselessness of the Great War, in which he fought from 1917–18. Yet Lewis's decision to limit himself to a rationalist worldview proved to be imaginatively sterile and uninteresting, leaving him existentially dissatisfied. It became clear to Lewis that pure reason offered him a bleak intellectual landscape that he could not bear to inhabit. Yet this, his reason insisted, was all that there was. To believe otherwise was pure fantasy. Lewis's imagination taught him that there had to be more. "Nearly all that I loved I believed to be imaginary; nearly all that I believed to be real I thought grim and meaningless."[6]

Lewis's study of English literature, especially the poetry of George Herbert, left him with gnawing doubts about his atheism. Herbert and others seemed able to connect up with a world that Lewis was tempted to dismiss as illusory, yet which haunted his imagination. "The two hemispheres of my mind were in the sharpest contrast. On the one side, a many-islanded sea of poetry and myth; on the other, a glib and shallow rationalism."[7] Might, Lewis wondered, the deepest intuitions of his imagination challenge the shallow truths of his dogmatic reason? And even triumph over it?

So how did Lewis break free from this rationalist prison? Lewis's understanding of the reasonableness of the Christian faith rests on a distinct way of grasping the rationality of the created order, and its ultimate grounding in God. Where some favour deductive arguments for the existence of God, Lewis offers his own distinct approach which is more inductive than deductive; more visual rather than purely rational.

Lewis's approach is difficult to simplify, as it is highly nuanced. But perhaps we could set out the key aspects of his approach as follows. The truths of the Christian faith lie beyond the reach of human reason; yet when those truths are presented and grasped, their rationality can easily be discerned. And one hallmark of that rationality is the ability of the Christian faith to make things intelligible.

It is clear that Lewis was drawn to Christianity because of both its intellectual capaciousness and its imaginative appeal. It made sense of things, without limiting itself to what could be understood or grasped by reason. Lewis, it seems to me, echoes a theme we find in the final canto of Dante's *Divine Comedy*, where the great Florentine poet and theologian expresses the idea that Christianity provides a vision of things—something wonderful which can be seen, yet which proves resistant to verbal expression:

> From that moment onwards my power of sight exceeded

---

6. Lewis, *Surprised by Joy*, 197.
7. Ibid.

That of speech, which fails at such a vision.[8]

For Lewis, there is always a sense of a "beyond," a "numinous"—something of enormous significance that lies beyond our reason, hinted at more by intuition than by logic. This point had been made earlier by G. K. Chesterton (whom Lewis greatly admired). "Every true artist," Chesterton argued, feels "that he is touching transcendental truths; that his images are shadows of things seen through the veil."[9] While the intellectual capaciousness of the Christian faith can be rationally analysed, Lewis hints that it is best imaginatively communicated.

Lewis invites us to see Christianity as offering us a standpoint (a Platonic *synoptikon*, if you like) from which we may survey things, and grasp their intrinsic coherence and interconnectedness. We *see* how things connect together. Lewis consistently uses a remarkably wide range of visual metaphors—such as sun, light, blindness, and shadows—to help us understand the nature of a true understanding of things. Where some argue that rationality concerns the ability of reason to give an account of things, Lewis frames this more in terms of our ability to see their relationships. This has two highly significant consequences.

First, it means that Lewis sees reason and imagination as existing in a collaborative relationship. Reason without imagination is potentially dull and limited; imagination without reason is potentially delusory and escapist. Lewis develops a notion of "imagined"—not imaginary—reality, which is capable of being grasped by reason and visualised by the imagination.

Secondly, it means that Lewis makes extensive use of verbal illustrations or analogies, to enable us to *see* things in a new way. Lewis's famous apologetic for the doctrine of the Trinity in *Mere Christianity* suggests that our difficulties arise primarily because we fail to see it properly. If we see it another way—as, for example, an inhabitant of a two-dimensional world might try to grasp and describe the structure of a three-dimensional reality—then we begin to grasp its intrinsic rationality. Lewis's apologetic often takes the form of a visual invitation: "Try seeing it this way!" The rationality of the Trinity needs to be shown, not proved—and it is shown by allowing us to see it in the right way.

Perhaps this helps us appreciate the special appeal of Lewis's Chronicles of Narnia, which present a way of seeing things, embodied within stories, which turns out to be rationally plausible and imaginatively attractive. Lewis's Oxford colleague Austin Farrer suggested that Lewis's apologetic approach might initially look like an argument, but on closer inspection,

---

8. Dante, *Paradiso* XXXIII, 55–56.
9. Chesterton, *The Everlasting Man*, 105.

it turned out to be an encouragement to see things in a new way, and thus grasp the rationality of faith. Lewis, Farrer suggested, makes us "think we are listening to an argument," when in reality "we are presented with a vision, and it is the vision that carries conviction."[10]

For example, consider Lewis's imaginative visualization of a theological truth—the entrapment of the human soul through sin in *The Voyage of the "Dawn Treader."* Lewis's opening line in this book is seen by many as one of its most memorable features: "There was a boy called Eustace Clarence Scrubb, and he almost deserved it." Eustace Scrubb is portrayed as a thoroughly unsympathetic character, whom Lewis develops as an example of selfishness. It's difficult to like him to begin with, and it's just as difficult to feel sorry for him when he changes into a dragon as a result of his "greedy, dragonish thoughts."[11]

The thoroughly obnoxious Eustace encounters some enchanted gold. He believes this will make him the master of all! But instead, it masters him. Lewis loved old Norse mythology, and borrowed the Norse story about the greedy giant Fáfnir, who turned himself into a dragon to protect his ill-won gain. So Eustace becomes a dragon. Now having become a dragon, how does Eustace stop being one? Lewis presents Eustace's initial transformation into a dragon and his subsequent "undragoning" as a double transformation that reveals both Eustace's selfish, fallen nature and the transforming power of divine grace.

The Voyage of the "Dawn Treader" provides a brilliant description of Eustace realizing, to his horror, that he has become a dragon. He doesn't like this at all, and he frantically tries to scratch off his dragon's skin. Yet each layer he removes merely reveals yet another layer of scales beneath it. He simply cannot break free from his prison. He is trapped.

But salvation lies to hand. Aslan appears, and tears away at the dragon flesh with his claws. And when the scales are finally removed, Aslan plunges the raw and bleeding Eustace into a well from which he emerges purified and renewed, with his humanity restored. The storyline is dramatic, realistic, and shocking. But the power of the narrative brings home the Christian themes that Lewis believed could not be described as effectively through a series of well-intentioned theological lectures. And while Lewis drew his dragon imagery from Norse mythology, the story of the "undragoning" draws on the rich ideas and imagery of the New Testament.

So what are we to learn from this powerful and shocking story, so realistically depicted? As the startlingly raw imagery of Aslan tearing at

---

10. Farrer, "The Christian Apologist," in *Light on C. S. Lewis*, ed. Jocelyn Gibb, 37.
11. For the narrative, see Lewis, *The Voyage of the Dawn Treader*, 91–92.

Eustace's flesh makes clear, Eustace has been trapped by forces over which he has no control. The one who would be master has instead been mastered. The dragon is a symbol, not so much of sin itself, as of the power of sin to entrap, captivate, and imprison. It can only be broken and mastered by the redeemer. Aslan is the one who heals and renews Eustace, restoring him to what he was intended to be.

The immersion in the water of the well is immediately familiar, picking up on the New Testament's language about baptism as dying to self and rising to Christ (Rom 6). (The omission of this aspect of the "undragoning" of Eustace in the recent movie version of *The Voyage of the "Dawn Treader"* was one of the more irritating and unnecessary of its many weaknesses.) Eustace is then tossed into the well by Aslan, and emerges renewed and restored.

You see my point. Lewis takes a classic theological doctrine, and transposes it into a narrative—a narrative that is embraced imaginatively, and not simply rationally understood. He breathes new life into a traditional doctrine by inviting us to *see* it. We are *shown* what sin is all about, not merely told about it.

Although some have tried to force Lewis into a purely rationalist way of thinking, this does not do him justice. Lewis does not try to prove the existence of God on *a priori* grounds. Instead, Lewis invites us to see how what we observe in the world around us and experience within us "fits" the Christian way of seeing things. Lewis often articulates this way of "seeing things" in terms of a "myth"—that is to say, a story about reality that both invites its "imaginative embrace," and communicates a conceptual framework, by which other things are to be seen.[12] The imagination embraces the narrative; reason consequently reflects on its contents.

So how does this approach to the reasonableness of faith work out in practice? Let's consider Lewis's celebrated "argument from desire," exploring both its rational structure and its apologetic appeal.

The starting point for Lewis's approach is an experience—a longing for something undefined and possibly undefinable, that is as insatiable as it is elusive. Lewis sets out versions of this argument at several points in his writings, including the Chronicles of Narnia. The most important statements of the argument, however, are the following:

1. *The Pilgrim's Regress* (1933), written shortly after his conversion to Christianity, in which Lewis sets out an allegorical account of his own conversion, focusing on the theme of desire.

12. For a detailed discussion, see McGrath, "A Gleam of Divine Truth: The Concept of Myth in Lewis's Thought," in *The Intellectual World of C. S. Lewis*, 55–82.

2. The university sermon "The Weight of Glory," preached in Oxford in June 1941, and subsequently published as an article in the journal *Theology*. This is the most elegant statement of the argument, which is here framed primarily in terms of the human quest for beauty.

3. The talk "Hope," given during the third series of Broadcast Talks for the British Broadcasting Corporation during the Second World War, and subsequently reproduced as a chapter in *Mere Christianity*. This is generally considered to be Lewis's most influential statement of the argument.

4. The autobiographical work *Surprised by Joy*, in which the theme of "Joy" plays a significant role in arousing Lewis's openness towards God.

In *Surprised by Joy*, Lewis described his childhood experiences of intense longing (which he names "Joy") for something unknown and elusive, triggered off by such things as the fragrance of a flowering currant bush in the garden of his childhood home in Belfast, or reading Henry Wadsworth Longfellow's poem in the style of the Swedish poet Esaias Tegnér. Lewis's epiphany of "Joy" bathed his everyday world of experience with beauty and wonder. But what did it mean—if it meant anything at all? What way of seeing it might help him to make sense of it? How was he to interpret it?

While an atheist, Lewis dismissed such experiences as illusory. Yet he became increasingly dissatisfied with such simplistic reductive explanations. His growing familiarity with what he termed the "Christian mythology"—Lewis here uses the term "myth" in the sense of a "narrated worldview"—led him to appreciate that these experiences could easily and naturally be accommodated within its explanatory framework. What if God were an active questing personal agent, as Christianity affirmed to be the case? If so, God could easily be understood as the "source from which those arrows of Joy had been shot at me ever since childhood."

In the 1941 sermon "The Weight of Glory," Lewis develops this theme further by exploring the human quest for beauty. Lewis argues that this is really a search for the *source* of that beauty, which is *mediated through* the things of this world, but not *contained within* them. "The books or the music in which we thought the beauty was located will betray us if we trust to them: it was not *in* them, it only came *through* them, and what came through them was longing."[13] Without a Christian way of seeing things, this longing remains "uncertain of its object." Its true goal remains to be identified and attained.

13. Lewis, *Essay Collection*, 98.

Christianity, Lewis declares, gives us the intellectual framework that both interprets the experience, and leads us to its true goal. In his own way, Lewis reworks the point so famously made by T. S. Eliot in *The Dry Salvages*:

> We had the experience but missed the meaning.
> And approach to the meaning restores the experience.

In *Mere Christianity*, Lewis sets out this approach in a somewhat different way, while still appealing to the elusiveness of our experiences of "Joy." The experiences he had in mind are shared across the human spectrum, often expressed in quotidian language as a sense of there being "something there." The great Russian novelist Fyodor Dostoyevsky, for example, spoke of "a nostalgic yearning, bordering at times on unendurably poignant sorrow," which he experienced in "the dreams of my heart and in the reveries of my soul."[14] Bertrand Russell, one of the most articulate and influential British atheist writers of the twentieth century, put a similar thought into words as follows:

> The centre of me is always and eternally a terrible pain . . . a searching for something beyond what the world contains, something transfigured and infinite—the beatific vision, God—I do not find it, I do not think it is to be found—but the love of it is my life . . . it is the actual spring of life within me.[15]

Russell's daughter, Katharine Tait, recalled that he was contemptuous of organized religion, dismissing its ideas mainly because he disliked those who held them. Yet Tait took the view that her father's life was really an unacknowledged, perhaps disguised, search for God. "Somewhere at the back of my father's mind, at the bottom of his heart, in the depths of his soul, there was an empty space that had once been filled by God, and he never found anything else to put in it." Russell was now haunted by a "ghost-like feeling of not belonging in this world."[16]

These are the kinds of experience to which Lewis appeals—a sense of hovering on the brink of discovering something of immense significance, linked with a sense of sorrow and frustration when what seemed to be so close tantalizingly disappears. Like smoke, it cannot be grasped. As Lewis puts it: "There was something we grasped at, in that first moment of longing,

---

14. Dostoyevsky, "The Dream of a Ridiculous Man," in *A Disgraceful Affair*, 172.

15. Letter to Colette O'Niel, 21 October 1916; in *The Selected Letters of Bertrand Russell: The Public Years 1914–1970*, 85.

16. Tait, *My Father Bertrand Russell*, 189.

which just fades away in the reality."¹⁷ So what does this sense of unfulfilled longing mean? To what does it point?

Some, Lewis concedes, might suggest that this frustration arises from looking for its true object in the wrong places; others that, since further searching will only result in repeated disappointment, there is simply no point trying to find something better than the present world.

Yet Lewis suggests that there is a third approach, which recognizes that these earthly longings are "only a kind of copy, or echo, or mirage" of our true homeland. Since this overwhelming desire cannot be fulfilled through anything in the present world, this suggests that its ultimate object lies beyond the present world. As he says in *Mere Christianity*: "If I find in myself a desire which no experience in this world can satisfy, the most probable explanation is that I was made for another world."

Here, as throughout his apologetic writings, the starting point of Lewis's approach does not lie with the Bible or the Christian tradition, but with shared human experience and observation. How do we make sense of them? Lewis's genius as an apologist lay in his ability to show how a "viewpoint" which was derived from the Bible and the Christian tradition was able to offer a more satisfactory explanation of common human experience than its rivals—especially the atheism he had once himself espoused.

Lewis's apologetic approach is to identify a common human observation or experience, and then show how it fits in, naturally and plausibly, within a Christian way of looking at things.¹⁸ For Lewis, Christianity provided a "big picture," an intellectually capacious and imaginatively satisfying way of seeing things. Lewis was always emphatic that nothing can be proved on the basis of observation or experience. Yet while such observations of nature or our own experiences *prove* nothing, they can suggest certain possibilities, and even intimate what they might mean. That's what Lewis was trying to express when he wrote:

> A true philosophy may sometimes validate an experience of nature; an experience of nature cannot validate a philosophy. Nature will not verify any theological or metaphysical proposition (or not in the manner we are now considering); she will help to show what it means.¹⁹

---

17. For what follows, see Lewis, *Mere Christianity*, 135–36.

18. Lewis's apologetic method is often misunderstood. For a correction of earlier accounts of his approach, see McGrath, "Reason, Experience, and Imagination: Lewis's Apologetic Method," in *The Intellectual World of C. S. Lewis*, 129–46.

19. Lewis, *The Four Loves*, 25.

That's what Lewis's mentor G. K. Chesterton was also getting at when he remarked that "the phenomenon does not prove religion, but religion explains the phenomenon."[20]

Lewis's approach could be framed like this: Christianity holds that the natural order—including our own reasoning—is shaped by the God who created all things. As Augustine of Hippo and Blaise Pascal had argued before him, Lewis affirms that the absence of God causes us to experience longing—a yearning for God, which we misinterpret as a longing for something located within the finite and created order. Conversion is thus partly about a semiotic transformation, in which we realize that something we believed to be pointing to one thing in fact points to something rather different.

We could set Lewis's argument out more formally as follows. We experience desires that no experience in this world seems able to satisfy. Yet Christianity tells us that we are made for another world. And when things are seen in this way, this sort of experience is exactly what we would expect. The appeal is not so much to cold logic, as to intuition and imagination, resting on an imaginative dynamic of discovery. Lewis invites his audience to see their experiences through a set of Christian spectacles, and notice how these bring what might otherwise be fuzzy or blurred into sharp focus. For Lewis, the ability of the Christian faith to accommodate our experience, naturally and easily, is an indicator of its truth.

As Lewis states this approach from desire, therefore, it is not really an argument at all; it is more about observing and affirming the fit between a theory and observation. It is like trying on a hat or shirt for size. How well does it fit? How many of our observations of the world can it accommodate, and how persuasively? Lewis's way of thinking also shows some similarity to a related approach within the natural sciences, now generally known as "inference to the best explanation."[21] This approach recognizes that there are multiple explanations of observations, and suggests how criteria might be identified to determine which such explanation is to be considered as "the best."

The same approach is found in Lewis's "argument from morality." This is sometimes portrayed in ridiculously simplistic terms—for example, "experiencing a sense of moral obligation proves there is a God." Lewis did not say this, and did not think this. As with the "argument from desire," his argument is rather that the common human experience of a sense of moral obligation is easily and naturally accommodated within a Christian framework.

---

20. Chesterton, "The Return of the Angels," *Daily News*.

21. For the importance of such approaches in relation to countering the "New Atheism," see McGrath, "The Boyle Lecture 2014: New Atheism—New Apologetics."

For Lewis, experiences and intuitions—for example, concerning morality and desire—are meant to "arouse our suspicions" that there is indeed "Something which is directing the universe." We come to suspect that our moral experience suggests a "real law which we did not invent, and which we know we ought to obey," in much the same way as our experience of desire is "a kind of copy, or echo, or mirage" of another place, which is our true homeland. And as we track this suspicion, we begin to realize that it has considerable imaginative and explanatory potential. What was initially a dawning suspicion becomes solidified as a growing conviction that it makes sense of what matters to us naturally and persuasively.

So what can be learned from Lewis's approach? Perhaps I could mention two points in bringing this lecture to a close.

First, Lewis helps us see that apologetics need not take the form of a slightly dull deductive argument, but can be understood and presented as an invitation to step into the Christian way of seeing things, and explore how things look when seen from its standpoint. "Try seeing things this way!" If worldviews or metanarratives can be compared to lenses, which of them brings things into sharpest focus?

And second, we need to realize that Lewis's *explicit* appeal to reason involves an *implicit* appeal to the imagination. Perhaps this helps us understand why Lewis appeals to both modern and postmodern people. I see no historical evidence that compels me to argue that Lewis deliberately set out to do this, constructing a mediating position between two very different cultural moods. The evidence suggests that he saw things this way naturally, and never formalized it in terms of a synthesis of these two very different modalities of thought. Lewis rather gives us a *synoptikon* that transcends the great divide between modernity and postmodernity, affirming the strengths of each, and subtly accommodating their weaknesses.

Yes, Lewis affirms the rationality of the universe—but does so without plunging us into an imaginatively drab world of cold logic and dreary argumentation. Yes, Lewis affirms the power of images and narratives to captivate our imagination—but does so without giving up on the primacy of truth. As the churches face an increasingly complex cultural context in which they must preach and minister, Lewis offers insights and approaches that are potentially enriching—and, I venture to suggest, culturally plausible and intellectually persuasive.

In the end, Lewis *tells* the truth by *showing* the truth. He offers us an intellectually capacious and imaginatively compelling vision of the Christian faith, perhaps best summed up in his lapidary statement at the end of his essay "Is Theology Poetry?" Using a powerful visual image, Lewis invites us to see God as both the ground of the rationality of the world, and the one who enables us to grasp that rationality.

> I believe in Christianity as I believe that the Sun has risen, not only because I see it but because by it I see everything else.[22]

This beautifully crafted sentence is a fitting memorial both to Lewis himself and his rich understanding of faith. How appropriate that it adorns the memorial to be unveiled in this Abbey tomorrow!

I must end. Let me do so by noting a parallel between Lewis and the great Genevan reformer John Calvin. Neither Lewis nor Calvin had any children, though both were stepfathers to children from their wives' earlier marriages. When Calvin was mocked by his critics for being childless, he offered an intriguing rebuttal. Anyone, he declared, who read his books and came to share his way of thinking was his child. And when seen that way, Calvin turned out to have rather a large family! I think the same is true of Lewis. Many of us find that our ways of thinking have come to be deeply shaped by Lewis; to put it another way, we share something of his intellectual DNA. Those of us gathered here today at Westminster are Lewis's children, meeting for a family celebration. Not one of us here today is a physical descendent of Lewis, but we are all linked to him through our imagination and reason. I think we all share in the delight of this family occasion, made possible both by the generosity and discernment of this great institution, Westminster Abbey, and by the genius and talent of C. S. Lewis himself. May both flourish in the next fifty years!

---

22. Lewis, *Essay Collection*, 21.

— 2 —

Telling the Truth through Imaginative Fiction

C. S. Lewis on the Reconciliation of Athene and Demeter

Malcolm Guite[1]

IN THE FOREGOING ESSAY in this volume, Alister McGrath explored the various ways in which C. S. Lewis appeals to reason in his apologetics, though he has pointed out that this appeal to reason and to what he calls "reasonableness" is, in fact, constantly interwoven with an appeal to imagination, a series of invitations to look at things in a new way, to imagine how a world might look if Christianity were the case. I agree with Dr. McGrath that in Lewis's mature work appeals to reason and imagination are complementary, balanced, and mutually enfolded. However, in this essay[2] I want briefly to distinguish from this interwoven thread the *imaginative* strand and to look specifically at the role imagination played both in Lewis's own *praeparatio evangelica* and in his subsequent apologetic writing, taking apologetics in its broadest sense to include both his fiction and his poetry.

---

1. The Revd. Dr. Malcolm Guite is Chaplain of Girton College, University of Cambridge. He is the author of *Faith, Hope and Poetry: Theology and the Poetic Imagination* (Ashgate, 2010) and of "Poet" in *The Cambridge Companion to C. S. Lewis* (Cambridge University Press, 2010). As a poet himself, he is the author of *Sounding the Seasons: Seventy Sonnets for the Christian Year* (Canterbury Press, 2012), and *The Singing Bowl* (Canterbury Press, 2013). He maintains a web presence at www.malcolmguite.wordpress.com.

2. A video of Dr. Guite's lecture is available online: https://youtu.be/lOxbeQLFX2k.

If we are to understand the special role played by imagination in Lewis's writing post-conversion, then it is essential to understand the very different way in which he configured the relations between reason and imagination before his conversion. What Lewis in fact experienced with deepening distress throughout the twenties was a profound divorce or bifurcation between what his reason told him, what he felt he could know and affirm philosophically, on the one hand, and the deepest intuitions or apprehensions of his imagination, on the other. As he puts it very starkly in *Surprised by Joy*:

> The two hemispheres of my mind were in the sharpest contrast. On the one side a many-islanded sea of poetry and myth; on the other a glib and shallow "rationalism." Nearly all that I loved I believed to be imaginary; nearly all that I believed to be real I thought grim and meaningless.[3]

Of course, this account of his dilemma was written post-conversion and many years after the period in his life that Lewis is describing. However, we have a much more contemporary document, a poem in which Lewis explores these same issues whilst they were still in suspension, still unresolved. The poem was published posthumously in Walter Hooper's edited collection *The Collected Poems of C. S. Lewis* and titled (by Hooper, not by Lewis) "Reason." But if Alister McGrath is right, as I think he is, first in dating this poem as early as 1925 and second in revising the date of Lewis's conversion to Theism to 1930,[4] then what we have in "Reason" is a poem, written about five years before he became even a Theist (let alone a Christian), in which Lewis lays out the fundamental dilemma, the deep gulf over which any effective Christian apologetics would have to throw a bridge or, to use a metaphor closer to Lewis's poem, the estranged powers of the soul which Christianity would have to reconcile. It seems to me that in this poem Lewis is identifying not simply a private dilemma, but is feeling deeply within himself a profound disjunction that was general to Western post-war culture and indeed more broadly, post-Enlightenment culture. For this reason it is worth examining the poem in some detail.[5]

The poem offers an extended metaphor of the soul as an inner Athens divided between the two goddesses, Athene, who represents Reason, and Demeter, who represents the Imagination:

---

3. Lewis, *Surprised by Joy*, 161.

4. For McGrath's datings, and his own account of Lewis's integration of reason and imagination, see McGrath, *C. S. Lewis. A Life*, 135–59.

5. For a fuller examination of this poem in the wider context of Lewis's poetry, see Guite, "Poet," *The Cambridge Companion to C. S. Lewis*, 294–308.

> Reason
>
> Set on the soul's acropolis the reason stands
> A virgin arm'd, commercing with celestial light,
> And he who sins against her has defiled his own
> Virginity: no cleansing makes his garment white;
> So clear is reason. But how dark, imagining,
> Warm, dark, obscure and infinite, daughter of Night:
> Dark is her brow, the beauty of her eyes with sleep
> Is loaded, and her pains are long, and her delight.
> Tempt not Athene. Wound not in her fertile pains
> Demeter, nor rebel against her mother-right.
> Oh who will reconcile in me both maid and mother,
> Who make in me a concord of the depth and height?
> Who make imagination's dim exploring touch
> Ever report the same as intellectual sight?
> Then could I truly say and not deceive,
> Then wholly say that I BELIEVE.[6]

So it opens with a vision of Athene:

> Set on the soul's acropolis the reason stands
> A virgin arm'd, commercing with celestial light,
> And he who sins against her has defiled his own
> Virginity: no cleansing makes his garment white;
> So clear is reason.

This opening makes it clear that any truth, however inconvenient, must be known and faced for what it is; there must be no flight from Reason, no refusal of fact. But on the other hand, imagination must also have a place, and the truths to which it bears witness, however apparently contrary to the truths made available by reason, must also be taken seriously. As Lewis goes on to say:

> But how dark, imagining,
> Warm, dark, obscure and infinite, daughter of Night . . .
> Tempt not Athene. Wound not in her fertile pains
> Demeter . . .

Then at the turn or "volta" of this extended sixteen-line sonnet Lewis asks the vital question:

> Oh who will reconcile in me both maid and mother,
> Who make in me a concord of the depth and height?
> Who make imagination's dim exploring touch

---

6. Walter Hooper (ed.), *The Collected Poems of C. S. Lewis*, 65.

> Ever report the same as intellectual sight?
> Then could I truly say and not deceive,
> Then wholly say that I BELIEVE.[7]

There are a number of remarkable things going on here, from the sense of inner space, of height and depth in the psyche itself, to the bodying forth of the soul's distinct powers of reason and imagination in the form of the two goddesses, Athene and Demeter. This is no glib classical allusion in the eighteenth-century manner, but a symbolic re-imagination of the inner self in which more than personal, perhaps more than human, powers are at work, and it is highly significant that at this point both these powers are figured as feminine. Lewis is sometimes caricatured as a bluff, masculine, conservative, probably misogynistic, bachelor don, yet here he is expressing his inner life by saying, in effect, "My problem is that I can't get my inner goddesses together!"

After exploring many paired contrasts—light and dark, armour and pain, standing and sleeping, virginity and fertility—the poem ends with a plea, which subtly summons the echoes of its own answer:

> Oh who will reconcile in me both maid and mother,
> Who make a concord of the depth and height?

From the later perspective of Lewis's conversion we can see that these lines point and give new significance to the paradox of incarnation, which is at the heart of the integrative faith that Lewis would later embrace. For it is, of course, the Christian figure of Mary who reconciles "both maid and mother." In and through her "Yes" to God, the archetypal assent of all faith, Christ the reconciler comes into the world, the one who not only reconciles man to God, and time to eternity, but is also in himself the concord of all depth and height, inner and outer. Furthermore Lewis's image of the depth and height seems to carry an echo of Paul's language in Ephesians:

> that ye, being rooted and grounded in love, may be able to comprehend with all saints what is the breadth, and length, and depth, and height; and to know the love of Christ, which passeth knowledge, that ye might be filled with all the fulness of God.[8]

These are of course anticipatory echoes: the poem as it stands witnesses to an impasse and points to a hoped for "concord," which has not yet arrived. Indeed this poem is itself an example of the way in which imagination can embody glimpses of a potential truth that has not yet become actual to

7. Ibid., 95.
8. Eph 3:17–19.

our reason, the "sacred power of self-intuition" to which Coleridge, who as we shall see is a very important figure for Lewis, points so presciently in *Biographia Literaria*:

> They and only they can acquire the philosophic imagination, the sacred power of self-intuition, who within themselves can interpret and understand the symbol, that the wings of the air-sylph are forming within the skin of the caterpillar; those only, who feel in their own spirits the same instinct, which impels the chrysalis of the horned fly to leave room in its involucrum for antennae yet to come. They know and feel, that the *potential* works *in* them, even as the *actual* works on them.[9]

The way Lewis found out of this personal impasse was at once spiritual, theological, and literary, and it brings us to the heart of both his Christian belief and his literary practice. For Lewis, Christ did indeed reconcile the broken parts and the severed dimensions of our divided being; the height and depth, outer and inner, reason and imagination.

This is why I don't think Hooper's suggested title of "Reason" does justice to this poem. Indeed I think it skews the way we read it, though equally to title it "Imagination" would do the same. The poem is not about exalting one of these faculties over the other, but rather about *reconciling them*. A better title for this poem might simply be "Who?" The real question posed by the poem is: Who is the reconciler? Reading the poem now it is easy for us to see that the answer is Christ. On the one hand, the story of his death and resurrection summons up the deepest imaginative and mythic response, but, on the other, the story of his incarnation brings imaginative myth and rational history together. For Christianity is, as Lewis came to believe, "myth made fact." As we have seen, the language of the poem, with its echo of Ephesians, points to a profound and integrative theology of incarnation and yet (assuming a 1925 date for its composition is correct) it was not until another five years had passed that Lewis was able fully to answer the question posed and whose answer is anticipated in this poem.

This is a clear example of the process of imaginative anticipation of truths to which reason has not yet attained, which Lewis describes more generally in *Surprised by Joy* by saying: "my imagination was in a certain sense baptized; the rest of me, not unnaturally, took longer."[10] And it is not surprising, therefore, that appeals to imagination are not simply a decorative extra, a sweetening of the doctrinal pill in Lewis's apologetic writing, but are

---

9. Engell and Bate (eds.), *Biographia Literaria*, 241–42.
10. Lewis, *Surprised by Joy*, 171.

woven essentially into the fabric of what he says. "The truth of imagination," as Keats called it, is part of the message.

At this point it is worth asking what Lewis himself meant by imagination, in what tradition is he standing when he speaks of it? Fortunately, we have a poem addressed to fellow-poet Roy Campbell and almost totally overlooked by Lewis scholars in which he sets out exactly what tradition he stands in, and it is the tradition of philosophical romanticism, in which Coleridge plays a central role:

> In England the romantic stream flows . . .
> . . . from Scott; from Coleridge too.
> . . . Newman in that ruinous master saw
> One who restored our faculty for awe,
> Who re-discovered the soul's depth and height,
> Who pricked with needles of the eternal light
> An England at that time half numbed to death
> With Paley's, Bentham's, Malthus' wintry breath.[11]

Indeed, in this poem we can see the key images of depth and height and even anticipate, if we wish, the glorious power of an imaginative Christ-figure who frees Narnia, "half-numbed to death" from a White Witch's "wintry breath." Though Lewis would have read Coleridge's *Biographia Literaria* as a matter of course, he was fortunate in having as a close friend and "wisest and best of my unofficial teachers,"[12] Owen Barfield, for whom Coleridge's understanding of imagination was essential for a complete renewal of the way we see the world. In this poem "To Roy Campbell" Lewis has already set out the kind of thing imaginative apologetics might be called on to do: to "restore our faculty of awe," to "help the soul re-discover its depth and height" and, in Lewis's telling and beautiful phrase, to "prick with needles of eternal light" a benumbed contemporary culture. But, perhaps the most helpful mapping of the terrain Lewis was to body forth and explore in books like the Ransom Trilogy and the Chronicles of Narnia and *Till We Have Faces* is to be found in the programme Wordsworth and Coleridge set themselves at the beginning of the Romantic movement, as it was later recalled by Coleridge in *Biographia Literaria*:

---

11. Lewis, *Poems*, 80. By citing Scott, and then Coleridge as read by Newman, Lewis is appealing to a particular understanding of imagination within a religious frame. For a fuller account of this tradition see Coulson, *Religion and Imagination* and Avis, *God and the Creative Imagination*. For my own discussion of the importance of this tradition see *Faith, Hope and Poetry*, 4–9.

12. Lewis, dedication of *The Allegory of Love*. First published Oxford 1936, 1953 ed.

> In this idea originated the plan of the lyrical ballads in which it was agreed that my endeavours should be directed to persons and characters supernatural, or at least romantic; yet so as to transfer from our inward nature a human interest and a semblance of truth sufficient to procure for these shadows of imagination that willing suspension of disbelief for the moment, which constitutes poetic faith. Mr. Wordsworth, on the other hand, was to propose to himself as his object, to give the charm of novelty to things of every day, and to excite a feeling analogous to the supernatural by awakening the mind's attention from the lethargy of custom, and directing it to the loveliness and the wonders of the world before us; an inexhaustible treasure, but for which, in consequence of the film of familiarity and selfish solicitude, we have eyes, yet see not, ears that hear not, and hearts that neither feel nor understand.[13]

We can see both these "endeavours," as Coleridge calls them, at work in Lewis's best writing. Certainly he procures for his "characters supernatural or at least romantic" just that transference and bodying forth of our "inward nature" that Coleridge was aiming for—whether the icy White Witch or the golden goodness of Aslan, whether the numinous *eldila* of the Ransom Trilogy or the beautifully embodied figures of Psyche and Orual in *Till We Have Faces*. But in some ways it is the Wordsworthian, more than the Coleridgean, side of his achievement that makes Lewis such an effective imaginative apologist: his power to "excite a feeling analogous to the supernatural" by "awakening the mind's attention" and "directing it to the loveliness and the wonders of the world before us." It has often been remarked that it is easier to portray evil than to portray goodness, but many people have noted that Lewis is an exception. The sheer goodness of his "good" characters (chiefly Aslan, of course), the sense of "solid joys and lasting treasure" (to quote Newton's famous hymn) that he evokes in "The Weight of Glory"[14] and sustains so beautifully throughout *The Great Divorce*—these are hard things to achieve as a writer. Michael Ward has drawn attention to the extraordinary imaginative skill and intertextual layering with which Lewis built up what he (Lewis) called the "kappa element" in his evocation of the "Donegality," or unique quiddity, of rich particularity and "inexhaustible wonder" of each of the seven Chronicles.[15] This power of re-enchantment, of removing the "film of familiarity" and "awakening the mind's attention" is something Lewis was striving for in his writing. He makes this clear in his important

---

13. Coleridge, *Biographia Literaria*, vol. 2, 6–7.
14. Cf. Walmsley (ed.), *C. S. Lewis Essay Collection*, 96–106.
15. Cf. Ward, *Planet Narnia*.

essay "On Three Ways of Writing for Children." In this essay Lewis makes a distinction between the kind of "fantasy" writing that is mere ego-pleasing and this-worldly wish-fulfillment—of which he says: "Its fulfilment on the level of imagination is in very truth compensatory: we run to it from the disappointments and humiliations of the real world: it sends us back to the real world undivinely discontented. For it is all flattery to the ego"[16]—and, by contrast, the kind of imaginative writing, "imaginative" in the Coleridgean sense, that he is aiming for. Of this he says:

> It would be much truer to say that fairy land arouses a longing for he knows not what. It stirs and troubles him (to his life-long enrichment) with the dim sense of something beyond his reach and, far from dulling or emptying the actual world, gives it a new dimension of depth. He does not despise real woods because he has read of enchanted woods: the reading makes all real woods a little enchanted.[17]

At its best, this is what Lewis's writing continually achieves, this re-enchantment upon return. We return from the Narnian woods to find all our real woods "a little enchanted." Indeed he makes this aim explicit, some would say a little too explicit, at the end of *The Voyage of the "Dawn Treader"* when Edmund and Lucy are told by Aslan that they cannot return to Narnia:

> "You are too old, children," said Aslan, "and you must begin to come close to your own world now."
> "It isn't Narnia, you know," sobbed Lucy. "It's *you*. We shan't meet *you* there. And how can we live, never meeting you?"
> "But you shall meet me, dear one," said Aslan.
> "Are—are you there too, Sir?" said Edmund.
> "I am," said Aslan. "But there I have another name. This was the very reason why you were brought to Narnia, that by knowing me here for a little, you may know me better there."[18]

Lewis may be in danger of making things too explicit here and breaking his own spell. A better emblem of the real imaginative enchantment he achieves, particularly through the art of story-telling itself, is the little episode in the same book where Lucy finds in the magician's Big Book a spell "for the refreshment of the spirit:"

> The pictures were fewer here but very beautiful. And what Lucy found herself reading was more like a story than a spell. It went

---

16. Walmsley (ed.), *C. S. Lewis Essay Collection*, 102.
17. Ibid., 103.
18. Lewis, *The Voyage of the Dawn Treader*, 222.

> on for three pages and before she had read to the bottom of the page she had forgotten that she was reading at all. She was living in the story as if it were real, and all the pictures were real too. When she had got to the third page and come to the end, she said, "That is the loveliest story I've ever read or ever shall read in my whole life."[19]

It is part of the magic that Lucy cannot turn the pages of the book backwards and repeat the experience or even remember the story, but when she meets Aslan at the end of this episode she asks:

> "Shall I ever be able to read that story again; the one I couldn't remember? Will you tell it to me, Aslan? Oh do, do, do."
> "Indeed, yes, I will tell it to you for years and years"[20]

Here Lewis offers the enchantment of imaginative story as both a bridge between reason and imagination and also an emblem of heaven itself.

Finally, let us return to the dilemma set out in the poem "Reason" and to the way it finally came to be resolved so fruitfully both in Lewis's actual conversion and in his subsequent writing. Lewis famously said, "For me reason is the natural organ of truth, but imagination is the organ of meaning."[21] We cannot have one without the other and in order to make them work together we must respect their differences. Lewis never published "Reason" in his lifetime, but had he been consulted towards the end of his life he might have wanted, from the perspective of those later works that appeal both to reason and imagination, to have challenged his own phrase "ever report the same" in that poem:

> Who make imagination's dim exploring touch
> *Ever report the same* as intellectual sight?

In one sense this phrase sets a false goal and betrays a failure of imagination, if it implies that the "reports" given to us by reason on the one hand and imagination on the other should be so exactly "the same" that each could be translated without loss into the other's terms. But if we mean by "report the same" not "bring back word for word the same report" but rather "report, in different ways and from different terrains, the same single reality, bring back news in different languages from the same far country," then indeed we will

---

19. Ibid., 144.
20. Ibid., 147.
21. Cf. "Bluspels and Flalansferes: A Semantic Nightmare," in Lewis, *Rehabilitations and other Essays*, 157.

be asking for something that Lewis's mature writing delivers to us in great and generative abundance.

And it is that generative abundance, that generosity of spirit, that lavish provision of infinitely suggestive image and metaphor, of stories that are mythopoeic, not allegories themselves, but as Lewis said of Tolkien's work, constantly suggestive of incipient allegory, that is his great legacy to us: stories and poetry that not only kindle the imagination for Christ, but constitute in themselves an open door, an invitation to new and yet more generative works of imagination.

I would like to conclude these remarks on Lewis and imagination, not in literary critical, nor even in theological mode, but with imagination and poetry. So I shall try to give scholarship the kiss of life with a verse, and sum up what I have to say in a sonnet:

C. S. Lewis

From "beer and Beowulf" to the seven heavens,
Whose music you conduct from sphere to sphere,
You are our portal to those hidden havens
Whence we return to bless our being here.
Scribe of the Kingdom, keeper of the door
Which opens on to all we might have lost,
Ward of a word-hoard in the deep heart's core,
Telling the tale of Love from first to last.
Generous, capacious, open, free,
Your wardrobe-mind has furnished us with worlds
Through which to travel, whence we learn to see
Along the beam, and hear at last the heralds
Sounding their summons, through the stars that sing,
Whose call at sunrise brings us to our King.

— 3 —

Panel Discussion

What Can Twenty-First Century Apologetics Learn from C. S. Lewis?

THE DAY-LONG SYMPOSIUM IN St. Margaret's Church ended with a Panel Discussion. It was introduced on behalf of the Westminster Abbey Institute by Canon Andrew Tremlett, chaired by Dr. Michael Ward, and closed by the Dean of Westminster, the Very Revd. Dr. John Hall. On the panel were William Lane Craig, Michael Ramsden, Jeanette Sears, Peter S. Williams, and Judith Wolfe. What follows is an edited transcript of the evening's proceedings.[1]

TREMLETT: On our panel tonight I am pleased to welcome:

> Professor William Lane Craig, Research Professor of Philosophy at Talbot School of Theology, California, the author of many books including *Divine Foreknowledge and Human Freedom*, and *God, Time and Eternity*.

> Michael Ramsden, Director of the Oxford Centre for Christian Apologetics and Honorary Fellow of Wycliffe Hall, Oxford.

---

1. A video of this discussion is available on-line: https://youtu.be/jgnbr-68Vws.

The Reverend Dr. Jeanette Sears, writer and speaker, who did her PhD at Manchester and post-doc at Harvard. She's the author of *A Murder in Michaelmas*, *Pig's Progress*, and has a special interest in the Inklings and Dorothy L. Sayers.

Peter S. Williams is philosopher-in-residence at the Damaris Trust and a writer and Christian apologist. He's the author of *C. S. Lewis vs. the New Atheists* and *A Sceptic's Guide to Atheism*.

Last but not least, Dr. Judith Wolfe, Fellow of St. John's College, Oxford; co-editor of *C. S. Lewis and The Church: Essays in Honour of Walter Hooper* and General Editor of the *Journal of Inklings Studies*.

Please, would you welcome our panel? *[Applause]*

WARD: Before we come to the questions, I'm going to ask each of the panellists to make a very brief opening statement about what they regard as especially valuable or interesting about Lewis's work in Christian apologetics and what we might learn from his legacy today. First, Bill Craig.

CRAIG: Thank you. Dr. Ward has invited each of us to say three hundred words, or less, about, quote, "those aspects of Lewis's apologetic work which we regard as especially valuable and especially worth learning from." Here are my 296 words. *[Laughter]*

C. S. Lewis lived through and wrote during the height of the positivist era in Oxford, the times of A. J. Ayer and Antony Flew, of verificationism and the alleged meaninglessness of religious, ethical, and metaphysical discourse. He lived to see the crumbling of positivism and the advent of post-modernism.

I am so grateful that Lewis never succumbed to the bullying of modernism or the blandishments of post-modernism. He was consciously and uncompromisingly a pre-modern man, a dinosaur, as he put it. "I am," he declared, "a rationalist." Reason can apprehend truth, and truth is objective and knowable. He bucked conventional wisdom by presenting a variety of arguments for God's existence. And he rejected the relativity of history, arguing for the historical veracity of the Gospels' record of the life of Jesus of Nazareth. Lewis was thus a champion of both natural theology and Christian evidences. As such he modelled for us a well-rounded Christian apologetic on behalf of what he called "mere Christianity."

If I may speak personally, my own approach has been inspired by Lewis' model. I have self-consciously focused on the defence of "mere Christianity," based upon the twin pillars of God's existence, as demonstrated by natural theology, and the resurrection of Jesus, as established by historical-critical studies of the New Testament.

Finally, on a practical level, Lewis has been a model to me of the ministry of the published word. I'm struck by the fact that through the legacy of the works he left behind, Lewis has reached far more people for Christ since his death than he ever did during his life. This has motivated me, personally, to try to produce, in my own small way, a body of published work, which I hope, in God's providence, may outlive me as well.

WARD: And now, Michael Ramsden.

RAMSDEN: Well, what I learned from Lewis—I'm now working as a full-time Christian apologist—was really very simple and was said so beautifully and so eloquently in the lectures here this afternoon. And in one sense it was very simple: Truth has a revelatory function. One of the functions of Truth, it helps you to see things as they are, rather like if someone comes and gives you a complicated lecture and you have no idea what they said and someone turns to you and in a couple of minutes tells you and sums it up beautifully. On receiving the explanation you normally respond by saying, "Oh, I see." Not just simply that you understand but you now see something you were unable to see before. And what I found through Lewis' writings was this: he helped me to see things as they were.

We don't even bother praying for that which we can't even imagine to be true and in a world of growing scepticism and the kind of hostility that's already been referred to, C. S. Lewis was a master at presenting the truth so as to help us see things as they are: about the person of Christ, about the world we live in, and about who we are.

And one of the ways he did that as well, which I know has stuck with me and has influenced my own apologetics immensely, is his love for language and the importance of words. It's hard to read almost any of his apologetic work and not realise he's spent a huge amount of time on the defence of words.

I'm sure this has affected me in all kinds of ways. I happen to own the twenty-volume *Oxford English Dictionary*, which I keep in my study and regularly use. As someone once said, it's not the most interesting book to read, but it does explain every word as you go through [*Laughter*], and it gives you a true sense of what these words mean. Where might that meaning have changed in my audience and how might I recover this vocabulary so that people can see the truth and respond to it?

WARD: Jeanette Sears.

SEARS: Thank you. Well, I love Lewis, not just because of who he was, not just for his writings, but also because of how he talked about his writings, how he described his methodology and gave us pictures of how to do it, which makes us feel that perhaps we can do it as well, which is really rather important.

And so, first of all, I love the way he describes his works of apologetic, his non-fiction, his popular theology, as "works of translation." I love the idea of "translation," that you're translating something that can seem quite complicated or dull or too deep, perhaps. People feel they can't understand Christian doctrine, the faith as it's been handed down, but Lewis translates it for us into words we can understand, into images, into wonderful stories we actually want to read.

And he said that this was really easy. In one of his letters he says that he wants to start a school of translation, that it's a trick that anybody can learn. We all ought to be able to do it! So I think that's really encouraging from him that he wants everyone to do that.

And then, secondly, I love the fact that he described his works of fiction as works of "supposition"—they're supposals—and that you can think, "Well, what if? What if something happened? What if there was another planet with different species on it but they were in the same trouble as we were and they needed saving?" Or, "What if there are talking animals in a medieval forest and they also have a king, who's one of the animals, who is like a dying and rising god and you can get to know him in that context?"

So I love the idea of supposals or supposition, the "what if" side of his stories. All writers are creating other worlds, and the "Other" with a capital "O" that he wants you to meet in *his* Other World really is God. I think he does that brilliantly in his works of supposition.

And lastly, another word ending in "-tion." You've had translation, supposition, and now imitation: because I think it's Lewis the man that we love, as well as his works, isn't it? We've even had films about his life. How many Oxford academics have films made about their love lives? [*Laughter*] It's not usually that interesting!

He himself did attempt to imitate Christ: the *imitatio Christi*. He attempted to live like Christ, and we all know that phrase, "What would Jesus do?" Well, I think you can often ask yourself, "What would Lewis do, or think, or say?" and often you'd be absolutely spot on. So, that's the third "-tion."

That leads to my admiration, my inspiration, perhaps emulation as well, but can we expect another Lewis? I don't know. Perhaps we will want to talk about that tonight. Perhaps it will be someone or something completely different to Lewis. Aslan did say to Lucy in *Prince Caspian* when she was wanting Aslan to come and save them with a big roar in exactly the way he had in the first story, he said to her, "Dear one, things never happen the same way twice." So perhaps God's got something very different for us.

WARD: Peter Williams.

WILLIAMS: Researching my book *C. S. Lewis vs. the New Atheists*, it struck me that Lewis had been the old-fashioned kind of atheist who takes philosophy seriously. As an atheist, Lewis rejected the scientism characteristic of modernity. One might say that the atheism of Lucretius saved Lewis from the positivism of A. J. Ayer. Moreover, Lewis didn't lurch from the mistakes of modernism to the mistakes of postmodernism. His love of philosophy produced neither a narrow rationalism nor a romantic anti-rationalism, but a pre-modern wisdom.

Lewis knew that Reason requires faith in rational insight and he recognised the value of empirical facts without rejecting the transcendent facts of Truth, Goodness, and Beauty.

Lewis attended to arguments against naturalism and for theism. In *Mere Christianity* he popularised the sort of moral argument for God developed in W. R. Sorley's Gifford lectures on *Moral Values and the Idea of God*. However, it's the reasons that Lewis gave for abandoning a naturalistic worldview that resonate most incessantly today. It's not only in reading, say, Alvin Plantinga's anti-naturalism argument from evolution that one is reminded of Lewis' anti-naturalistic apologetic in *Miracles*; it's frequently in reading non-theistic scholars like Thomas Nagel, Anthony O'Hear, or Raymond Tallis.

One can't separate Lewis's philosophy from his fiction. His philosophy often uses story to elicit rational insight. Consider his "Meditation in a Toolshed." His fiction fleshes out a philosophical skeleton, allowing us to drink in the atmosphere of a philosophy. I particularly enjoy *The Abolition of Man* through *That Hideous Strength*.

Lewis teaches us the importance of being nourished by a community of scholarship, including voices of dissent jointly dedicated to following the argument wherever it leads.

Finally, Lewis helps us transcend the "chronological snobbery" of our own age through the reading of old books—not least those by Lewis himself.

WARD: And now, Judith Wolfe.

WOLFE: Thank you. I was struck by something that Richard Dawkins said in a recent debate with Rowan Williams at the Sheldonian Theatre in Oxford. A member of the audience asked him what sense he could he make of the senseless tragedy of the violent death of a young child? And Richard Dawkins stared at her and said: "I don't see any problem or tragedy here. It might be sad for the mother, but it's nothing other than the workings of evolution."

And I think Lewis came to the same conclusion that, for the purely evolutionary thinker, there is no problem of evil because there is nothing that qualifies *as* evil. The natural evolutionary order gives us no standards of justice or goodness and, therefore, also nothing that can count as violating them and therefore constituting evil. And so for the purely evolutionary thinker our very deeply human responses of outrage or indignation at evil must be written off as pure illusions.

So, when Lewis came to God I think it was not so much as a fool-proof answer to the problem of evil, or other problems like it, but rather as a reality that accommodated, made possible, our feelings in their full range of outrage and indignation and so forth; something that made the problem of evil, and others like it, possible in the first place.

And I think that this approach to apologetics, of not starting from pre-packaged abstract, nicely arranged, rational arguments but rather from attentiveness to the full-range of what makes us human and seeing what view of the world can accommodate that, is something that we should emulate as apologists and, indeed, as Christians more generally.

WARD: Thank you all very much. Now to our questions: and the first question is one that Canon Vernon White, despite having lost his voice, managed to croak out to me during one of the breaks [*Laughter*], and it relates to a very important aspect of Lewis's thought. Perhaps his most serious work of apologetics was *Miracles: A Preliminary Study*, and Canon White was asking about what the panel thought of Lewis's argument in *Miracles* as regards the apologetic value of Reason itself, and how Reason may be understood as *relatively* supernatural to our material organisms and therefore indicative, perhaps, of something which is *fully* supernatural. So, panel, what do you make of *Miracles*?

WOLFE: Do the philosophers want to start?

WILLIAMS: It was something that I mentioned in my opening remarks: how very contemporary Lewis's discussion of the problems of a naturalistic worldview in trying to account for the nature of human rationality is. It's something that's still very much being discussed in philosophical literature today. The most recent edition of the world's biggest circulating philosophy of religion journal, *Philosophia Christi*, for example, had an article in it by a contemporary philosopher defending C. S. Lewis's argument from *Miracles* and interacting with Alvin Plantinga's similar argument—which he gave a number of years ago, in *Warrant and Proper Function*, where Alvin Plantinga specifically footnoted that his argument bore some similarities with the argument that Lewis had given.[2]

So, it's still very much alive and, as I say, it's actually, I think, increasingly a point of tension that you can see atheist writers recognising within a naturalistic worldview. If you read Thomas Nagel's recent book, *Mind and Cosmos*, there you see passages that read like, "Good grief! Am I reading *Miracles* by C. S. Lewis?" No, I'm reading a book by an atheist philosopher wrestling with how do I, how can you, put Reason into a naturalistic worldview?—and saying in the end, "We don't know how to. I don't see how to."

WOLFE: And then indeed he says, "I really hope that God is not the answer to this."

WILLIAMS: "But..."

WOLFE: "But I don't know what else is!"

WILLIAMS: But he's really struggling to try and find a way of doing it.

WOLFE: Very much so, yes.

RAMSDEN: I remember speaking in an Oxford University college about eighteen years ago and the Master of the college had started out life in that place as an undergraduate student, done his post-graduate degree there, became a lecturer there, went up through the ranks, ended up as Master of the college

---

2. Cf. Goetz, "The Argument from Reason," *Philosophia Christi* 15.1 (2013).

and, um, I was speaking in chapel that Sunday evening and he happened to be there and it was full and at the end he said, "Could you come back to my study for a drink?" So I thought, either I'm going to be told off or asked a question.

Thankfully, it was a question and as he handed me a glass of port he simply said, "You know, when I was a young academic here we all used to make fun of C. S. Lewis and we even had a debate in this college about shutting down the chapel because it was obsolete and we thought we should convert it into a second library. It would be useful to the students who were here."

In my sermon one of my points had been from *Miracles* and C. S. Lewis's argument about Reason and how do we account for the process of Reason and how can we trust Reason itself?

And then he said to me, "You know, we used to make fun of him. But today in the chapel it was filled. There wasn't a single spare seat." And he said, "If you went into the Senior Common Room of my college, every don I know is reading a C. S. Lewis book right now."

So I think this is one of the remarkable legacies of Lewis. We think of people as being "prophetic," and we often use that term in the sense of telling the future. Any good Old Testament scholar will tell you, "That's a minor use of the word 'prophecy.' Biblically, it's not about telling the future, it's about interpreting the times, and I think Lewis was able to interpret the times by revealing things as they really were and just show naturally where it would go. And I think that's one of the reasons why he's still so contemporary, and why almost any book on apologetics you pick up today is almost bound to have a Lewis quote. As a matter of fact, maybe someone should write a book on apologetics *without* a Lewis quote in it [*Laughter*] and see what would happen.

I remember to my shame on the Reason question that you raise, coming up with this myself one day as a postgraduate student with my professor of philosophy, who described himself as a "born again atheist." We were at 2 a.m. and I came up with this argument from Reason and I was so impressed with myself and thought, "Wow, I could write this up!" And then I realised at about 3 a.m., having finished the conversation, that actually Lewis had already said that and I just momentarily forgot where he'd put it [*Laughter*]. So, I think that just demonstrates how he gets into your mind and imagination, even when you're not conscious that he's necessarily with you.

WARD: Thank you. Bill Craig?

CRAIG: Well, I would just say that one thing that we need to keep in mind with respect to these arguments—and I think this is such a perfect illustration—is that contemporary Christian philosophy, which is experiencing a tremendous renaissance, stands on Lewis's shoulders and moves beyond him. It's not as though we should simply read C. S. Lewis as the final thought on these arguments. Alvin Plantinga, in particular, has developed this evolutionary argument against naturalism with a tremendous rigour and precision that Lewis didn't have.

What Lewis grasped in a kind of rough and ready way, Plantinga has developed in a very meticulous and rigorous way, to show that, if our cognitive faculties are the product of naturalistic evolutionary processes, then we cannot have any confidence in the reliability of our cognitive faculties. But if that's true, it's self-defeating, because you can't have any confidence in the reliability of those faculties in telling you that naturalism is true or that this argument is correct. So, Plantinga says that naturalism has a built-in defeater and so cannot be rationally affirmed; and so I would just encourage all of us who are studying apologetics not to take Lewis as the final word, but to use him as a springboard for further reflection, further advancement, in developing these arguments.

SEARS: And what I would like to add to that as well is that when I read *Miracles* in my teens, I was reading a book of really quite sophisticated philosophy as a teenager who normally would be reading about pop music or rock stars or whatever, and Lewis was such a brilliant communicator that I was absolutely riveted and it felt like the most exciting subject I'd ever read. It was great to know that, as a Christian, Reason was on my side somehow. Instead of it being "Reason versus Faith," I, as this young tiny Christian, as it were, could actually have Reason on my side when I was relating with non-Christians. And so it was a tremendous encouragement on that level too.

WARD: Thank you. All right: from the value of Reason we turn to the dangers of Imagination. This is a question from Sarah de Nordwall, who describes herself as a poet: "What do we have to do to ensure that our imaginations don't lead us into spiritually dangerous places?" Who would like to come in on that?

SEARS: Well, I think Lewis was a great believer in intellectual chastity. I think that's probably how he would put it. Our minds have to be open to God and God's Spirit, and I think it's part of our daily spiritual discipline, you know, what we open our minds to is incredibly important. And I think Lewis was a very disciplined person and certainly took this very seriously, what he fed his mind on, and so I think he would place it in our daily spiritual disciplines, probably, wouldn't he? Because the visual was so important to him: what we look at is incredibly important and, of course, it becomes part of our brains forever, so we have to be very careful what we look at, ensuring that it's something in line with what God would want.

WARD: Yes, in fact he talked about discipline—disciplining his imagination—even before he was a theist, let alone a Christian. If I myself may make a brief comment on this point: I think one of Lewis's own ways of answering this question would be to say that the Imagination needs to be operated in consort with the Reason. Imagination that just runs amok without any rational control over it is not true Imagination, as Lewis understands it; it's merely the "imaginary." It has no necessary value in itself. It's just like the muddle of visions that floods through our minds at night in our dreams. The "organ of meaning," the Imagination, needs to submit its findings to the "natural organ of truth," Reason, for an adjudication to be made about the value of those meanings. Are they true? Are they false?

WOLFE: And that, of course, is the substance of his "Great War" with Owen Barfield, his good friend, who believed that the Imagination could apprehend truth that Reason was not capable of reaching. C. S. Lewis made the very clear distinction that we heard about earlier this afternoon, that Reason is the natural organ of truth, whereas the Imagination is the organ of meaning, but the Imagination has to submit to the judgment of Truth.

And I think that when he became a Christian later on, he saw this organ of truth not only as Reason but also as Revelation and so an adherence to revealed doctrine was always something that he held on to as a means of disciplining his imagination and keeping it in its bounds, just as Coleridge, of course, does when he frets about his "wayward imagination" in the *Eolian Harp*, for example, and then goes back to doctrine as reining it in.

WARD: Thank you, Judith. Anybody else?

RAMSDEN: Dr. Guite—it's funny *we're* all up here: we've got people in the audience who know more about this than we do; who've *forgotten* more about this than we ever learned in the first place!—Dr. Guite addressed this question specifically in his lecture, I think, very, very well. So, I'm going to refer you back to that recording and claim that I had all of those thoughts in my head before he presented them so eloquently this afternoon. [*Laughter*]

WARD: Let's move on to our third question, from Jenny Peterson, which rather picks up on the point that Jeanette was just making about the importance of what we look at. The question asks: "Lewis wrote and broadcast before the current era with its cultural dominance of visual media in film and television. In what ways might these new visual media inhibit or enhance Christian apologetics?"

CRAIG: I can say something about the way in which it can enhance the reach of Christian apologetics. I think that YouTube is an incredible tool for apologetics and world evangelisation, because through the internet these materials get into all sorts of contexts where persons would never read a book or have access to library materials. And I have found that making a YouTube archive of talks, debates, interviews, panels of this sort, will reach thousands, sometimes hundreds of thousands of people through YouTube.

So we, as Christian apologists, need to be very aggressive and pro-active in using YouTube and the internet to disseminate these materials.

RAMSDEN: I have to admit I've been very sceptical about the new media, you know, fuelled by the comment that YouTube, Twitter, and Facebook were going to merge into a new URL: You-Twit-Face-dot-com. [*Laughter*] I think maybe that's coming from seeing the irresponsible use of it.

And it's quite interesting, I guess, if you look at Lewis's life: he became a voice to the nation through his broadcast talks during the Second World War when actually there were no competing media, which is why he became such a household name. And he did so responsibly, without a glib apologetic, but speaking in a situation where hundreds of thousands of people were dying and the cost was very high, which I think gave a reality to what he did.

Then I think, sadly, maybe a lot of irresponsible and sensationalist voices came into the media and I think a lot of Christians sort of recoiled from that slightly, thinking, "I don't want to be tarred with that brush." Maybe there was a bit of a vacuum left.

I have a feeling if he were here, he might well say, "Look, nobody knew much about radio back then. It was quite a new medium for this kind of thing, and you should fully engage with it." I think that's what he would he would say. I mean, you may have a better insight than . . .

WARD: No, I'm sure you're right. I mean, Lewis was one of the first "media dons" wasn't he? He and his Magdalen colleague, A. J. P. Taylor, they were a new breed, and yes, it was a very modern medium—the wireless, I mean. Not the radio, the *wireless*. [*Laughter*] What do we mean by "wireless" now? Something quite different!

WILLIAMS: A word as well about Christian use of media in the less overt way: I mean, Bill's talking about the sort of overt Christian apologetics and the way in which you can communicate that into different situations through YouTube and so on. But I think that our engagement with, say, Christian film-writers and film-makers and so on, especially, can take a leaf out of Lewis's book of "supposals"; of doing things not in the sort of direct "here's a gospel presentation with an altar-call at the end" kind of way, but in that way of teasing the imagination with the little "spears of sunlight" that Malcolm was talking about earlier today, to get people thinking in terms of the big, the deep, spiritual, moral issues of "life, the universe, and everything."

To get people thinking about Christ, first you have to get them to think. Getting people thinking about life, the universe, and everything, opening up those issues, that in itself is a really positive part of the engagement that I think Christians are called to in today's media.

SEARS: And of course we're not just wanting people to think, we're wanting them to love. If we're going to be Christians in the new media, the irony is that we want to portray God's love and loving relationships, in visual and written media, for people who perhaps only look at that in order for them to then *leave* it and actually be involved in real relationships with God, with other people in the church, and so on . . .

WILLIAMS: . . . following in Lewis's footsteps by giving media portrayals of goodness that are interesting and captivating.

SEARS: Yes.

WARD: This, er, what was it? You-Twit-Face-dot-com? [*Laughter*] This new media phenomenon which results to a large extent in globalisation, with national boundaries now meaning much less than they did, touches upon our next question from Rod Miller: "Is Lewis really growing mainstream in Britain besides the Poets' Corner Memorial, and, if so, is there a particular aspect of his writing or thinking that is fuelling the growth? In a related point, why is Lewis more popular in the U.S. than in the U.K?"

We have one American and four Brits on the panel. I don't know, Bill, if you would like to touch on the popularity in the U.S?

CRAIG: I think Alister McGrath is probably right when he says in his biography of Lewis that what happened in the United States is that Lewis connected with southern American evangelical Christianity.

Since about 1948, in the United States, with Billy Graham, Carl F. H. Henry, Harold Arkingate, and so forth, evangelicalism was born and has come to displace the old mainline Protestant denominations in the United States as the most culturally significant expression of Christianity. Evangelicals connected with C. S. Lewis and, rightly or wrongly, they saw him as one of them, in a sense, and I think that has fuelled his enormous popularity in the United States.

Lewis's *Mere Christianity* transcends denominational boundaries as well and makes him appealing. I understand from discussions with some of my colleagues that Lewis is tremendously popular in the Mormon Church and that a good many Mormon people are moving away from traditional LDS doctrine, which thinks of God as a physical humanoid being on a planet in outer space, to a more classical theism of God as a transcendent creator of the universe. So, Lewis has had an incredible influence even within so unexpected a denomination or confession as the Mormon Church.

WOLFE: I think there are two points to make about the British reception of Lewis. One is that now that he's been dead for fifty years he's moved from a very annoying or almost threatening contemporary to a classic writer, whom one can appreciate from a distance, almost as a primary source, so to say, about which one can debate and so forth. So there's a certain distance and classical status that allows people to talk about him in new ways.

But the second point I think is that, as you said, it's not so much that more people are reading him, but rather that it's become more suitable for polite society to talk about it.

I think that people have been reading him in their closets, and academics in particular have been reading him in their closets all this time, but now that people like Rowan

Williams or Alister McGrath and some others have stepped up and engaged with him publicly and on a rigorous level, it's suddenly possible to talk about him, as I say, in polite society.

To look slightly further afield, it's also interesting to note that in countries like Germany, for example, where there is a strong division—and speaking now as a theologian—in countries like Germany where there is a strong division between Lutherans or Protestants and Catholics, it seems to be mainly the Catholic academics who are engaging with Lewis and doing so in a more lively way than the Lutherans, because for the Catholics he is a champion of a natural theology, an approach to God as in some way continuous with human reason. Whereas the Protestant theologians, who are very strongly emphasising a theology of the cross, of *dis*continuity between God and the world, are quite wary of him. So there's a much stronger confessional divide, I think, at least among theologians, in those countries than here.

WARD: Jeanette?

SEARS: I'm tempted to agree with Lewis now being a classic and so having a different status and that making a big effect. I'm tempted to say that people become popular when someone can make money out of them and it's certainly the case with the films now. We all know that the films of the Narnia Chronicles came on the back of the Tolkien films in many respects, and obviously huge amounts of money were being made out of those—and of course, they're very filmic stories—so that makes a lot of sense.

But probably the writer who has been the main Christian novelist recently in this country has been G. P. Taylor, who has written Christian novels and originally got a huge amount of money for them. But as soon, he says, as soon as he started to be called "the next C. S. Lewis," he was dropped like a hot brick by the media. So, it's a two-edged sword really.

WARD: Thank you. In addition to the written questions that have been submitted, I've asked two people in the audience to ask a question, and I've asked them because they each represent a very significant Lewis institution in the United States.

So let's start with a question from Dr. Stanley Mattson, who is President of the Lewis Foundation. The Foundation have, over many years, restored Lewis's home, The Kilns, and run many successful Oxbridge conferences. So, Stan, what question do you have for the panel?

MATTSON: Thank you, Michael. I pondered your invitation to ask a question and, as I did, I was somewhat surprised with the particular question that I came up with, but it is a sincere question and it has to do with this: I think one of the things that most amazes me about Lewis is simply the extraordinarily prodigious nature of his work: over forty published books; thousands of letters, largely written with a pen. With a pen, mind you! I don't know how in the world a human being, who was not a professor with a big endowed Chair, but who, in fact, was a tutor, working with students one-on-one, and all the while so incredibly engaged in life, whether with the Inklings, hiking, attending services, or broadcasting on the BBC, did it. I marvel at it, I really do. The phrase that came to me was "incarnational apologetics," in that his life was so invested in every idea, in every person. I wonder if you'd comment on that? If you've had that experience of being overwhelmed, knowing yourself how diligent one has to be to write just one book, let alone forty, and yet find such time for others. Would one of you like to comment?

WARD: Thank you very much. So I think the question might boil down to emulation. How can we possibly consider emulating someone who's a giant among men? Is it possible? Should we even try?

SEARS: Yes, . . . well: we need to listen to God. We need to be like the Green Lady on Perelandra who, before she answers a question she's quiet and she's listening to Maleldil and she only answers when she knows what Maleldil wants her to say. So I'm tempted just to sit here quietly until the Lord shows me what to say. [*Laughter*] It's a question of calling, isn't it? And when God gives a calling, He also empowers you to do what

He's asking you do to. And so, thank God that He did call Lewis to that work and that He empowered him to do it.

And we all have different callings. And it's possible that even if we only wrote one book, that might be *the* thing that converts thousands. We only have to think of the Lord Jesus himself who never wrote any of his stories down and . . . look at the effect He's had! [*Laughter*]

WARD: Bill?

CRAIG: John Wesley once distinguished, in an address to his Methodist ministers, between what he called "innate abilities" and "acquired abilities" and, if you don't have the innate abilities that a C. S. Lewis had, you're not going to be able to produce that kind of body of work.

Nevertheless, there are acquired abilities that we can all strive for, and I'm thinking here of things like self-discipline, time-management, setting of priorities, having a vision for writing, if that's what we feel called to do. And I think that these kinds of abilities can be acquired and can help us to be surprisingly productive.

One method that I've adopted in my work is what my wife Jan and I called the Tortoise Method. In the story of the Tortoise and the Hare, the tortoise, just by steady, slow, plodding, eventually wins the race. And so if you can just write a paragraph one morning, or a few pages that day, it's incredible how, after the weeks go by, it begins to accumulate. So I do think that through these kinds of self-disciplining activities one can maximise whatever innate potentialities the Lord has given us so as to try to produce a body of written work, for those of us who are called to be writers, that will hopefully be read even after we are gone.

RAMSDEN: I've had a working relationship with Professor Alister McGrath now for fifteen years and when that started I thought, "Gosh, every time he writes something I should really buy it and read it"—and the dear man's almost bankrupted me. [*Laughter*] So, I think some people have a natural writing gift. Some people you pray that they wrote slightly less. [*Laughter*]

But I think we as a culture and maybe sometimes even as a church, we haven't always encouraged people in the expression of their faith through the arts. Not as an illustration of something else, but as a vehicle of communication for that something. And I think we've paid the price for that in some ways. We haven't recognised the role of the arts as the vehicle by which this can happen. You look at Jesus Christ, who in many senses was a metaphorical theologian: he wasn't making complex theological points and then illustrating them with simple stories for children. The parables he told were the very vehicle by which he was delivering his theology. The parables weren't an "illustration" of something else.

And I think that's something that the arts are uniquely gifted to do. Art becomes the medium and the vehicle by which things can be passed on and I think that's the one part of Lewis's example that we really need to see encouraged, so that people can find the theological expression *through* poetry, *through* novels, *through* short stories, *through* plays; to really engage with people out there, through that medium where the message is embedded.

WILLIAMS: I'd just like to pick up on that in talking about Lewis's embrace of the transcendental values of Truth and Goodness and Beauty. I think that the church historically here has been pretty good on keeping the importance of Truth and the Word of God and so on, and of course, Goodness and morals and ethics. The church is very big on talking about ethics but has, frankly, largely dropped the ball on Beauty.

But Beauty encompasses the other two and Beauty is that which is truly worthy of being admired, and incorporates Truth and Goodness, and the widest transcendental value is Beauty. I think Lewis should be a prod and a reminder to the Western church to not take our eye off the place of Beauty in church, in liturgy, in communication, in apologetics.

WARD: Thank you. Judith, do you want to add anything to that?

WOLFE: Well, I completely agree with Peter. I mean, if we look at Lewis's productivity, I think emulating him will become a very frustrating task, but if we look at the habits of mind and of heart that he cultivated then those are something that we certainly can emulate: the attentiveness to others that you mentioned, Stan, the self-discipline and so forth. And what fruits arise from that is not up to us, but we can certainly cultivate those habits and see what comes.

WARD: Thank you. One thing that occurs to me is this: Michael Ramsden, you're in charge of the Oxford Centre for Christian Apologetics and I teach in an apologetics program for Houston Baptist University—we're trying to train up young apologists, but it occurs to me that Lewis never went though apologetic training. In fact, he was a bit of a lone wolf. For a couple or three years of his most formative period in his middle teens, he wasn't even schooled in the English Public School system, but was privately tutored, one-to-one, by William Kirkpatrick. He wasn't part of a school. And I think that's not unimportant in understanding Lewis's abilities, that he was to a certain extent a "Free Thinker"; he wasn't trammelled by expectations and conventions in the same way that most of his contemporaries were.

I read once that, of the top ten patent holders at ICI, who hold the greatest number of patents, four out of those ten had *not* received a university education. Which is extremely interesting. There can be a way in which we squelch originality by over-training people. So it may be that the great new apologist who's going to wow the twenty-first century is not even at a school. Who knows?

The second question from the audience is going to come from Dr. Jerry Root. Jerry is a representative of the Wade Center at Wheaton College, Illinois. The Wade Center is the primary collection of Lewis's papers and documents; it was established first of all in the 1960s by Professor Clyde S. Kilby and it's now the central place in the world if you want to study anything to do with Lewis. Jerry is on its Advisory Board. So, Jerry, what is your question?

ROOT: This is picking up on Dr. Mattson's question. The book *C. S. Lewis: Defender of the Faith* concludes, "Lewis himself was his greatest apology; the apologetic that walked in shoes." Could you comment about his humility, his magnanimity, his willingness to shoulder the weight of his neighbour's glory, and how this lends to his persuasiveness as an apologist and as a Christian?

WARD: Who would like to come in on that?

RAMSDEN: I feel, as the most humble member of the panel, I should comment first. [*Laughter*] I think the point you make is a very good one. If the gospel is true, it should be seen as well as heard and, most of all, seen in the life of the Christian. And it's very interesting that, if we were to say, "Look, close your eyes and imagine a thoroughly uncompromised and uncompromising Christian" and then we were to say, "What figure came to mind?" the answer is probably someone who was quite difficult, awkward, hard, thoroughly outspoken, maybe. If you look at the book of Galatians, which we know to be one of the earliest of all the epistles and the books that we have in the New Testament, Paul there has several concerns, one of which is, "What is the real gospel? And what isn't the real gospel?" But then he has another concern, the apostle Paul, in Galatians, which is, "What is the true characteristic of a Christian?" And he tells us how to tell the true person who is a Christian from the fake. In Galatians 5:22 he says there's a fruit of the spirit, just one fruit, and when you taste that fruit, it should taste of love, joy . . . you don't need me to recite it. Some of you know little songs that you've learned by heart, listing all of those characteristics.

Now, I find that really interesting. What the apostle Paul is saying there is, "Bite me," but in a very nice way. [*Laughter*] And he's saying, "Look, if someone is claiming this is true and real in their life, you should be able to taste it in their life and what you should taste should be this love and this peace and this joy and this gentleness," and so on.

If, however, what you taste is murder, envy, lust, strife, you have the right to question their claim to have had this transforming, life-changing encounter with the person of Christ.

I think that's one of the reasons why we like people like C. S. Lewis. I also have the privilege of working very closely with a guy called Professor John Lennox who, you know, if you ever heard him speak you feel half way through his talk that you want to go up onto the platform and give him a big hug [*Laughter*] because he's so gentle, and his demeanour and his manner of delivery is very attractive. I think it's something that we need to recover and maybe become even more challenging at times as Christians ourselves, to say, "Well, what does the church look like? What, what does it taste like? Does it taste like this?" Because that's what we're told it should.

And so let's not be compromising about that. Let's be thoroughly uncompromising when it comes to things like, "Is this fruit? Does it taste like this in our life?" And I think the church would be a lot stronger and have a much larger platform for its message if we were.

So I'm sure it was part of how Lewis commended his own message—through his own lifestyle and embodied by all those letters he wrote. I think it was a general principle, wasn't it? He tried to respond to every letter he got. I mean, I struggle responding to my emails! I would love to know what he would've made of email! Maybe he would've seen that as some form of demonic attack. I don't know. That's how I feel, but . . . [*Laughter*] . . . but it just shows how he valued the person. They had taken time to write to him: he wanted to write back to them. And he did.

SEARS: Speaking as someone who did actually give John Lennox a hug once . . . . [*Laughter*] As I get older and lots of my friends are having to care for elderly relatives and as my own mother gets older and so on, the word "carer" is starting to take on a whole new meaning. I'm starting to see Lewis as a carer. He cared for so many people throughout his life, obviously, for Mrs. Moore as she got older; for his wife, Joy, when she was ill; and for lots of neighbours and relatives and, particularly, his brother as well. And for animals, he loved animals and he cared about nature.

And there's just that caring attitude, that taking responsibility for someone who's got a need. If you're there, you're the one who looks after that person, despite what it means clearing up off the floor, or whatever. Lewis was really right there in his caring.

WOLFE: And I think that one important thing about humility in particular is that, for Lewis, humility was not just a spiritual virtue, it was also an intellectual virtue. It was not something that you had to tie yourself in some sort of spiritual knot to achieve, making yourself seem worse than you really are or anything like that, but rather he emphasises again and again in his writings that a good writer is one who makes you not look at him but rather makes you see through the lens that he is seeing through.

And this outward movement of the mind and of the eyes towards the reality out there and our way of seeing it, rather than looking at ourselves, is something that he valued very much in literature and in scholarship and, therefore, also embodied in his life quite naturally, I think.

WILLIAMS: The famous aphorism on humility just sprung to mind, which is this: "Humility is not thinking less of yourself but thinking of yourself less."

WARD: Bill, do you have anything to add to that?

CRAIG: Well, I think Jerry is right in reminding us that we've got to walk the walk as well as talk the talk, but I have to say I think it's striking, really, how little of C. S. Lewis's personal life comes through in his works, apart from, say, *Surprised by Joy*.

He doesn't put himself forward. He doesn't tell anecdotes about "I was walking in the quad the other day and spoke to this professor" or "a student said this and that to me." Really, you can appreciate his apologetic works without knowing anything about Mrs. Moore or his brother or his life. So I don't think it's true that the effectiveness of his work depends upon "his living it out in his personal life." I was really surprised by a lot of his personal life when I read McGrath's biography of Lewis. His works stand on their own, I guess, is what I'm trying to say, independent of life, because in most cases the man doesn't intrude into his books in a personal way, which is perhaps a mark of humility itself.

WARD: Yes, I think he deliberately tried to keep himself off stage as much as possible and that's part of what *Mere Christianity* is about, isn't it? Because he's not wanting to say, "This is *my* religion," he's wanting to say "This is the broad central mainstream of the Faith to which pretty much every Christian could subscribe."

"But I, myself," he says, "am not anyone special. I'm a very ordinary layman of the Church of England"—which is a vast understatement! [*Laughter*]

But would that we were all that way, in a sense. You see what he's trying to say: that he's not extraordinarily virtuous; he's just ordinary. He's neither particularly High nor particularly Low nor particularly anything else. He's not trying to convert you to a particular brand of Christianity or, indeed, a particular churchmanship within Anglicanism; he's just wanting to give you something beyond all the denominations, or within all the denominations.

We have our last question now, after which I will ask Professor Don King to come and read a closing poem. This final question comes from A. J. Finch: "What particular books or articles of Lewis have impacted the panellists especially and should be better known today?"

CRAIG: Wow, we're all going, "Gosh, where do we begin?" you know!

WILLIAMS: Can I jump in?

WARD: Of course.

WILLIAMS: *The Abolition of Man*: a very short book, three lectures. *The Abolition of Man*, I think, is one of those very prophetic books about our times; it should be read next to Aldous Huxley's *Brave New World* for understanding the modern world. I like it for its defence of the objectivity of Beauty, of Knowledge, but also for not wanting to go into the sort of shallow rationalism that we've talked about, for seeing the way through this modernist/post-modernist dilemma that the world has got itself into. The way he resolves that and his defence of objective values (which you also find in essays like "The Poison of Subjectivism" and "De Futilitate") makes it a particular favourite of mine.

WARD: There's an interesting book about *The Abolition of Man*, which is too little known. It's by Lord Hailsham, sometime Lord Chancellor, who thought very highly of *The Abolition of Man* himself, and wrote this little book about it called *Values: Collapse or Cure?* So you're right there with Quintin Hogg, Peter! Anybody else want to come in on this?

WOLFE: I think that there are some essays and works of Lewis that have gained new popularity through being mined quite a lot recently, and I think "De Futilitate" and "The Poison of Subjectivism" and so forth belong to those—having been worked up by people like Alvin Plantinga in very interesting and rigorous ways.

I think that there are some other essays whose main argument or idea hasn't really been touched upon very much at all by academia, and I think that "Transposition," in particular, and "The Funeral of a Great Myth" as well, are some of those and I'm waiting to see whether people will pick those up and make something of them in the way that things like *Miracles* have been made something of. So those would be some of my recommendations, I suppose.

WARD: Thank you. Jeanette?

SEARS: I would say almost any of his letters, really. I've been amazed, reading through his letters, how I can read them almost like *Lectio Divina*, where it's like contemplative reading. There is so much of his faith in there, so much good advice, so much of God. And he can't write a dull sentence! It's fantastic.

WARD: Michael?

RAMSDEN: My most surprising Lewis learning experience by far was buying a copy of *The Screwtape Letters* read aloud by John Cleese. [*Laughter*] I never thought Basil Fawlty would teach me theology [*Laughter*]! I tried reading the book and I think I read the first six letters in one day and it was almost too rich. I put it down and forgot about it. Then I discovered those recordings and I listened to them one per day in my car and had to discipline myself to press "stop" and not go any further. It was a remarkable experience.

Both hearing them read out, and also just thinking and reflecting on how much was packed in there, really surprised me. They're deceptively simple but actually much deeper, and I think they open up the whole question of, "Is there a spiritual realm to life and does it interact with us?" "Is there a battle and struggle that's going on around us that we're not aware of?" I don't know if you can get hold of it anymore, but try John Cleese reading *The Screwtape Letters*.

WARD: It's being read this week, isn't it, on Radio 4 by Simon Russell Beale?

WOLFE: Really?

WILLIAMS: They should have got Michael McIntyre. [*Laughter*]

WARD: There's also a recording by Andy Serkis. Evidently, lots of actors are wanting to take the part.

Do we have any offerings from this side of the panel?

CRAIG: For me, as I shared in my opening remarks, it hasn't been so much any particular work of Lewis that has been influential as it has been his serving as a role model for Christian apologetics. As a young student, for me, Francis Schaeffer and Edward J. Carnell were more shaping influences on my thought and then later Alvin Plantinga; but Lewis as a role model, I think, has been important in his defence of *Mere Christianity* and his endorsement of the project of natural theology and Christian evidences in defence of the Christian faith. And in that model I follow and try to emulate Lewis.

WARD: Thank you. Answering for myself, I would say one of Lewis's works that ought to be better known is the essay with the title "Bluspels and Flalansferes: A Semantic Nightmare," which has actually been quoted from several times today, in the definitions of Imagination as the organ of meaning and Reason as the natural organ of truth.

It's a terribly titled essay. If Lewis had called it "The Importance of Metaphor in All Our Knowing," everybody would have flocked to this essay. It's a very deep and seminal case that he makes and it should be better known.

As regards my own favourite work, I think I would probably cite his last novel, *Till We Have Faces*. Lewis himself regarded it as easily his best work. I understand that Rowan Williams thinks most highly of that title, among all of Lewis's works, and I share his opinion. It's an amazingly deep, rich, mysterious novel, which is hard to conceptualise, hard to understand except while you are reading it because it is truly mythic, I think. In order to understand it you have to read it ... and re-read it. [*Laughter*]. And then *re*-re-read it. [*Laughter*]

We're approaching our last few minutes so I think at this juncture I shall ask Professor Don King to come and close proceedings for us by reading the poem: "The Apologist's Evening Prayer," after which we can draw the whole event to an end.

KING: As one who's been reading Lewis's poetry for forty years I would add: some of you might want to begin reading Lewis's poetry!

"The Apologist's Evening Prayer" wasn't published until 1964, but it appears in a letter in 1942, and I think it picks up on the question that Jerry Root asked a few moments ago.

"The Apologist's Evening Prayer"

From all my lame defeats and oh! much more
From all the victories that I seemed to score;
From cleverness shot forth on Thy behalf
At which, while angels weep, the audience laugh;
From all my proofs of Thy divinity,
Thou, who wouldst give no sign, deliver me.

Thoughts are but coins. Let me not trust, instead
Of Thee, their thin-worn image of Thy head.
From all my thoughts, even from my thoughts of Thee,
O thou, fair Silence, fall, and set me free.
Lord of the narrow gate and the needle's eye,
Take from me all my trumpery lest I die."

WARD: Thank you, Don. For those who may not know, Don King is the editor of a new critical edition of the collected poems of C.S. Lewis, published by Kent State University Press, and the author of a study of Lewis's poetry, entitled simply *C.S. Lewis, Poet*, also from Kent State. It seemed appropriate, on the eve of the unveiling of Lewis's memorial in Poets' Corner, and at the end of this discussion of his apologetic legacy, to conclude with one of his own poems, in which he meditates so self-critically on the experience of being a Christian apologist. So, thank you again, Don. And, please, everyone, as we close, thank the panel. [*Applause*]

HALL: Ladies and gentlemen, as the panel leaves, on behalf of the Dean and Chapter, I'd like to express our thanks to Michael Ward in particular, who has been a key agent of this whole project. Vernon has driven it as far as we're concerned, but since Michael has asked us to thank the panel, may I ask you in turn to thank Michael? [*Applause*]

I'm thrilled to be looking forward to dedicating the Memorial to C. S. Lewis tomorrow in Poets' Corner, but this has been a wonderful curtain-raiser and a wonderful inspiration for many of us who don't know Lewis as well as we might and are now determined to get to know him better.

As one who read *The Screwtape Letters* and other titles when I was a teenager, and was very inspired by them and very much encouraged by them, it's wonderful to have been brought back to C. S. Lewis in this way. I'm myself grateful for today and looking forward to tomorrow. [*Applause*]

PART TWO

— 4 —

Memorial Service

Westminster Abbey

A SERVICE TO DEDICATE
A MEMORIAL
TO
C. S. LEWIS
WRITER, SCHOLAR, APOLOGIST

Friday 22nd November 2013
Noon

"In reading great literature I become a thousand men and yet remain myself. Like the night sky in the Greek poem, I see with a myriad eyes, but it is still I who see. Here, as in worship, in love, in moral action, and in knowing, I transcend myself; and am never more myself than when I do."

C. S. Lewis

Clive Staples "Jack" Lewis
1898–1963

THE C. S. LEWIS MEMORIAL STONE

*I believe in Christianity as I believe that the Sun has risen,
not only because I see it but because by it I see everything else.*

Of the countless fine phrases that Lewis spoke and wrote, this one has been chosen as the inscription on his memorial in Poets' Corner. It links together many areas of his life and work.

The sentence comes from an address entitled "Is Theology Poetry?" The answer Lewis gives to his own question is that although Christian theology is not *merely* poetry it is still poetic and therefore must be received with an imaginative, as well as a rational, embrace.

Millions of readers who have moved about the worlds of Narnia, Perelandra, and Glome know the ripe fruits of his imaginative engagement with theological themes and the power of his poetic prose.

The address was one of many he gave to the Socratic Club, the forum for debate between Christians and non-Christians, of which he was President. Thus the inscription points to his role as an apologist who publicly—and not without professional cost—defended the faith, "following the argument," as Socrates said, "wherever it should lead." Lewis was a rationalist as well as a romantic.

The sentence is straightforwardly confessional, marking the centrality of his faith at a personal level. "I never knew a man more thoroughly converted," remembers Walter Hooper, to whom thanks are especially due at this anniversary time for doing so much over the last half century to keep Lewis's memory green.

The Sun is there, aptly enough, for "the heavens are telling the glory of God," in the words of the psalm that Lewis regarded as the psalter's greatest lyric. "Everything else" is there too, because his vision was all-embracing. Angels, poached eggs, mice and their tails, Golders Green, birdsong, buses, Balder, the great nebula in Andromeda: all are there and all may be redeemed for us in Christ—as long as the Cross comes before the Crown.

That Lewis spoke these words at a debating society in Oxford reminds us also of his long association with that university and of his distinguished academic career. If Oxford could have been picked up and deposited in his native County Down, he said, it would have realised his idea of heaven. He lived in Oxford all his adult life—even while happily employed as a professor at Cambridge—and died there three years after his beloved wife, Joy, at his home, The Kilns, on this day in 1963.

The 22nd November is the feast of St. Cecilia, patron saint of music and musicians. Lewis's great comedic character, Screwtape, despises music as a direct insult to the realism, dignity, and austerity of Hell. Lewis himself believed its joy to be the serious business of Heaven. He had, in the words of Donne, "tuned his instrument" at Heaven's door and knew with greater intensity than most the longing to cross the threshold and join the heavenly harmony. Fifty years ago, the door on which he had been knocking all his life opened at last.

"Nothing makes a man so noticeable as vanishing!" Lewis once observed, but he had not envisioned how true this would be in his own case. In conversation with Walter Hooper, he predicted that sales of his works would decline steeply after his death. Hooper countered, "No, they won't. And you know why? Your books are too good, and people are not that stupid." It was one of the rare occasions when Lewis's foresight failed him. Hence, it may be safely assumed that he would find today's service completely surprising, but also, it may be hoped, not wholly displeasing.

Come, let us worship God, wonderful in his saints!

Dr. Michael Ward,
Senior Research Fellow,
Blackfriars Hall,
Oxford.

Members of the congregation are kindly requested to refrain from using private cameras, video, or sound recording equipment. Please ensure that mobile phones, pagers, and other electronic devices are switched off.

The church is served by a hearing loop. Users should turn their hearing aid to the setting marked T.

The service is conducted by The Very Reverend Dr. John Hall, Dean of Westminster.

The service is sung by the Westminster Abbey Special Service Choir, conducted by James O'Donnell, Organist and Master of the Choristers.

The organ is played by Martin Ford, Assistant Organist.

Music before the service:

Peter Holder, Organ Scholar, plays:

Rhapsody I Op 17	Herbert Howells (1892–1983)
Sonata in F minor Op 65 no 1	Felix Mendelssohn (1809–47)

The Lord Mayor of Westminster Locum Tenens is received at the Great West Door by the Dean and Chapter of Westminster. Presentations are made. All stand, and then sit.

Hymns covered by Christian Copyright Licensing (Europe) Ltd are reproduced under CCL no 1040271.

ORDER OF SERVICE

All stand as the Collegiate Procession moves to places in Quire and the Sacrarium.

The Choir sings

THE INTROIT[1]

VENI, Sancte Spiritus, et emitte caelitus lucis tuae radium. Veni, pater pauperum, veni, dator munerum, veni, lumen cordium. Amen.

Come, Holy Spirit, and send the heavenly radiance of your light. Come, Father of the poor; come, giver of gifts; come, light of all hearts. Amen.

George Fenton (b 1950)   *from the Sequence for Pentecost Stephen Langton (c 1150–1228).*

All remain standing. The Very Reverend Dr. John Hall, Dean of Westminster, gives:

THE BIDDING

FIFTY years after the death of C. S. Lewis, we assemble to give thanks for his life and work. We celebrate his work as a scholar, as one of the most significant Christian apologists of the twentieth century, and as the author of stories that have inspired the imagination and faith of countless readers and film-goers.

Here are buried or memorialised over three thousand men and women of our country and of the Commonwealth and of the English-speaking world. Today the name of C. S. Lewis will join that distinguished roll when we dedicate a permanent memorial to him near the graves and memorials of poets and other writers in the South Transept.

As we celebrate C. S. Lewis, so we shall pray that scholars, writers, and apologists may be inspired by his example, and that his work will continue to exercise an influence for good on young and old alike.

---

1. Composed by George Fenton for the opening credits of the movie *Shadowlands* (1994). Available online: www.youtube.com/watch?v=5orh6mHT0AY.

All sing

THE HYMN

He who would valiant be,
'gainst all disaster,
let him in constancy
 follow the master.
There's no discouragement
shall make him once relent
his first avowed intent
 to be a pilgrim.

Whoso beset him round
with dismal stories,
do but themselves confound,
 his strength the more is.
No foes shall stay his might,
though he with giants fight,
he will make good his right
 to be a pilgrim.

Since, Lord, thou dost defend
us with thy spirit;
we know we at the end
 shall life inherit.
Then, fancies, flee away!
I'll fear not what men say,
I'll labour night and day
 to be a pilgrim.

Monk's Gate 372 NEH   John Bunyan (1628–88)
adapted from a traditional English melody
by Ralph Vaughan Williams (1872–1958)

All sit. An excerpt is played

from BEYOND PERSONALITY: THE NEW MEN

Voice of C. S. Lewis
in the sole surviving recording
of his broadcasts for BBC Radio
(that became Mere Christianity[2])

AT the beginning of these talks I said there were Personalities in God. Well, I go further now. There are no real personalities anywhere else. I mean, no full, complete personalities. It's only when you allow yourself to be drawn into His life that you turn into a true person. But, on the other hand, it's just no good at all going to Christ for the sake of developing a fuller personality. As long as that's what you're bothering about, you haven't begun. Because the very first step towards getting a real self is to forget about the self. It will come only if you're looking for something else. That holds, you know, even for earthly matters. Even in literature or art, no man who cares about originality will ever be original. It's the man who's only thinking about doing a good job or telling the truth who becomes really original, and doesn't notice it. Even in social life you never make a good impression on other people until you stop thinking what sort of impression you make.

That principle runs all through life from the top to the bottom. Give up yourself and you will find your real self. Lose your life and you will save it. Submit to death, submit with every fibre of your being, and you will find eternal life. Look for Christ and you will get Him, and with Him everything else thrown in. Look for yourself and you will get only hatred, loneliness, despair, and ruin.

Dr. Francis Warner, C. S. Lewis's last pupil, reads

ISAIAH 35:1–7, 10

THE wilderness and the solitary place shall be glad for them; and the desert shall rejoice, and blossom as the rose. It shall blossom abundantly, and rejoice even with joy and singing: the glory of Lebanon shall be given unto it, the excellency of Carmel and Sharon, they shall see the glory of the Lord, and the excellency of our God. Strengthen ye the weak hands,

---

2. Available online: https://youtu.be/m3jYLGcDUFE. Lewis amended the text of this address before he published it as part of *Beyond Personality: The Christian Idea of God* (1944). He amended it again before incorporating it into *Mere Christianity* (1954).

and confirm the feeble knees. Say to them that are of a fearful heart, Be strong, fear not: behold, your God will come with vengeance, even God with a recompence; he will come and save you. Then the eyes of the blind shall be opened, and the ears of the deaf shall be unstopped. Then shall the lame man leap as a hart, and the tongue of the dumb sing: for in the wilderness shall waters break out, and streams in the desert. And the parched ground shall become a pool, and the thirsty land springs of water: in the habitation of dragons, where each lay, shall be grass with reeds and rushes. And the ransomed of the Lord shall return, and come to Zion with songs and everlasting joy upon their heads: they shall obtain joy and gladness, and sorrow and sighing shall flee away.

All remain seated. The Choir sings

PSALM 19

THE heavens declare the glory of God: and the firmament sheweth his handy-work.

One day telleth another: and one night certifieth another.

There is neither speech nor language: but their voices are heard among them.

Their sound is gone out into all lands: and their words into the ends of the world.

In them hath he set a tabernacle for the sun: which cometh forth as a bridegroom out of his chamber, and rejoiceth as a giant to run his course.

It goeth forth from the uttermost part of the heaven, and runneth about unto the end of it again: and there is nothing hid from the heat thereof.

The law of the Lord is an undefiled law, converting the soul: the testimony of the Lord is sure, and giveth wisdom unto the simple.

The statutes of the Lord are right, and rejoice the heart: the commandment of the Lord is pure, and giveth light unto the eyes.

The fear of the Lord is clean and endureth for ever: the judgements of the Lord are true, and righteous altogether.

More to be desired are they than gold, yea than much fine gold: sweeter also than honey, and the honey-comb.

Moreover, by them is thy servant taught: and in keeping of them there is great reward. Who can tell how oft he offendeth: O cleanse thou me from my secret faults.

Keep thy servant also from presumptuous sins, lest they get the dominion over me: so shall I be undefiled, and innocent from the great offence.

Let the words of my mouth, and the meditation of my heart: be always acceptable in thy sight, O Lord: my strength, and my redeemer.

Glory be to the Father, and to the Son: and to the Holy Ghost;
as it was in the beginning, is now, and ever shall be: world without end.
Amen.

Edward Hopkins (1818–1901)

Professor Helen Cooper, Professor of Medieval and Renaissance English, University of Cambridge (Chair held by C. S. Lewis 1954–63), reads

2 CORINTHIANS 4: 5–END

WE preach not ourselves, but Christ Jesus the Lord; and ourselves your servants for Jesus's sake. For God, who commanded the light to shine out of darkness, hath shined in our hearts, to give the light of the knowledge of the glory of God in the face of Jesus Christ. But we have this treasure in earthen vessels, that the excellency of the power may be of God, and not of us. We are troubled on every side, yet not distressed; we are perplexed, but not in despair; Persecuted, but not forsaken; cast down, but not destroyed; Always bearing about in the body the dying of the Lord Jesus, that the life also of Jesus might be made manifest in our body. For we which live are always delivered unto death for Jesus's sake, that the life also of Jesus might be made manifest in our mortal flesh. So then death worketh in us, but life in you. We having the same spirit of faith, according as it is written, I believed, and therefore have I spoken; we also believe, and therefore speak; Knowing that he which raised up the Lord Jesus shall raise up us also by Jesus, and shall present us with you. For all things are for your sakes, that the abundant grace might through the thanksgiving of many redound to the glory of God. For which cause we faint not; but though our outward man perish, yet the inward man is renewed day by day. For our light affliction, which is but for a moment, worketh for us a far more exceeding and eternal weight of glory; While we look not at the things which are seen, but at the things which are not seen: for the things which are seen are temporal; but the things which are not seen are eternal.

All remain seated. The Choir sings

THE MOTET

during which the Procession moves to the memorial stone

LIKE as the hart desireth the water-brooks: so longeth my soul after thee, O God.
My soul is athirst for God, yea, even for the living God: when shall I come to appear before the presence of God?
My tears have been my meat day and night: while they daily say unto me, Where is now thy God?

Herbert Howells (1892–1983)   Psalm 42: 1–3

Douglas Gresham, younger stepson of C. S. Lewis, reads

from THE LAST BATTLE

"FURTHER up and further in!" roared the Unicorn, and no one held back . . . . And soon they found themselves all walking together—and a great, bright procession it was—up towards mountains higher than you could see in this world even if they were there to be seen. But there was no snow on those mountains: there were forests and green slopes and sweet orchards and flashing waterfalls, one above the other, going up for ever. And the land they were walking on grew narrower all the time, with a deep valley on each side: and across that valley the land which was the real England grew nearer and nearer.

The light ahead was growing stronger. Lucy saw that a great series of many-coloured cliffs led up in front of them like a giant's staircase. And then she forgot everything else, because Aslan himself was coming, leaping down from cliff to cliff like a living cataract of power and beauty . . . .

Aslan turned to them and said: "You do not yet look so happy as I mean you to be." Lucy said, "We're so afraid of being sent away, Aslan. And you have sent us back into our own world so often." "No fear of that," said Aslan. "Have you not guessed?" Their hearts leaped and a wild hope rose within them. "There was a real railway accident," said Aslan softly. "Your father and mother and all of you are—as you used to call it in the Shadowlands—dead. The term is over: the holidays have begun. The dream is ended: this is the morning."

And as He spoke He no longer looked to them like a lion; but the things that began to happen after that were so great and beautiful that I cannot write them. And for us this is the end of all the stories, and we can most truly say that they all lived happily ever after. But for them it was only the beginning of the real story. All their life in this world and all their adventures in Narnia had only been the cover and the title page: now at last they were beginning Chapter One of the Great Story which no one on earth has read: which goes on for ever: in which every chapter is better than the one before.

C. S. Lewis

All stand for

THE DEDICATION OF THE MEMORIAL

L-R: **Walter Hooper, The Very Revd. Dr. John Hall, Dr. Michael Ward, Douglas Gresham**

Dr. Michael Ward, Senior Research Fellow, Blackfriars Hall, Oxford, says:

I ASK you, Mr. Dean, to receive into the safe custody of the Dean and Chapter this memorial in honour and memory of C. S. Lewis.

The Dean replies:

TO the greater glory of God and in thankful memory of C. S. Lewis, I dedicate this memorial: in the name of the Father, and of the Son, and of the Holy Spirit. **Amen.**

Flowers are laid on the memorial stone by Walter Hooper, Trustee and Literary Adviser, the Lewis Estate.

The Dean says:

ALMIGHTY God, Father of lights and author of all goodness: we give thee humble praise for the life and work of thy servant, C. S. Lewis, and beseech thee that, as he has helped us look to a world beyond this world and to hopes better than our own, we may come with him to the fullness of everlasting joy which thou hast prepared for them that truly love thee, in the heavenly courts of thy Son, our Lord Jesus Christ.
Amen.

All sing

THE HYMN

ALL creatures of our God and King,
lift up your voice and with us sing
    Alleluia, alleluia!
Thou burning sun with golden beam,
thou silver moon with softer gleam:
    O praise him, O praise him,
    Alleluia, alleluia, alleluia!

Thou rushing wind that art so strong,
ye clouds that sail in heaven along,
    O praise him, Alleluia!
Thou rising morn, in praise rejoice,
ye lights of evening, find a voice:

Thou flowing water, pure and clear,
make music for thy Lord to hear,
    Alleluia, alleluia!
Thou fire so masterful and bright,
that givest man both warmth and light:

And thou, most kind and gentle death,
waiting to hush our latest breath,
    O praise him, Alleluia!
Thou leadest home the child of God,
and Christ our Lord the way hath trod:

Let all things their Creator bless,
and worship him in humbleness,
 O praise him, Alleluia!
Praise, praise the Father, praise the Son,
and praise the Spirit, three in One:

Lasst uns erfreuen 263 NEH *St Francis of Assisi (1182–1226)*
Ralph Vaughan Williams (1872–1958) *translated by William Draper (1855–1933)*
after a melody in
Geistliche Kirchengesäng Cologne 1623

THE ADDRESS

by

The Most Reverend and Right Honourable
The Lord Williams of Oystermouth

THE scene is the planet Mars. In the presence of the angelic ruler of the planet and representatives of its races, the wicked scientist Dr. Weston is trying to explain to the Martians exactly why it would be right for the human race to colonize the rest of the universe. Unfortunately, Dr. Weston has all the skill in foreign languages characteristic of British academics, and so has to find a translator. His translator is the philologist Ransom. And we watch, as the scene unfolds, and Weston's vastly complicated, verbose, highfalutin' words are rendered into plain Martian by Ransom.

Weston will talk about the manifest destiny of the human race, how its capacities lead it to ever-ongoing expansion and elevation at the expense of those less gifted and less powerful. And Ransom is able to render this in plain terms, telling the Martians that, since the human race thinks it is bigger and cleverer than them, it has the right to kill them. Weston, who is beginning to get a few words of the native language, interrupts at one point to try to explain that the human race is constantly moving onwards and upwards, constantly becoming greater and more complex, and moving into an unknown future. Sadly, the only words in Martian he can come out with are "strange," "big." It's not a very compelling moral case.

But this wonderful and eloquent satirical scene is very typical of one aspect of Lewis's apologetic that we sometimes overlook: his profound, sophisticated, and witty sense of the terrible things we do to language. You might even say that, for Lewis, the abuse of language is one of the things which would tell you immediately that you couldn't trust someone, that the person you were listening to didn't understand what it was to be human.

Lewis is interested in de-mystifying the myths that we tell ourselves—the myths about the intrinsic nobility of the human race, entitled to exploit not only its own planet but every other one in the universe; the myths we tell ourselves about how our will and our imagination can somehow make us more than human. And in spelling that out, he shows us how the aspiration to become more than human leaves us profoundly less than human.

The jargon-spouting Dr. Weston ends up, in the second volume of Lewis's science-fiction trilogy, as the terrifying Un-man, the de-humanized, diabolical figure that Ransom fights with in the caves of the planet Venus. But we can see the same interest at work in the third volume of Lewis's science-fiction trilogy, *That Hideous Strength*, in the climactic scene of the banquet, where the skills of language and intelligence desert the speakers. Now we have most of us been at banquets where something rather like that appears to have happened; but this is a more drastic instance. This is High Table choreographed by Quentin Tarantino. One by one, the speakers begin to lose the capacity to make sense and utter sense, and the disguised Merlin stands up in the midst of them, and cries out loudly, in Latin, that because they have turned their backs on the Word, the Word has abandoned them. Intelligence has left them. Not the least impressive aspect of that narrative is how very slowly some people realize that the speakers are talking nonsense. But that's another story.

But in these two vignettes from the science-fiction trilogy, Lewis puts before us two of the most typical and most disturbing abuses of language that we can suffer from. There is the language we use to hide from ourselves, to tell ourselves that our ignoble habits and our selfish aspirations are really elevating and moral; and there is the language that prevents us, truly, from thinking about things, about reality, language turning in upon itself in an endless spiral of nonsense. And for Lewis, our delivery from those two kinds of error and corruption is an intrinsic part of the delivery and the renewal of our very humanity. The liberation of words is essential to the liberation of our human nature. Indeed, we could say that it is part of our growing into that humanity where, as Lewis says in his last and perhaps greatest fictional work, we have faces. We uncover ourselves to the truth. Because God sees us in the face, we discover we have a reality, a truth, a face, and words to speak. And even as we grow into having words to speak that are honest and truthful and undefended, we are drawn nearer and nearer to that point where, as Lewis says in *Till We Have Faces*, "questions die away";[3]

---

3. Lewis, *Till We Have Faces*, Part Two, chapter iv.

where we have nothing to say because there is too much to say; where, as we heard in that wonderful passage from *The Last Battle*, "the things that began to happen . . . were so great and beautiful that I cannot write them."[4]

All through Lewis's work these themes seem to recur. To try to be more than human is to become less than human. To try to put speech between ourselves and our reality or the reality of the world is to be condemned to nonsense. And perhaps it's that suspicion of putting speech, language, between ourselves and the world, that explains something of Lewis's aversion to literary modernism. His critical judgments in this area were not, I think, infallible. But one can understand his deep anxiety over an interest in words that could actually stop us thinking about—indeed, seeing—things. And it explains, too, his apparently rather odd indifference to the beautiful and majestic language of the King James Bible. It is, he says, so beautiful and so majestic, that it can actually get in the way of our realizing what the language is about. And we need a Moffatt, a Knox, or a J. B. Phillips, to startle us again with the freshness of what Scripture is saying.

And all of that also, perhaps, helps us to make sense of one of the strangest bits of apologetic in all of Lewis's books. And that is the great testimony offered by Puddleglum, the marsh-wiggle, in *The Silver Chair*. Puddleglum, you remember, and the children who are at the centre of the story are deep underground in the stronghold of the Witch, and the Witch is explaining to them that the only reality that there is is this underground world, lit by a lamp. There is no outside world. There is no sun in the sky. The sun in the sky is just an imaginative projection from the lamp that hangs in the cave. There is no fresh air, there is no natural light. All that is is here, in this self-enclosed cavern. And Puddleglum, resisting both the strength of her rhetoric and the fumes of the intoxicating herbs that have been burned in the cave, protests that, whether or not she's telling the truth, there is something about the very idea of an outside world that is more appropriate to life and joy and, yes, truth-telling, in a certain sense, than what the Witch is saying. And isn't it odd that our imagination can produce so much more real and interesting a world than this narrow and impoverished cave?

Puddleglum is appealing not to reasoned argument here, but to a deep, inarticulate sense that we are in touch, that we are connected, that our language and our ideas are not everything, that we are summoned and prodded and lured into life, into knowing, into speaking. Something is given, something calls, something draws us onwards and outwards. What Puddleglum argues is that the self-enclosed world is just not good enough and not interesting

---

4. Lewis, *The Last Battle*, chapter 16, "Farewell to Shadowlands."

enough to keep us thinking, talking, loving, and enjoying. Somehow, that self-enclosed, lamp-lit underground reality has to be exploded.

Lewis wanted above all to remind us that our very reality, our very life, depended on the life and reality of God. He wanted to remind us that there was no truth, no joy, no life that did not come to us unexpectedly from beyond. Think about yourself, think about, God forbid, your "spiritual life," think about the beauty and solemnity and emotional quality of the words you are using, and you will stay in your prison. It's the man who is only thinking about doing a good job or telling the truth who becomes really original and doesn't notice it.

So to become free enough to notice our own self-deceptions, to notice the seductions of jargon, to notice how very easily we settle down in the underground chamber—that is one of the great works of grace. And to be reconnected with the world for which we can't always find appropriate words, where we're searching, reaching, sometimes stumbling—that is the gift of the God who became, for us, and for ever, part of that real world in the flesh and blood of Jesus.

Lewis's interest in words and what they tell us about humanity is one reason—not the only reason, but one significant reason—to remember today the fact that we honour him in Poets' Corner; that we honour him as somebody who, in the words of a poet with whom he had a rather fraught relationship, "purifies the dialect of the tribe."[5] Lewis believed that to become human was to become a speaker of honest truth, and that that could only happen in the face of the God who helps us, who enables us, to drop our masks and our delusions and have faces in His presence. He shares, perhaps surprisingly, with George Orwell a deep diagnostic accuracy about jargon. He shares, even more surprisingly, with Dietrich Bonhoeffer an awareness of how even the most orthodox and polished religious language can become stale and cease to change anything internally or externally. Only the Word, the Word incarnate with the most capital of "W"s, can save us, not only from nonsense, but from the self-consuming boredom of endless inhumanity, Un-manhood. And when we allow the Word to speak in us and to us, that is when—as he says in a paper of the 1940s—we learn how "to lay our ears closer to the murmur of life as it actually flows through us at every moment and to discover there all that quivering and wonder and (in a sense) infinity which the literature that we call realistic omits."[6]

---

5. Eliot, *Four Quartets*, "Little Gidding," II, iv, line 50.

6. Lewis, "Hedonics," *Time and Tide*, 16 June 1945. Reprinted in *C. S. Lewis, Essay Collection and Other Short Pieces*, ed. Walmsley, 688.

All remain seated. The Choir sings

THE ANTHEM[7]

LOVE's as warm as tears,
Love is tears:
Pressure within the brain,
Tension at the throat,
Deluge, weeks of rain,
Haystacks afloat,
Featureless seas between
Hedges, where once was green.

Love's as fierce as fire,
Love is fire:
All sorts—infernal heat
Clinkered with greed and pride,
Lyric desire, sharp-sweet,
Laughing, even when denied,
And that empyreal flame
Whence all loves came.

Love's as fresh as spring,
Love is spring:
Bird-song hung in the air,
Cool smells in a wood,
Whispering "Dare! Dare!"
To sap, to blood,
Telling "Ease, safety, rest,
Are good; not best."

Love's as hard as nails,
Love is nails:
Blunt, thick, hammered through
The medial nerves of One
Who, having made us, knew
The thing He had done,
Seeing (with all that is)
Our cross, and His.[8]

7. Available online: https://youtu.be/dOHlrgCizJI.

8. C. S. Lewis, "Love's As Warm As Tears" (undated). See *The Collected Poems of*

Paul Mealor (b 1975) C. S. Lewis
Specially commissioned for this Service

All kneel or remain seated. The Reverend Dr. James Hawkey, Minor Canon and Sacrist of Westminster, leads

THE PRAYERS

In thanksgiving, let us pray to the Lord and giver of life.

The Reverend Philip Hobday, Chaplain, Magdalene College, Cambridge, says:

LET us praise God for his revelation of truth and transcendent beauty to C. S. Lewis: for Lewis's longing for God, and his perception of divine reality, and for his deep appreciation of the strength and freshness of God's love in ordinary situations.
Let us bless the Lord:
Thanks be to God.

The Reverend Professor Vernon White, Canon Theologian, says:

LET us praise God for Lewis's Christian vocation to inspire and to teach: for his love of debate and discussion, for his commitment to reason and the discovery of the truth, and for his passion to commend the credibility and reality of God.
Let us bless the Lord:
Thanks be to God.

Professor Simon Horobin, Professor of English Language and Literature, University of Oxford, and Tutorial Fellow of Magdalen College, Oxford, says:

LET us praise God for Lewis's academic life: for his contribution to scholarly research, for his commitment to the imaginative and literary worlds which shaped his own writing and communication, and for his respect for the power of great literature to open new horizons.
Let us bless the Lord:
Thanks be to God.

C. S. Lewis: A Critical Edition, ed. King, 421.

The Reverend Adrian Dorrian, Rector, St. Mark's, Dundela, says:

LET us praise God for Lewis's vision and creativity: for his imagination and ability to communicate lucidly to children and adults alike, for his care as a correspondent, for his skill as an author, poet and broadcaster, for his understanding of the human condition, and his joy in the glorious vitality of creation.
Let us bless the Lord:
Thanks be to God.

The Reverend Tim Stead, Vicar, Holy Trinity, Headington Quarry, says:

LET us pray for all those who take inspiration from Lewis's life and work: for teachers and apologists, catechists and mystics, playwrights, film-makers, novelists, and poets, and for those seeking after God, or pondering the mysteries of existence. Lord, hear us:
Lord, graciously hear us.

The Reverend David Stanton, Canon in Residence, says:

ALMIGHTY God, who hast proclaimed thine eternal truth by the voice of prophets and evangelists: direct and bless, we beseech thee, those who in our generation speak where many listen, and write what many read, that they may do their part in making the heart of the people wise, its mind sound, and its will righteous; to the honour of Jesus Christ our Lord. Amen.

The Sacrist concludes:

Watching in hope for the coming of Christ's Kingdom, we are bold to pray:

OUR Father, who art in heaven, hallowed be thy name; thy kingdom come; thy will be done; on earth as it is in heaven. Give us this day our daily bread. And forgive us our trespasses, as we forgive those who trespass against us. And lead us not into temptation; but deliver us from evil. For thine is the kingdom, the power, and the glory, for ever and ever. Amen.

All stand to sing

THE HYMN

A - men, a - men.

O PRAISE ye the Lord!
praise him in the height;
rejoice in his word,
   ye angels of light;
ye heavens adore him
   by whom ye were made,
and worship before him,
   in brightness arrayed.

O praise ye the Lord!
   praise him upon earth,
in tuneful accord,
   ye sons of new birth;
praise him who has brought you
   his grace from above,
praise him who has taught you
   to sing of his love.

O praise ye the Lord!
   all things that give sound;
each jubilant chord,
   re-echo around;
loud organs, his glory
   forth tell in deep tone,
and, sweet harp, the story
   of what he has done.

O praise ye the Lord!
   thanksgiving and song
to him be outpoured
   all ages along:
for love in creation,
   for heaven restored,
for grace of salvation,
   O praise ye the Lord! Amen, Amen.

Laudate Dominum 427 NEH   *Henry Williams Baker (1821–77)*
Charles Hubert Hastings Parry (1848–1918)   *after Psalm 150*
from Hear my words, ye people

All remain standing. The Dean pronounces

THE BLESSING

GO forth into the world in peace; be of good courage; hold fast that which is good; render to no man evil for evil; strengthen the faint-hearted; support the weak; help the afflicted; honour all men; love and serve the Lord, rejoicing in the power of the Holy Spirit; and the blessing of God almighty, the Father, the Son, and the Holy Spirit, be among you and remain with you always. **Amen.**

All remain standing as the Choir and Clergy depart.

Music after the service:

Allegro maestoso *from* Sonata in G Op 28   *Edward Elgar*
                                                                                            (1857–1934)

Members of the Congregation are requested to remain in their places until invited to move by the Stewards.

A retiring collection will be taken in aid of the C. S. Lewis Scholarship in Medieval Literature.

SCHOLARSHIP IN MEDIEVAL LITERATURE[9]

The Professorship of Medieval and Renaissance English at the University of Cambridge, first held by C. S. Lewis, reflects Lewis's conviction that the Middle Ages made possible many of the great achievements of the early modern period—especially in the field of writing. Shakespeare's and Spenser's works, for example, were as replete with the princes, damsels and troubadours as were Chaucer's and Dante's.

C. S. Lewis, too, drew from the rich tapestry of medieval literature in his writings, and taught his students that they must "keep the clean sea breeze of the centuries blowing through [their] minds," something which could only be done "by reading old books." It is thanks to him that Medieval and Renaissance Literature thrives as a study subject on every academic level, but it cannot be denied that its study in this country is on the decline. At present, there are many more British medievalists in the United States than there are in the United Kingdom. The new scholarship scheme will enable a brilliant young scholar to study medieval literature at the University of Cambridge, and help future generations to continue reading the "old books" so beloved by Jack Lewis.

Enquiries about the C. S. Lewis Scholarship Fund should be sent to database@alumni.cam.ac.uk.

---

9. Cf. "C.S Lewis: 50 years after his death a new scholarship will honour his literary career": www.cam.ac.uk/research/news/cs-lewis-50-years-after-his-death-a-new-scholarship-will-honour-his-literary-career.

───────────

Warm gratitude is extended to all those who helped make possible the Poets' Corner memorial to C. S. Lewis through their kind contributions.

The individual donors are too numerous to mention by name, but their generosity is appreciated just as much as that of the following institutions who gave their support:

Azusa Pacific University, California
(University Library Special Collections)

George Fox University, Oregon

Houston Baptist University, Texas
(Department of Apologetics)

Magdalene College, Cambridge

The Marion E. Wade Center, Wheaton College, Illinois

The Oxford University C. S. Lewis Society

Taylor University, Indiana
(The Center for the Study of C. S. Lewis and Friends)

───────────

Printed by
Barnard & Westwood Ltd
23 Pakenham Street, London WC1X 0LB
By Appointment to HM The Queen, Printers and Bookbinders
& HRH The Prince of Wales, Printers
Printers to the Dean and Chapter of Westminster[10]

---

10. A pdf of the Order of Service is available online: http://static.westminster-abbey.org/assets/pdf_file/0011/69275/27999-C-S-Lewis-service-web.pdf.

PART THREE

Reflections on the Westminster Commemorations

— 5 —

Reflections on Composing
Love's As Warm As Tears

Paul Mealor[1]

THE REASON I FIRST came across the works of C. S. Lewis? I nearly drowned when I was nine.

I grew up on the Isle of Anglesey in North Wales and one day, tagging along after my older brother who was going canoeing, I managed somehow to fall into the river. Not being the best swimmer, I was soon in difficulties, trying to get out of the water, but failing repeatedly, and being carried along by the current. I kept going under and coming up again and this gradually got more and more serious. It probably lasted less than a minute or so, but it felt like a long time. Eventually there came a moment when I remember thinking to myself, "I'm dying," and at the same moment I had the sensation of unbelievable warmth. There was suddenly no fear at all. It was an utterly remarkable feeling. In fact, it was a religious experience. All at once I somehow "knew that God existed," if I can put it like that. I just knew that death wasn't to be feared, though what I probably said to myself at the time was something like, "This isn't so bad."

An elderly couple happened to be passing by on the riverbank, and they reached in and pulled me out. My brother came running, and I was taken home, where I mentioned the strange sensation I'd had. My father

---

1. Paul Mealor is Reader in Composition at the University of Aberdeen. 2.5 billion people heard his motet *Ubi caritas* performed by the choirs of Westminster Abbey and Her Majesty's Chapel Royal at the wedding of Prince William and Catherine Middleton in Westminster Abbey on 29th April 2011. He maintains a web presence at www.paulmealor.com.

asked me if I'd ever read the Narnia Chronicles and I said no, but soon afterwards began to do so, starting with *The Lion, the Witch and the Wardrobe*. And I began to find some answers to the questions I was asking at that stage about the nature of the experience I'd been through. Lewis became important to me, and when I finished reading Narnia, my father bought me a copy of Lewis's collected poems. I would have been about eleven by this point. Looking back at the copy he got me, I see that I scribbled ideas next to particular lines and phrases, indicating passages that I might one day set to music. One was this, from the "Prologue" to *Spirits in Bondage*:

> In my coracle of verses I will sing of lands unknown . . .
>
> Sing about the Hidden Country fresh and full of quiet green.
>
> Sailing over seas uncharted to a port that none has seen.

So, when, many years later, the invitation came from James O'Donnell [Director of Music] to write something for the Lewis memorial service at Westminster Abbey, I was more than delighted. The Dean, John Hall, suggested three possible poems that might be set to music and the one he liked best was also the one I preferred, "Love's As Warm As Tears."[2]

I spent about four weeks reading it over and over, feeling the words and sensing the stresses of the phrases, meditating upon it. I fell in love with the poem for its beautiful, warm expression of Christian life and love. And, as always when I'm setting words to music, I tried to find ways of bringing light, musical light, to what I was reading. The danger is that you take something away from the poem when you set it, but my aim is always to add something new, something that brings out the inner contours of the piece.

There are some poets and poems where I just can't find a way of doing this. I've been trying for twenty years to set Yeats's "An Irish Airman Foresees His Death," and I simply can't do it! Perhaps it's me, or perhaps it's because there's already so much musicality in Yeats's language. Blake is another poet I find hard; his work is so full of images. And anything in the Welsh language is also difficult, I find, unless I do it very very simply. You're wanting to "colour" the words, and if they're already very densely coloured, it can be tricky. Lewis's poem suited me well because it's quite straightforward in terms of imagery. It has depths of meaning, of course, but the individual images aren't too complicated.

Meditation leads to music eventually, and in this case I knew I wanted to make a big thing of the second stanza—"Love's as fierce as fire." The idea is to suggest emotional flames flickering, cascading upwards in a huge gathering counterpoint, and exploding. I even put a deliberate wrong note in one

---

2. Available online: https://www.youtube.com/watch?v=dOHlrgCizJI.

of the chords, to suggest something fierce and uncontrollable. And I also knew I wanted a big tenor solo in the final stanza, "Love's as hard as nails."

The only part of the poem that I felt didn't quite fit, at least not within the four-to-five minute limit I was trying to observe, was the third stanza. A single line can take thirty seconds or more to develop fully and, although I did actually write music for the whole of stanza 3, I felt it was better to leave part of it out of the finished version. You don't want your musical gestures to outstay their welcome. It's a delicate game to play.

I'm very pleased with how it sounds now and people seem to like it, I'm glad to say. I've already attended eight or so different performances in different places, including Canada and New York, and I'm sure it's been performed on other occasions when I haven't been present, so it seems to be finding a home in the repertoire. Although it's not the easiest piece to sing, it should be within the range of most half-decent choirs. I certainly want it to be sung, and I'm hoping I may be able to include a recording of it in a future album. We'll see. At any rate, I'm proud that this is, as far as I know, the first ever musical setting of Lewis's poetry. Maybe I'll do more in the future. The other two poems on the Dean's list ["The Naked Seed" and "After Prayers, Lie Cold"] would certainly go well.

I'm always keen to find opportunities to compose. It's what I'm put here for, I feel, because music helps us get in touch with wonder. It makes connections with something beautiful, something beyond us—like that beautiful sensation when I nearly drowned. We all want that, I think, like Lucy pushing through the fur coats and discovering Narnia. I could never express it in words, like Lewis did. Words are too hard-edged for me; I need the fluidity of music as my medium. But I think we're all in search of that "hidden country," and it's not limited to Christians, by any means. I'm a Christian—an Anglican—and value very much the link between music and faith, and I'm glad that that seems to be something you can talk about more these days. When I listen to the St. Matthew Passion or Tallis's "Salvator Mundi," it touches the core and reawakens me to that larger dimension.

And my atheist friends are just as open to the way music can transport us into other realms. You don't have to be a Christian to be awed and moved by the St. Matthew Passion, any more than you have to be a Communist to be moved by a Bertolt Brecht play.

Music's been important for me ever since I was a choirboy at St. Asaph's Cathedral. I remember hearing Gibbons's "See, See the Word Is Incarnate" and thinking that that was the whole New Testament packed into seven minutes! Mahler is another great inspiration and he was probably the first composer I ever seriously listened to. My grandfather played Mahler *at* me, and I was blown away. Who wouldn't be! Later I got into Vaughan Williams and Britten; and American composers like Morten Lauridsen have been key for me too.

In my own work, I've just completed my first symphony, entitled "Passiontide," for orchestra and chorus, and I'm close to completing my second, which will be an orchestral symphony. I may preface it with those words from Lewis about the coracle seeking the Hidden Country fresh and full of quiet green. We'll see . . . .

— 6 —

Mystery Worshipper: Westminster Abbey

Acton Bell[1]

The church:

Collegiate Church of St. Peter at Westminster, London.

Denomination:

Church of England. Westminster Abbey is a Royal Peculiar.[2]

---

1. Acton Bell is the *nom de plume* of the anonymous reviewer reporting for the website, Ship-of-Fools.com. "We're here for people who prefer their religion disorganized," says the website's editor, Simon Jenkins. "Our aim is to help Christians be self-critical and honest about the failings of Christianity, as we believe honesty can only strengthen faith." One regular feature of the site is the "Mystery Worshipper." Since the year of its founding, 1998, Ship-of-Fools has been sending Mystery Worshippers to churches worldwide. Jenkins describes their purpose as follows: "Travelling incognito, they ask those questions which go to the heart of church life: How long was the sermon? How hard the pew? How cold was the coffee? How warm the welcome? The only clue they have been there at all is the Mystery Worshipper calling card, dropped discreetly into the collection plate." The Lewis Memorial Service report is available online: http://shipoffools.com/mystery/2013/2627.html.

2. A Royal Peculiar is a church that does not fall under the jurisdiction of the bishop in whose diocese it is located, but rather comes under the direct jurisdiction of the Sovereign. In 1534, the Act of Supremacy declared King Henry VIII to be "the only supreme head on earth of the Church of England." Westminster Abbey became a Royal Peculiar in 1560, during the reign of Henry's daughter, Elizabeth I, and remains so under the present Queen, Elizabeth II.

The building:

Westminster Abbey has probably been Mystery Worshipped more often than any other church in the world! Since the service I attended was to dedicate a monument in Poets' Corner, let me limit my description of the building to that particular feature.

The south transept, which abuts some of the oldest parts of the Abbey, is commonly referred to as Poets' Corner. Geoffrey Chaucer was the first poet to be buried there, but that wasn't at all because he was a writer, but rather because he lived nearby and was the Clerk of Works. It took several centuries before another writer joined him, namely Edmund Spenser, author of the incomplete epic poem *The Faerie Queene*. Others followed. By the eighteenth century the tradition to bury authors in this particular space, or to erect monuments to those buried elsewhere, was firmly entrenched. The memorials vary in style from a simple stone slab to intricately carved memorial busts. Some include eloquent epitaphs, often tinged with irony, such as that of the poet Samuel Butler, who died in poverty: "He ask'd for bread, and he received a stone."

Memorialisation sometimes occurs years after death, such as that of Lord Byron (died 1824, monument dedicated 1969) and even William Shakespeare (died 1616, monument dedicated 1740). Today's service was held to dedicate a monument to C. S. Lewis, author of The Chronicles of Narnia, among many other works, who died in 1963.

The church:

There is something about Poets' Corner that smacks a bit of the absurd. As early as the eighteenth century, commentators were remarking on how crowded Westminster Abbey as a memorial site had become, and specifically Poets' Corner, with memorial after memorial very tightly packed together. Ben Jonson was buried standing up in a wall in the nave, as he, too, died penniless and his friends couldn't afford a proper coffin. His epitaph reads "O Rare Ben Jonson," which is thought by some to be "*Ora re Ben Jonson*" ("Pray for Ben Jonson") in somewhat ungrammatical Latin. Occasionally, one bone or another pops out during renovations or reconstructions. I can't help thinking that this mighty army of dead authors may one day rise up, pens in hand, to protest some particularly annoying modern day innovation (text messaging, perhaps?).

The neighbourhood:

The Palace of Westminster, more commonly known as the Houses of Parliament, is nearby, linking the Abbey visually and culturally to the very centre of Government.

The cast:

The Most Revd. and Rt. Hon. The Lord Williams of Oystermouth (former Archbishop of Canterbury, Rowan Williams) was the preacher. The service was conducted by the Very Revd. Dr. John Hall, Dean of Westminster. Also taking part were the Revd. Vernon White, Canon Theologian at Westminster Abbey; the Revd. David Stanton, Canon Treasurer and Almoner, Westminster Abbey; the Revd. Philip Hobday, Chaplain, Magdalene College, Cambridge; the Revd. Adrian Dorrian, Rector, St. Mark's, Dundela; the Revd. Tim Stead, Vicar, Holy Trinity, Headington Quarry; Francis Warner, PhD, Emeritus Fellow of St. Peter's College, Oxford (one of C. S. Lewis's last pupils); Helen Cooper, PhD, Professor of Medieval and Renaissance English, University of Cambridge (chair held by C. S. Lewis 1954–63); Simon Horobin, PhD, Professor of English Language and Literature, University of Oxford, and Tutorial Fellow of Magdalen College, Oxford; Michael Ward, PhD, Senior Research Fellow, Blackfriars Hall, University of Oxford; and Douglas Gresham (younger stepson of C. S. Lewis).

The date & time:

Friday 22nd November 2013, Noon.

What was the name of the service?

A Service to Dedicate a Memorial to C. S. Lewis, Writer, Scholar, Apologist.

How full was the building?

From where we were seated, directly across from the pulpit in the crossing, it was difficult to judge exactly how many were in attendance, since we couldn't really see much of the quire. My rough estimate would be 400.[3]

---

3. The number of people in attendance was actually about 1,000.

Did anyone welcome you personally?

Yes. A very friendly verger greeted me with a smile and directed me to one of the Abbey ushers, who were identifiable by the ribbon and badge they wore around their necks. The usher who helped me was quite friendly and suggested I move to a better seat so as to see the pulpit better. I felt very welcome.

Was your pew comfortable?

It was a folding chair that wasn't too uncomfortable. I doubt I'd want to do the Easter vigil sitting in it, but for an hour it was fine. We also weren't very tightly spaced, which was a pleasant surprise. I wasn't left feeling like a sardine and could stretch out within reason.

How would you describe the pre-service atmosphere?

Anticipatory is, I think, the best way to describe it. A very tweedy type came rushing up to my row and demanded, in very plummy tones, "Just a few 'graphs for the magazine, anyone? Yes?" I don't think she was talking to me. I was also approached by a woman with a heavy Northern Irish accent who asked me why I was attending. She didn't introduce herself, and I had to resist the urge to be a real New Yorker and ask her why she wanted to know. I was also surprised to hear a wailing bairn, wondering who in their right mind brings a baby to such a service, but so be it. Cell phones and babies seem inescapable these days, no matter where you are (what must the residents of Poets' Corner think, I wonder?).

What were the exact opening words of the service?

"Fifty years after the death of C. S. Lewis, we assemble to give thanks for his life and works." This had been preceded by a sung introit, *Veni, Sancte Spiritus*.

What books did the congregation use during the service?

A really lovely, four-colour service bulletin on heavy card stock, with the Abbey's seal on the front cover and a large picture of Lewis on the inside cover.

What musical instruments were played?

The organ. The service was sung by the Westminster Abbey Special Service Choir, which was made up of about twenty-five men and women, who were just about perfect.

Musically the service was pretty traditional, with lots of Herbert Howells in the mix. The motet, Howells's *Like as the Hart Desireth the Waterbrooks*, was quite evocative, and I noticed quite a few wiping away the odd tear.

An anthem written especially for this service by the Welsh composer Paul Mealor (b. 1975), with a text from Lewis's poem "Love's As Warm As Tears," was noteworthy.

Did anything distract you?

There were so many distractions it would be hard to count: a woman quietly weeping, the vergers rushing to and fro, people moving chairs, and the Abbey itself—it is such an incredible space, it is easy to get lost looking for something previously unseen. I did have a head scratch at Douglas Gresham's outfit, which consisted of white jeans, a leather jacket, jackboots, pectoral cross, and a turtleneck turned down so low as to look suspiciously like a clerical dog collar.

Was the worship stiff-upper-lip, happy clappy, or what?

About as stiff as it gets before hopping off into Latin, I suppose, although there was a dash of Latin in the beginning with the sung introit. The Dean delivered the bidding, which was followed by the hymn "He Who Would Valiant Be" (which my tone-deaf self finds nearly impossible to sing). Then came a recording of Lewis reading from "Beyond Personality," which was broadcast on the BBC in 1944 and is the only surviving recording of the weekly broadcasts Lewis later included in his book *Mere Christianity*. Readings from Scripture and others of Lewis's works followed. The memorial plaque was unveiled and flowers were laid thereon. That old standby "All Creatures of our God and King" was sung with great gusto by the choir and congregation and was followed by Lord Williams's address. The anthem, prayers, the Lord's Prayer, and more hymns followed. The service concluded with a blessing and the Allegro maestoso movement from Edward Elgar's *Sonata in G* for organ.

Exactly how long was the sermon?

Eighteen minutes.

On a scale of 1-10, how good was the preacher?

10. I could listen to Rowan Williams read Chinese take-out menus hour after hour on a continuous loop. He is, hands down, one of the most brilliant preachers I've ever encountered.

In a nutshell, what was the sermon about?

Lord Williams began by describing Lewis not so much as a Christian apologist but as a writer, speaking to his demand for precision in language and holding the belief that words should indeed mean what they say. Sacrifice and belief, he argued, are commonly held to be the hallmarks of Lewis's oeuvre, and they are indeed there, but they are nothing without clarity and precision because they clear away the cobwebs of self-delusion and are thus essential to any understanding of Lewis's works. Obviously the *Narniad* and *A Grief Observed*, his two most well-known works, detail what could arguably be the most honest descriptions of loss and its relationship to Christianity, but one can find those themes throughout Lewis's works.

Which part of the service was like being in heaven?

The service was held on the fiftieth anniversary of Lewis's death, so I was surprised and moved that such a public service held very private meaning for the several close associates of Lewis present. There were many who were visibly touched during the service, and it was hard not to be struck by how deeply Lewis's literary executor [Walter Hooper] appeared to feel the emotions of the moment. It was a great reminder that these events aren't just public "dumbshows," but have real meaning—an idea I think Lewis would appreciate.

And which part was like being in ...er...the other place?

I had always thought it too fantastical to be believed when, in Victorian novels or the like, a character dies after a long and painful illness caused by sitting exposed to a cold draught for any length of time. I am now convinced that such a plot device is entirely plausible. The temperature inside the Abbey was positively arctic! I am sure I face death.

What happened when you hung around after the service looking lost?

No chance of looking lost with the Abbey ushers on hand. Everyone was directed to see the newly unveiled plaque, which caused a bit of a traffic jam. Ultimately I had to give up, as I had to get back to the office for a meeting.

How would you describe the after-service coffee?

Unfortunately I couldn't attend the gathering afterwards—pressing demands at the office—but I did have a nice word with the Dean of Westminster on the way out.

How would you feel about making this church your regular (where 10 = ecstatic, 0 = terminal)?

5. I think if I knew that one day I'd be included in the Corner or even a dim wall off in some nook like Ben Jonson, I'd have a different rating. But since there's not a chance in Hades, I'll have to stick with a 5. They do the big events flawlessly, but since I'm no big event, I doubt I'd make it my parish church.

Did the service make you feel glad to be a Christian?

Absolutely! Lewis is inspirational, and I can't think of a more suitable person to memorialise in Westminster Abbey.

What one thing will you remember about all this in seven days' time?

Rowan Williams speaking so eloquently about Lewis as a writer. I still think it is fascinating to hear a religious figure give literary criticism of a literary figure whose focus was religious. There's a perfect symmetry there that I think even Lewis would appreciate.

— 7 —

C. S. Lewis's Memorial Service

Jeanette Sears[1]

AFTER BEING AT THE C. S. Lewis memorial events at Westminster Abbey this week—listening to lectures on C. S. Lewis, speaking at the C. S. Lewis Symposium, meeting up with C. S. Lewis fans and friends, and finally attending the C. S. Lewis service itself—I felt like having a bit of a day off today to recover, preferably on activities nothing to do with C. S. Lewis. Especially as I've also spent the last few weeks reading Lewis's novels and writing talks about Lewis, some non-Lewis reading seemed in order, much as I love him.

But, as usually happens when I'm trying to escape a subject, the very thing I pick up instead drags me back to it—or, to put it more positively, gives new insight and perspective on the forbidden subject. This morning, as an escape, I picked up at random an old murder mystery by Ngaio Marsh called *False Scent* (1960). It concerns the death of a famous actress. And after being with the thousands who turned up to honour Lewis this week, I couldn't help but resonate with the opening words of Ngaio Marsh's story:

> When she died it was as if all the love she had inspired in so many people suddenly blossomed. She had never, of course, realised how greatly she was loved, never known that she was to be carried by six young men who would ask to perform this

---

1. The Revd. Dr. Jeanette Sears is a writer and speaker, with a special interest in Lewis, Sayers, and Tolkien. Formerly Curate at St. Aldate's Church, Oxford, and for seven years lecturer in Christian Doctrine and Church History at Trinity College, Bristol, her books include the novels *Pig's Progress* and *A Murder in Michaelmas* and the tour-guide *The Oxford of J. R. R Tolkien and C. S. Lewis*. She maintains a web presence at www.jeanettesears.com, where the original version of this article first appeared.

last courtesy: to bear her on their strong shoulders, so gently and with such dedication. Quite insignificant people were there . . . the family nurse . . . her dresser . . . the stage doorkeeper . . . Crowds of people whom she herself would have scarcely remembered but upon whom, at some time, she had bestowed the gift of her charm. All the Knights and Dames, of course, and The Management, and . . . the great producer who had so often directed her. Bertie Saracen who had created her dresses since the days when she was a bit-part actress and who had, indeed, risen to his present eminence in the wake of her mounting fame. But it was not for her fame that they had come to say goodbye to her. It was because, quite simply, they had loved her.

That was exactly how I felt! I, surely, was one of those "insignificant people" who had turned up to honour Lewis on the fiftieth anniversary of his death. As a speaker at one of the commemorative events, I did have a place in the Quire of the Abbey and so was closer to the "action" and so felt doubly blessed, and I'm sure I wasn't alone in thinking along the lines of "Why has this happened to me, that the mother—or at least a great author—of my Lord comes to me?"—if I can reapply Elizabeth's words to Mary.

The service was stunning and moving, beginning with the oh-so-appropriate opening hymn "He Who Would Valiant Be," based on *Pilgrim's Progress*, then a recording of Lewis himself speaking about "getting a real self." How strange and affecting to hear his voice in that setting!

Dr. Francis Warner, one of Lewis's pupils, read from Isaiah 35 (including the wonderful phrase "the habitation of dragons," putting one in mind of "that record stinker" named Eustace Clarence Scrubb, who almost deserved it!), and Professor Helen Cooper, who holds Lewis's old Chair at Cambridge, read 2 Corinthians 4 (with its reference to the "eternal weight of glory" that gave Lewis the title of his greatest sermon).

There followed a particularly telling reading as Douglas Gresham, Lewis's stepson, gave us Aslan's welcoming of the children into his land forever after their earthly deaths in *The Last Battle*—hard not to shed a tear at that point if you hadn't already.

Dr. Michael Ward led the dedication of the memorial that he has done so much to bring about, and Walter Hooper, Lewis's friend and secretary and the editor of his works, laid beautiful white flowers above Lewis's name. The Most Reverend and Right Honourable Rowan Williams (now "The Lord Williams of Oystermouth"—who knew?) gave a brilliant sermon on Lewis's defence of language and the human, and the choir sang Paul Mealor's flowing arrangement of his poem, "Love's As Warm As Tears"—another opportunity for tears from the congregation. The prayers were led by a wonderful array of clergy representing the geography of Lewis's life, and the service ended on an uplifting note with the hymn, "O Praise Ye the Lord!"

There was then the chance for us to actually see the memorial in the stone floor of Poets' Corner, cut with his own words: "I believe in Christianity as I believe that the Sun has risen, not only because I see it but because by it I see everything else."

People sometimes go to services at Westminster Abbey just to see the magnificence of the building without paying the usual £18 entrance fee (there's a tip for you!); and some may have been tempted to attend this Memorial Service simply because Lewis is now a celebrity—as opposed to the very few who went to his funeral in 1963. But I actually don't think either of these things would have been the case with many or even any people yesterday, the 22nd November 2013. If I can adapt the words of the Ngaio Marsh story: "It was not for his fame that they had come to say goodbye to him. It was because, quite simply, they had loved him."

— 8 —

Stonecrop: Lewis Takes His Place in Poets' Corner

Holly Ordway[1]

On 22ⁿᵈ November 2013, the fiftieth anniversary of his death, C. S. Lewis was honoured with a memorial in the celebrated Poets' Corner of Westminster Abbey. I had the privilege of being present—knowing that this Memorial and its attendant Symposium were events of international, and lasting, significance for Lewis studies, English letters, and Christian apologetics.

The Poets' Corner Memorial was a labour of love by Dr. Michael Ward, whose idea this was and who led the effort from the beginning, including being in charge of the fundraising: every penny of the £20,000 required for the Memorial and Service was raised through private donations—and every individual and institution who donated, no matter how big or small the amount, is listed in the records of the Oxford C. S. Lewis Society, archived in the Bodleian Library, so that future Inklings scholars will be able to see the global reach and depth of Lewis's readership. Dr. Ward, my colleague in the Apologetics Department at Houston Baptist University, attended to every last detail to the final minute; he joined with many others in making

---

1. Dr. Holly Ordway is Professor of English and Director of the MA in Apologetics at Houston Baptist University, Texas. She is the author of *Not God's Type: An Atheist Academic Lays Down Her Arms* (Ignatius Press, 2014) and of "Charles Williams, *Descent into Hell*" in *C. S. Lewis's List: The Ten Books that Influenced Him Most* (Bloomsbury, 2015). She is the Charles Williams subject editor for *The Journal of Inklings Studies* and maintains a web presence at www.hollyordway.com, where the original version of this article first appeared.

these commemorations something that would truly honour this great man, C. S. Lewis, and extend his legacy.

The Symposium

Thursday 21st November was the occasion of a Symposium on Lewis's works, focusing on his contribution to Christian Apologetics. Professor Alister McGrath and Dr. Malcolm Guite spoke, respectively, on his use of Reason and Imagination—an approach that felt particularly relevant for us at HBU, since our approach to apologetics deliberately integrates rational and imaginative approaches. Professor McGrath's address was on "Telling the Truth through Rational Argument," and Dr. Guite's was on "Telling the Truth through Imaginative Fiction."

After the lectures and a service of Evensong at Westminster Abbey, we reconvened to hear a panel discussion on "What Can Twenty-First Century Apologetics Learn from C. S. Lewis?" chaired by Michael Ward. The panel included novelist Jeanette Sears, theologian Judith Wolfe, and apologists William Lane Craig, Peter S. Williams, and Michael Ramsden.

The Service

It was glorious and all-too-brief. There will never be another event like this one—at which were gathered many of those still living who knew C. S. Lewis personally. The British people welcomed Lewis as one of their own (at last!). Though Lewis is popular in America and indeed around the world, it was most fitting that this commemoration was conceived of and organized by British people, and held in Westminster Abbey, England's coronation church, which has been at the heart of national life for the last thousand years. Almost every aspect of Lewis's life and work was honoured in some way, through the choice of readings and indeed the choice of readers, the music, the hymns, and the quotations selected for the Order of Service and for the Memorial itself.

The sermon was given by the former Archbishop of Canterbury, the Most Reverend Rowan Williams—a brilliant exposition of Lewis's understanding of the significance of language, and the corruption of language.

The Service was also the occasion of the world premiere of a new choral anthem, commissioned especially for this anniversary, by noted composer Paul Mealor, who composed the motet for the Royal Wedding. The text was taken from Lewis's poem "Love's As Warm As tears"—and it was stunning. If this first performance is any guide, it seems likely the piece will become a permanent fixture of the English choral repertoire; it certainly deserves to be!

Continuing Lewis's legacy: the closing collection at the Service went to support a new scholarship in Medieval and Renaissance Literature at the University of Cambridge, where Lewis finished his professional career. It reminded me that Lewis's beneficent influence extended to his interactions with his students and colleagues. Without Lewis's unfailing encouragement, for instance, one of those colleagues, his fellow-medievalist friend Tolkien, would never have finished his masterwork, *The Lord of the Rings*.[2]

But before the close of the Service came its climax when Dr. Ward unveiled the Memorial Stone itself. Alongside Lewis's name and dates was the inscription: "*I believe in Christianity as I believe that the Sun has risen, not only because I see it but because by it I see everything else.*" Walter Hooper, who has done more than anyone else over the past fifty years to preserve and tend Lewis's literary legacy, then placed flowers at the head of the Stone. I later discovered the thinking behind the choice of flowers: sixty-four white roses (one for each year of Lewis's life); seven sprigs of holly berries (one for each of the Narnia Chronicles); three sprigs of rosemary (one for each novel of the Ransom Trilogy); and a single red rose (for the *Roman de la Rose*, the great medieval poem, signifying his academic career as a literary critic and historian).

When the ceremony was concluded, I went and stood by the Memorial and read its inscription, reflecting on all that Lewis had accomplished in his life and all that his work has meant to so many people. I thought in particular of his influence on Tolkien—who, in turn, has had such a transformative effect on my own life. The reference to the Sun, combined with the beautiful flowers, put me powerfully in mind of Frodo and Sam at the Cross-Roads:

> Suddenly, caught by the level beams, Frodo saw the old king's head. . . . [A]bout the high stern forehead there was a coronal of silver and gold. A trailing plant with flowers like small white stars had bound itself across the brows as if in reverence for the fallen king, and in the crevices of his stony hair yellow stonecrop gleamed.
> "They cannot conquer for ever!" said Frodo. And then suddenly the brief glimpse was gone.[3]

---

2. "The unpayable debt that I owe to [Lewis] was not 'influence' as it is ordinarily understood, but sheer encouragement. He was for long my only audience. Only from him did I ever get the idea that my 'stuff' could be more than a private hobby. But for his interest and unceasing eagerness for more I should never have brought the L[ord] of the R[ings] to a conclusion," *The Letters of J. R. R. Tolkien*, ed. Carpenter, 362.

3. Tolkien, *The Two Towers*, Book IV, chapter 7, "Journey to the Cross-Roads." Dr. Ordway is currently working on a study of *The Lord of the Rings*, entitled *Tolkien's Modern Sources*.

— 9 —

The Best Tale Lewis Ever Told

Sarah Clarkson[1]

ON THE DAY of the C. S. Lewis Symposium at Westminster, we got to the doors of St. Margaret's almost an hour before they opened. I tightened my scarf and watched the line grow; we queued in our hundreds in the chilly November air, present to honour an author whose words had helped form us, in mind and heart and soul.

My attendance at these commemorative events came as somewhat of a pilgrimage, to give thanks for a man whose writings shaped my faith almost from its inception. He may have died long before I was born, but Lewis's books reached me like letters from a kind, witty, and child-hearted godfather. Narnia companioned my childhood. Talking stars and valiant mice and swaying dryads peopled my dreams. When my siblings and I rigged up the oak tree in our front yard and called it a ship, it was the *Dawn Treader* I was sailing. And it was Aslan's country I desired to find.

Ah, Aslan ... Good, but never safe. "Not a *tame* lion."

As I grew up and began to wrestle with the reality of an untameable God, Lewis's works came often to my aid. His written voice guided me through doubt, assuaged my frustration, and called me back from the brink of disbelief. His stories evoked the kind of beauty that gave me powerful reason to hope, cause to continue trusting the lion-like God I was learning to love. If Lewis had still been living, I would gladly have trekked half the

---

1. Sarah Clarkson is the author of four books, including *Read for the Heart* (Apologia Press, 2009), and is currently studying for a degree in Theology at the University of Oxford where she serves as President of the Oxford C. S. Lewis Society. She maintains a web presence at www.thoroughlyalive.com, which is where the original version of this article first appeared.

world round to see him, so England didn't seem too far to celebrate his legacy. But I was amazed that day, as the crowd steadily swelled, to realize how many others felt the same.

I clapped my hands against the cold and watched my breath etch the frosty air. As the line lengthened behind me, a question formed in my mind: Why, I wondered, is the draw of C. S. Lewis so strong? What power in his self or his works summoned us from around the globe, from all walks of life, to honour his legacy and study his thoughts? What was the particular quality that so influenced me as a young reader and Christian? His books are famous, yes, but so are countless others. Novelists we have aplenty. Apologists too. And though his status as an Oxford don intrigues us, it's really not enough to kindle the kind of love that lasts for decades and links the hearts of countless different souls.

I ruminated on this throughout the day. As I listened to the excellent Symposium talks, I glimpsed the fact that part of the allure was the extraordinary way in which Lewis reconciled reason and imagination, engaging both faculties in his readers. His sheer writing genius is also, of course, part of his power, in books that continue to captivate with their richly imagined truth, their clarity of argument, their vivid fictional atmospheres. But even after these obvious qualities, I felt there was another element still to identify. I mulled it as I walked home that night, discussed it over dinner with my family, and returned to it as I rode the Tube back downtown for the Memorial dedication next morning. Perhaps most of all, I wondered as I sat in my stall waiting for the service to begin; for the Abbey itself is the kind of place in which such a question may well be pondered.

There are few places so shaped to shelter questions of legacy as the wide grey height of Westminster Abbey, with its spacious, motherly, encompassing embrace. A thousand years of prayer have risen amidst these pillars, this taut reach of stone; and a jeweled rain of light still falls from the high stained-glass. Myriads of busy people are always there in an eddy and flow, but the gentle talk and shuffle of steps is the run of a little river through a formidable old canyon. As I sat, I was deeply aware of a silence and shadow engraved by the passing of many centuries, hallowed by countless saints living and dead, a stillness that hovered above the sound of any modern voice.

The Abbey is a house of faces. They meet you at every step, at every turn, for this great church is, in many ways, a hall of heroes, a carved memorial to the kings and heroes, warriors, artists, and statesmen who have crafted the story of England. I felt almost haunted that day. In each alcove, grave sculpted faces arrested my glance. Emperors glared a challenge down at me from their pedestals; martyrs wailed their faith with eloquent eyes. I dropped my gaze to the floor, and remembered that the words of poets and novelists, priests and composers were cut in the very stones at my feet. I lifted my eyes and found the face of Christ, calm, fierce, lovely, reflected through figures glimmering and dancing in a hundred coloured windows. *So great a cloud of witnesses* . . . . The words from the Epistle to the Hebrews sang in my head.

The first strains of music signaled the start of the service. I thought again of Lewis as I studied the wise, knowing eyes of those statues and imagined the strong acts of compassion, battle, or creation that stood as the story and cause behind each silent figure. Each face was set in that place because the living soul it represented had thought or felt or fought its way to some vital truth about the world, a truth that compelled them to craft a life and work that embodied the treasure they had found.

Perhaps it was then, as I pictured Lewis in company with that multitude, that I first perceived his continuing power to draw and shape so many. After two hours of a marvelous service crammed with the truths that Lewis himself had found and striven to tell, all spoken into the air of that storied, sacred place, echoing down the decades to us, I began to understand.

We came because Lewis *lived* a great story. The best tale that Jack Lewis ever told was the tale of his own life and that story lends a power to his words that time cannot dispel. In his essay "On Stories,"[2] Lewis wrote of the "atmosphere" imbuing his favorite "romances." Some tales were steeped in a certain air beyond the cycle of mere events, an air that struck the reader with a sense of otherness, a sense of something beyond a plotted sequence. Whether the long, awful dark of "Outer Space," or the chill, pure sky of Northern myths, the greatest stories let us enter, for a moment, a "sheer state of being" that stirs our souls to life with hunger, awe, or wonder.

Human lives have atmospheres as well. Some lives, like those tales Lewis loved, are marked by a vibrancy so potent that we taste the numinous in their presence or their telling. The life of C. S. Lewis is a romance in and of itself.

His story bears the smell of pipe smoke, the taste of beer, the atmosphere of hearthsides and shabby college rooms in which fast friendships formed and strong opinions volleyed forth with brusque good humour into the small hours. In his tale, the fresh air of long walks and longer thoughts blows free. His elements are tea and common sense and high learning and the call of distant hills.

But into this lively picture flows an even fresher wind from the vast beyond, the heady skies of imagination. Who would have thought that an Oxford don skilled in logic, the "best read man" of his generation, whose

---

2. Lewis, *On Stories, and Other Essays on Literature*, ed. Walter Hooper.

intellect cowed countless students (and peers), could countenance a fairy tale? The atmosphere of Lewis's story grows rich and strange as we marvel that the mind at work in *Miracles* wove also the tale of a little girl named Lucy and the love she had for a lion. Walking trees and tea-drinking fauns peer round the corners of Lewis's life. Dragons roar through his dreams and give his story an atmosphere in which any number of wonders might take place. We relish his life because it gives us hope that our own stories too could quicken with the wind of imagination—and with a spirit yet more glorious still.

In his pithy *Experiment in Criticism*, Lewis identifies a number of key qualities belonging to the kind of story that he calls a "myth." He describes myth as a story that is "a permanent object of contemplation—more like a thing than a narration—which works upon us by its peculiar flavour or quality." Myth, he contends, is a story not dependent on literary finesse or narrative twists. A tale of absolutes, it deals with "impossibles and preternaturals." "Myth," says Lewis "may be sad or joyful but it is always grave." Last, and most important of all, Lewis believed that in reading myth we encounter some facet of Reality itself. We come up against something, clothed in story, which "will move us as long as we live."[3] In tales of dying gods or kings returned or great sea-faring heroes, we apprehend some aspect of eternal Reality. Myth, at its best, gestures to Christ.

The life of Lewis was the best kind of myth. Not because he was sinless or brilliant, not because he was a legend, but because he turned—or tried to turn—every facet of himself to the love of God; and that makes a person mythic in the end. Lewis did nothing by halves. From the point of his conversion onwards he followed every logical conclusion demanded by faith. He shirked nothing. His books are certainly marked by reason, by beauty, by vivid imagination. But they are also shaped by an eminently practical faith. With frank, good-humored obedience he worshipped and prayed, confessed his sins, and loved his neighbour by succouring the poor (giving away most of his royalties) and bearing with the difficult (especially the ageing Mrs. Moore and those "lame ducks" who wrote to him, endlessly). And so, unwittingly, he made his life into "a permanent object of contemplation." His was a heroic virtue, the "impossible or preternatural" virtue that comes through Christ, lived on the scale of the every day. The longer he lived, the more his own story was subsumed into the divine drama. His life took on the form he had described as a literary critic, that of an intentionally patterned *objet d'art* gesturing toward a fuller Reality.

---

3. Lewis, *An Experiment in Criticism*.

Anyone who spends many years loving God with heart, soul, mind, and strength will begin to grow mythic in the end. The lines become clearer the longer you follow the Master. Sin gets sloughed away. The soul grows crystalline with love, and the light of Christ shines through, "lovely to the Father in the features of men's faces."[4] Lewis practised what he preached in his sermon "The Weight of Glory," and "conducted all his dealings" in such a way that his life was the slow becoming of "everlasting splendor."[5]

The way was not without pain and doubt. His works detail the depths of inner dilemmas and temptations. He knew the struggle that comes with truly learning to love. And after death took his wife, Joy, the book that he wrote about his bereavement voiced the anguished abandonment all lovers know in loss. He understood from within the way that God Himself seems to change when suffering obscures one's sight. But I remember how Bishop Simon Barrington-Ward described him in the months after Joy's death: as if he had fought a battle that cost him everything. And yet, "there was almost a light upon his face."[6]

I don't believe that the stories Lewis told or the truths he argued could wield such power today without the bedrock story of his faithful life. His writings were rooted in the primary story of his life. He chose God and lived for Him at every turn, and his life became a living story pointing toward that Love.

When Lewis's legacy is considered, people often wonder who the next Lewis will be. Young Christians are encouraged to pursue rigorous training in reason and apologetics, or aim for the best kind of literary education at a prestigious university. These are fine pursuits for those who hope to emulate Lewis's genius at cultural engagement and imaginative apologetics. But if we really want to raise up another Lewis or two, I think we have to start with our own hearts and follow the advice of Lewis himself:

> Give up yourself and you will find your real self. Lose your life and you will save it. Submit to death, submit with every fibre of your being and you will find eternal life. Look for Christ and you will get Him, and with Him everything else thrown in. Look for yourself and you will get only hatred, loneliness, despair, and ruin.[7]

Those words pounded down the aisles and echoed in the arches of Westminster Abbey on the day of the memorial service. They came to us in

---

4. "As Kingfishers Catch Fire," Gerard Manley Hopkins.

5. Lewis, *The Weight of Glory*.

6. Simon Barrington-Ward, "What I Learnt from C. S. Lewis," address to the Oxford University C. S. Lewis Society, 21st February 2012.

7. Lewis, *Beyond Personality*.

Lewis's own recorded voice, and they opened the service with a challenge. Everything that followed—the tributes and songs, the prayers and readings honouring his life—was framed by his own ringing description of what he thought it meant to die well, and thus live well. He confronted each of us present at the service with an invitation: to join the best story that has ever been told; to live the one true myth of Christ.

Lewis once said that "you could never find a book long enough"[8] to suit his taste. Like Lucy in *The Voyage of the "Dawn Treader,"* who found the best tale ever told within the house of a great magician and wished she could read it forever, Lewis himself hungered from childhood to get inside the great myths that he loved. And the great, joyous fact of his existence was that he actually did. In his love of Christ, Lewis entered the one true myth of the world. He got right inside the best story ever told and his life became a living image of its beauty. And he calls to us, through the stories he left behind, to join him.

"Further up and further in!"[9] said Aslan . . . said Lewis. Shall we follow?

---

8. Lewis, *Of This and Other Worlds*, ed. Walter Hooper, 9.
9. Lewis, *The Last Battle*.

PART FOUR

Cambridge Conference

— 10 —

Rhetoric, Doctrine, and the Ethics of Language

C. S. Lewis on *Paradise Lost*

Rowan Williams[1]

———

A PREFACE TO PARADISE LOST[2] has been described as "Lewis at his very best"[3]: "Here is evidence of a mind abundantly stocked with reading which the author has enjoyed—effortlessly, intelligently, and selflessly enjoyed— and he wishes to communicate this enjoyment to us."[4] Generations of readers would echo A. N. Wilson's judgement; this is a book of wide-ranging learning but, most strikingly, of relaxed and confident exposition, *conversational* exposition as Wilson says, and commonsensical but by no means conventional judgement. It has worn well as an introduction to aspects of Milton (I can recall reading it with delight as a schoolboy in the late sixties, and younger readers still find it both accessible and illuminating); but it also serves as an introduction to some of Lewis's own favourite themes as critic and as moralist. In this brief introduction to the book, I hope to suggest some of those ways in which it helps us read Lewis as well as Milton. We shall look at what Lewis has to say about rhetoric, at his distinctive typol-

---

1. Dr. Rowan Williams (Lord Williams of Oystermouth) is Master of Magdalene College, Cambridge. He served as Archbishop of Canterbury (2002–12) and Lady Margaret Professor of Divinity at Oxford (1986–91). He is the author of numerous books, including *Faith in the Public Square* (Bloomsbury Academic, 2012) and *The Lion's World: A Journey into the Heart of Narnia* (Oxford University Press, 2013).
2. Oxford University Press 1942, reprinted in paperback 1960.
3. Wilson, *C. S. Lewis. A Biography*, 171.
4. Ibid.

ogy of epic narrative, and finally, briefly, at the moral analysis offered of the characters of Milton's poem. A great deal more could be and needs to be said about the direct and generously acknowledged influence on Lewis of Charles Williams's writing and lecturing on Milton,[5] and about the extent to which the *Preface* is shaped by Lewis's concern to push back at Eliot's verdicts on Milton (his references to Eliot are a masterpiece of respectful hostility); and since 1940 there has been no shortage of studies of Milton's theology, so that Lewis's sparring in the *Preface* with the work of Denis Saurat reflects a situation long since past.[6] But I believe it is worth simply looking at the frontier country between criticism and theology as it emerges in Lewis's book, with an eye to seeing how the *Preface* can show us connections within Lewis's own thought; and that is the purpose of this short exploration.

Rhetoric

The *Preface* could be read as in large part a defence of the very idea of rhetoric. Chapters 7 and 8 of the book examine the style of epic in general, arguing forcefully that the last thing this genre needs is sustained originality. The point of the language used in this kind of composition is to evoke "stock" responses—by which Lewis means not what happen to be demographically prevailing attitudes but the deep continuities of cultural intelligence. With a typical zest for paradox, he maintains that "stock" responses have to be learned; they are "a delicate balance of trained habits, laboriously acquired and easily lost, on the maintenance of which depend both our virtues and our pleasures and even, perhaps, the survival of our species."[7] We need to be educated in appropriate response to our environment; it is a massive error to think that we have truthful or reliable instincts that will save us from disaster, and the science of rhetoric, in its proper context, is a necessary part of this educative process. Yes, it "manipulates," it seeks to produce results in action, and because of this function it is inevitably selective. Yet selectivity is vital to seeing certain things truthfully ("Certain things, if not seen as lovely or detestable, are not being correctly seen at all"[8]). Poetry may not have as its primary purpose the moving of souls to action, but it is unintelligible if

---

5. Lewis refers specially to Williams's introduction to the 1940 World's Classics edition of *The Poetical Works of Milton*, but frequently alludes in his letters to the impact on himself and others of Williams's Oxford lectures on the poet.

6. For a very good recent essay with ample reference to the literature, cf. Myers, *Milton's Theology of Freedom*.

7. Lewis, *Preface*, 56–57.

8. Ibid., 53.

it has no element of seeking to change readers' minds—otherwise it would be written for the delectation of the writer, and "Himself is the very audience before which a man postures most and on whom he practises the most elaborate deception."[9]

Here as elsewhere, what Lewis has in the sights of his artillery is the notion that sincerity or transparency is a naturally available and unequivocal good in human dealings. He is a writer deeply preoccupied with truthfulness, and, as this last quoted comment shows, has a ruthless eye for self-deception, especially the deceptions we commit by telling ourselves they are "natural." To be truthful, let alone "sincere," is a matter of protracted learning and constant self-challenge. It requires a *moral culture*. It is no accident that the chapter following his defence of epic rhetoric deconstructs the idea of an "unchanging human heart," a repository of culturally unmediated, "innocent" and timeless perceptions or moral insights, available to any sensible person's introspection. And in this rather neglected aspect of his critical work, Lewis is in fact a good deal ahead of his time, refusing any suggestion that there are language-free or culture-free levels of the imagination that are not always already entangled with a culturally-shaped intelligence. But what makes him something other than a postmodernist denier of the *hors-texte* is, of course, that he believes there are culturally mediated perspectives that correspond to what is not at our disposal, what is abidingly the case in a moral universe—so that there is such a thing as corrupt or erroneous speech/culture, and it is simply and objectively bad for us. If there are no such perspectives, rhetoric is solely about power (as Plato fully understood); there is nothing but contestation, and rhetorical "manipulation" becomes entirely to do with who is to be master (to borrow the prescient phrase of Lewis Carroll's Humpty-Dumpty).

Epic is a publicly significant kind of narration, so Lewis argues in his opening chapters; and this means that there are some stories we corporately need to hear over and over. If this is so, such stories must be clothed with appropriate ritual, with "solemnity" (and Lewis is excellent on what this word does and does not mean[10]), and this in turn entails finding the correct "register" for public speech, since this will secure the right kind of hearing, absorbing, sensing, seeing, and, ultimately, acting. And to recognize this is to begin to be liberated from the autocracy of a self constantly seeking transparency to its own limpid interiority. If the *Preface* is a defence of rhetoric, it is also a not-too-covert polemic against a cult of sincerity that effectively leaves us with the

---

9. Ibid., 54.

10. "Easter is *solempne*, Good Friday is not. The *Solempne* is the festal which is also the stately and the ceremonial, the proper occasion for *pomp*" (ibid., 17).

dangerous fiction that our ideal audience is, indeed, ourselves—when we have been told by Lewis in no uncertain terms just how corrupting this particular audience is. In this sense, to defend rhetoric and to attack simplistic ideas of sincerity is no more and no less than to defend the inescapably *linguistic* character of human identity itself: we do not talk primarily to ourselves, and it is tempting to think that Lewis would have grasped something of what Wittgenstein's critique of "private language" was about.

But, as some of Lewis's own colleagues and friends insisted, this is not without its problems. Owen Barfield, in a tantalisingly brief introduction to a commemorative collection of essays by Lewis's friends, recalls his impatience with Lewis's unembarrassed fluency in pastiche; and he also records his impression in regard to a poem of Lewis's that "it left me with the impression, not of 'I say this,' but of 'This is the sort of thing a man might say.'" Lewis's initial response was that he was not sure of the difference.[11] Barfield grants that in fact the distinction is not at all so obvious, but persists in worrying at the underlying question: does Lewis actually think there is a proper place for spontaneity or personal authenticity, in word or act? Granted that everything is at some level a "performance," do we not need ways of distinguishing between performances that are authentic and inauthentic, as in fact we do when we think about stage performances? To bring it back to the *Preface*, is Lewis's strong reaction against sentimental individualism being pushed too hard, so that we begin to lose the criteria by which we might judge between good and bad performance—in the sense that a performance may be the act of someone seeking transparency to her basic convictions and direction, or of someone whose aim is purely and simply control for its own sake? How do we express and recognize an ethic of *self-surrender* in the act of performance? And once this has been formulated as a question, we have to think about the ambiguities of the way the *will* is involved in performance; as Barfield says, the element of the *voulu* in Lewis's public persona, the deliberate adoption of a style and position self-consciously in opposition to the fashionable, leaves a nagging concern, which might be formulated as a concern about the conscious concealment of a self not at peace with itself, or still uneasily in search of a language not defensive or evasive. As Barfield makes plain, this is emphatically not to accuse Lewis of "insincerity" but to identify a serious question to which the answer is not at all clear—a question about the very nature of the "personal," and a question as to whether Lewis's consistent and bracing repudiation of the self as an object of *interest* can be the whole story.

11. *Light on C. S. Lewis*, ed. Jocelyn Gibb, x–xi.

So to read the *Preface* as an apology for rhetoric opens up a number of larger questions in the reading of Lewis. It underscores the importance for him of challenging the self-evident good of "sincere" or "original" poetic language if this is simply an attempt to circumvent the absolute givenness of culture and so of cultural *formation* and so of the need for rhetoric. It raises the issue of the metaphysical or theological assumption behind all Lewis's criticism—and much of his broader social comment on linguistic degradation[12]—that speech should aim to nurture appropriate response ("stock" response) to the world, that, in other words, there are morally proper and morally improper ways of seeing phenomena, or to put it still more strongly, natural and unnatural responses. This conviction is—as we have seen—completely separate from an argument that such "natural" response can be deduced from a majority vote at any given moment, though it does make appeal (as Lewis spells out in works like *The Abolition of Man*) to some sort of very diffuse cross-cultural consensus. And the consideration of rhetoric also, ultimately, prompts questions about the very nature of the speaking self, as we shall see further in the third section of this essay. But not the least interesting feature of the *Preface* is that, in its tracing of the evolution of the epic form, it suggests how the register of narrative itself carries a kind of moral charge. How we tell significant stories shows what we think of the universe we inhabit; and teasing out the different styles of epic narrative can clarify aspects of a developing ethical awareness as well as a developing sense of *history*—of an ordering of events and epochs. It is out of these basic considerations about the place of rhetoric that Lewis's typology of epic emerges.

Epic

The *Preface* begins with a consideration of what Milton himself thought about epic. Lewis is admirably clear about the need to settle what exactly Milton thought he was doing before attempting any judgement on *Paradise Lost*, and he refers to Milton's own subdivisions of epic style in his Preface to Book II of his *Reason of Church Government*:[13] Lewis (rightly, I think) concludes that Milton is working with a broad division into "classic" and "romantic" types of epic—those working with a "single action," everything focused on one episode and set of relations, and those which deal serially

---

12. See, for example, the essay on "The Death of Words," published in *The Spectator* in September 1944; *C. S. Lewis: Essay Collection and Other Short Pieces*, ed. Walmsley, 447–49.

13. Lewis, *Preface*, 3–8.

with many adventures, in Spenserian or Italianate style. Milton's awareness of these diverse options is itself, Lewis argues, a measure of Milton's stature as a writer, conscious of the tension between possible styles, all of which appeal to him and all of which he is capable of handling. But once we recognize his choices, we understand more precisely what he thinks he is doing in *Paradise Lost*; and it is clear that he has turned his back on the "Spenserian" mode in order to write something more closely approaching a unified, *durchkomponiert* work. This does not mean a commitment to brevity, as is plain from Milton's—and Lewis's—discussion; it is rather a commitment to a poem that has one setting, one cast of characters, even one decisive episode. In this sense, Homer and Virgil exhibit a unity lacking in Spenser or Tasso.

But Lewis proposes a further refinement of typology, distinguishing between "primary" and "secondary" epic.[14] It is not an evaluative distinction, privileging the primitive over the more sophisticated (Lewis would obviously have no truck with romantic primitivism, for all the reasons implied in our earlier discussion); what it points to is more a distinction in both subject matter and moral tenor. Primary epic—the *Iliad*, *Beowulf*—does not deal with events or even personalities that are intrinsically significant, with "great" subjects: in the mentality of a Heroic Age, "No one event is really very much more important than another."[15] This may sound counter-intuitive: surely the whole point of early epic is to celebrate exceptional events or deeds? But Lewis persuasively turns this around. Primary epic does indeed narrate acts of outstanding heroism, or strength, or cruelty; but they are events that change nothing in the climate of the world in which they are set. The famous standard Homeric epithets for persons and features of the natural world ("rosy-fingered dawn" and so on) have the effect of repeatedly drawing us back to the sense of a background that never alters; just as the poignant simile in *Odyssey* VIII.523 ff. referring to a woman's laments over a dying husband killed in battle tell us that this is inexorably and unalterably the kind of world this is. All action is in a sense futile, yet there is nothing else for human beings to do but enact the immutable script of violence. The emotional force of such poems comes from the tension between the felt intensity of suffering and triumph here and now and the steady background both of the natural world and the pointless flux of conflict. Lewis quotes Goethe's chilling characterization of the *Iliad*—that its message is that "on this earth we must enact Hell."[16] A few years later, he might have referred to Simone Weil's great essay on the *Iliad* as a poem of "force," spelling out the "gravitational"

---

14. Ibid., chapters 3–7.
15. Ibid., 30.
16. Ibid., 31.

effect of violence in human action, the way in which violent conflict reduces human interaction to a "geometry" of forces seeking equilibrium so that there is never any significance for the participants in another point of view, another subject's perspective that has to be weighed or felt.[17]

In contrast, secondary epic *does* look to events that alter the course of things. Virgil is the paradigm for this kind of epic narrative, in which the temporal horizon of the story extends backwards and forwards in a way unthinkable in Homer, framing the actions under immediate review against a background of foreshadowings and prefigurings. The hero's action is called, mandated; it is the embodiment of a purpose not his own, apprehended both as duty and as desire.[18] But as such it is also something with which the hero must struggle, precisely because it is not blind fate. As Lewis says, Aeneas is nothing if not an *adult* who has to negotiate competing goods and desires, who has to think about the cost of actions and learn to live in compromised and to some degree guilty self-awareness. Lewis's analysis of Virgil, brief as it is, is one of the best things in the *Preface*, making one regret that he never devoted a whole book to the subject;[19] and its heart is the contention that secondary epic is inevitably in some important sense tragic—involved with sacrifice and collision of values. But to understand the style of secondary epic—the need for the rhetoric we have already been thinking about—we have to grasp that this more reflective narration, lacking as it does the physically and publicly ritual trappings of primary epic (music and ceremony in the mead hall or whatever), has to work that much harder for its effects; and Lewis eloquently argues that Milton's very syntax is an aspect of the rhetoric, carrying us along in its complex grammatical flow so that we internalise the long perspective and the connectedness of temporally remote things. There is, he says, a "facade of logical connexions" overlaying the emotional connections that are the main point;[20] Milton both quarries the remotest areas of learning for similes pregnant with more than their surface shows, and, through the apparent indeterminacy that his Latinate style so often presents—highly complex constructions, grammatical patterns that do not immediately yield their sense—moves us along with what can seem like an

---

17. There is a translation ("The *Iliad*, Poem of Might") in Weil, *Intimations of Christianity among the Ancient Greeks*, ed. and trans. Geissbuhler. cf. Winch, *Simone Weil: "The Just Balance,"* 143–46, for a good discussion of the text.

18. Lewis, *Preface*, 38.

19. The fragments of his translation of the *Aeneid* along with some critical/expository material have been published, edited by Reyes as *C. S. Lewis's Lost* Aeneid.

20. Lewis, *Preface*, 42.

almost dreamlike immediacy that is also rapidly shifting and slipping away; an "indivisible, flowing quality."[21]

All this is superbly presented and argued. But again it leaves a substantial question: does the subject matter of *Paradise Lost* actually lend itself to the techniques identified as those of secondary epic? On Lewis's showing, epic of this kind focuses on an episode whose significance is prepared for long beforehand and felt long afterwards; and we can hardly deny that "Man's first disobedience" is arguably such an episode. But part of the difficulty many readers have discovered in Milton's epic is that the events surrounding this central drama (in which, as Lewis argues,[22] it is possible to see elements of a will confronted with conflicting goods) are described as if the heavenly battle between the loyal angels and Satan were a series of contingent happenings whose outcome was uncertain—as if God could in principle be defeated. Lewis, in chapter 15 of the *Preface*, mounts a stout defence of the relative coherence of Milton's view of angelic corporeality; but, even granting that Raphael, in narrating (in Book V) to Adam and Eve the war in heaven, excuses his use of routinely material language and categories to give an impression of "invisible exploits," there is something bizarre about the entire enterprise of *narrating* the rebellion of Satan; and something worse than bizarre about depicting God's involvement in it as a sort of clinching military intervention. And Lewis himself winces at the Homeric mockery of Satan's defeat[23] and the "Olympian" anthropomorphism of some of the depictions of heaven.[24] Lewis rightly sees some of these passages as simply poetically tactless, not just theologically misplaced; but they reflect one of the underlying difficulties in Milton's exercise as Lewis defines it. Secondary epic requires the delicate double vision of a contingent series of events unfolding and a fixed destiny and purpose shaping them, and this is none too easy to apply to the extra-historical setting of primordial spiritual conflict, let alone the interaction of the persons of the divine Trinity. It is as though the central action of *Paradise Lost* had proved inadequate in drama for its author and had to be supplemented with a drama imported from elsewhere, artificially sustained with the trappings of Renaissance militarism.

Lewis has characterized Virgilian tragedy wonderfully well earlier in the book when he writes of Aeneas having to seek "something more important than happiness" and of the inescapable unhappiness of those who are

---

21. Ibid., 48.
22. Ibid., chapter 18.
23. Ibid., 95.
24. Ibid., 131.

left damaged in the wake of this vocationally directed quest.[25] But if secondary epic is about a destiny intermittently seen and pursued at tragic cost, what exactly is there about the narrative of the Fall that is Virgilian? The vocation of Adam and Eve is crystal clear; the following of it is not intrinsically shadowed with unavoidable loss. I suspect that Lewis's admirable clarity in expounding and defending what we might call the post-Virgilian aspects of Milton's rhetoric and idiom somewhat diverts our eyes at first from the extreme difficulty of representing Milton's subject matter in Virgilian terms. This is related to but not quite identical with the question of whether a genuinely tragic perspective is possible for a Christian artist—a larger issue than I can hope to tackle here. But if we read the war in heaven as an essential part of the poetic labour of "justifying" God's ways, the critical and theological embarrassments will not go away in a hurry. What Milton is saying is, in effect, that the apparently causeless act of disobedience by Adam and Eve in Eden is in fact the effect of Satan's rebellion; the narrative of a will struggling with unsought choices is projected from Eden to heaven. But the two great imaginative difficulties this faces are, first, that it is, by definition, impossible for us to imagine the interiority—and so the narrative trajectory—of the unfallen mind (more on this a little later); and second, that the war in heaven simply shifts the problem of causeless disobedience to another level. The minds of both angels and unfallen human agents are not narratable in the way in which we habitually narrate growing and deciding; they cannot be dealt with as if they were like Aeneas. Lewis's insightful and lucid anatomy of epic and its language turns out not quite to fit the Miltonic case; and, rather ironically, the lack of fit appears most clearly in Lewis's analysis of the post-Fall psychology of Milton's figures.

Moral Analysis

The chapters in which Lewis analyses the moral discourse of Satan and the fallen angels—and indeed of the fallen Adam and Eve (13, 14, 18)—are among the most lively and entertaining in the *Preface*. In many ways, they mirror the exactly contemporary enterprise that Lewis was involved in, the composition of *The Screwtape Letters*. The analysis of the "diabolical" mind requires us to try to see virtue itself through the lens of falsehood, holiness through the lens of unqualified self-absorption; and Lewis clearly believed that such an analysis could be an important stimulus to proper moral self-awareness. Follow through the implications of routine selfishness and idleness and this is where you end, in the ingenious but wholly sterile perspective

---

25. Ibid., 38–39.

enjoyed (not the right word, of course) by the devil and his angels—and also in the vulgarity of emotion and utterance displayed by the fallen Adam and Eve ("The father of all the bright epigrammatic wasters and the mother of all the corrupting female novelists are now both before us"[26]). These chapters, like *Screwtape*, remain a useful exercise for anyone looking to identify more clearly their own habits of moral evasion and self-deception; but their place in the *Preface* is, as Lewis explains,[27] nonetheless a matter of *critical* understanding. He is not, he says, "merely moralizing"; the *aesthetics* of Satan's language and that of the other fallen angels is bound up with their moral tenor and function. If we are concerned with issues of rhetoric, we need to learn how to read these utterances. They are illustrations of what language can do faced with intractable reality, examples of how we may be persuaded not to see what is in front of our eyes. For dramatic purposes, the devils are locked into a frame of self-reference that cannot be changed (because only they can change it and they choose not to): how do you speak, how do you configure the world and persuade others, when you are irreparably out of touch with reality? That is the question Milton addresses, according to Lewis, in the demonic speeches of Book II of *Paradise Lost*.

We noted earlier that a refusal to take rhetoric seriously in its metaphysical and moral context left us with a picture of human affairs as no more than a contest about power, detached from any idea of a substantive and common moral good. The chapters on the rhetoric of the devils can be read as a spelling-out of the same point: imagine a situation in which there is no sense of a set of moral goals independent of the will, and then imagine what could be *said* in such a situation. As in many other contexts,[28] Lewis's underlying concern is to show that the very idea of reasoned discourse takes for granted a "something" that is being talked about, and that without this there is only the clash of wills. For him, an inextricable aspect of the critical task itself is to expose what is going on when language becomes no more than such a contest of power. And to understand the general importance of knowing how rhetoric works—which is, as we have seen, a major motive in the *Preface*—is essential in conserving any notion of what linguistic integrity means; without a grasp of what it is for language to embody its purpose

---

26. Ibid., 128.

27. Ibid., 104.

28. Notably the unforgettable passage in *Out of the Silent Planet* where Ransom attempts to translate into the language of the planet Malacandra the aspirations of the Faustian scientist Weston, cast as they are in what turns out to be untranslatable cliché; and in the bloody and grotesque climax to *That Hideous Strength*, in which the power of coherent speech is taken away from the villains who have consistently abused and distorted language itself.

in its form, the form of any utterance becomes exactly what some kinds of postmodern theory insist it must be, a coding for power. And, lest we should be under any illusion about what this means, Lewis very characteristically insists that it means an infinity of boredom. In chapter 13 he notes how Satan is depicted as repeatedly "stating his own position";[29] any and every aspect of his environment has to become grist for the mill of his self-defence and self-reference, and, says Lewis, this monomania "is a necessity of the Satanic predicament,"[30] the fundamental refusal of a reality not at the mercy of the will.

Lewis admits the risk of "trespass[ing] beyond the bounds of purely literary criticism" in what he has to say about Satan;[31] and most readers will probably feel that these chapters, though superbly engaging, are really a coda to the properly literary discussion of earlier pages. It is certainly true that Lewis is letting his hair down somewhat; but it is a mistake to think that he is stepping away from the main themes of the *Preface*. What this analysis has sought to draw out is the way in which a set of arguments about genre and style are, for Lewis, inseparably connected with a robustly moral view of what criticism itself is for. This needs to be stated carefully: as his own later *Experiment in Criticism*[32] was to argue at greater length, the point is not that criticism as such enables moral and aesthetic judgements to be made more decisively and authoritatively than "ordinary" reading but that the good critic will help you see more clearly what a writer is saying and intending—what the writer values, despises, wants to persuade you about. Criticism is thus always a moral science to the degree that writing, like other forms of human speech, is out to make a difference—to make the reader want something other than he or she might have wanted left to themselves. The critic shows you with greater clarity *what is to be judged* rather than prescribing the judgement to be made. Thus Lewis can, in effect, say in the *Preface* that he is not insisting on a moral condemnation of the language of the fallen angels on critical grounds; he is simply spelling out what the fallen angels are in fact saying. That he himself manifestly, eloquently, and entertainingly regards this as poisonous nonsense he does not attempt to conceal; but he does try to distinguish between the critical task of explaining what it is that Milton's epic as a whole, and the dramatic speeches of the devils in particular, are as a matter of fact saying, and what a sensible person ought to think about what they are saying. The somewhat porous boundary between

29. Lewis, *Preface*, 102.
30. Ibid.
31. Ibid., 94.
32. Cambridge University Press, 1961.

these two exercises is of course part of the appeal of the book, even for those who do not agree with Lewis about either question.

But, to return for a moment to the issue touched on at the end of the previous section, the manner in which the fallen angels are depicted in *Paradise Lost* and the characterization of the post-Fall Adam and Eve highlight the central difficulty in Lewis's attempt to persuade us to read Milton in a Virgilian way. The speeches of the fallen angels and humans represent exactly what Lewis's Virgil opens up for us: they are about choice and loss, all the more poignantly, of course, because the speakers do not recognize the choices they are making or the losses they are incurring. As we have just seen, one of the functions of criticism is to clarify, at least for the reader, what those choices and losses amount to. But in the context of *Paradise Lost*, these are matters that arise in the wake of the Fall itself: the devils and Adam and Eve now have psyches like ours, we might say, inner lives about which we can tell a story. The fallen psyche is able to represent to itself its own position, its history, its location in regard to other egos; that is why it is able at worst comprehensively to ignore the pressure of reality and to create its own world. This is the nature of its inalienable freedom; or rather, this is what becomes of created freedom once it has discovered its capacity to talk about itself. (It is no accident that in *Perelandra* the equivalent to the biblical temptation of Eve involves the agent of evil presenting the Eve figure with a mirror.) That capacity is the source both of destructive falsehood and of healing repentance (and sanity-inducing irony); it is what makes both tragedy and comedy possible. The complete erosion of this would be just that reduction of language to contests of power that Lewis helps us identify—a purely diabolical language. The problem of Satan's followers in chapter 14 of the *Preface* is, you might say, that they haven't yet become diabolical enough for their own stability; they still resent and suffer because of the truth. It is a question Lewis leaves open whether there could be absolute and final deadness to truth, with not even a vestige of the pain that is both recognized and denied in the speeches of the fallen angels. But at the other end of the spectrum, something similar holds. We cannot imagine tragedy or comedy in the lives of unfallen angels or humans; and this is not so much a theological point as a "grammatical" one. The very idea of unfallen consciousness in this imaginative world is of an awareness so transparent to reality that it is not capable of being *interested* in itself. Remember that, as we saw in the first section of this essay, Lewis sees all forms of such interest—the whole business of being a self-aware "personality"—as ambiguous at best. And the unavoidable conclusion of all this is that the most an epic about the Fall could do would be to dramatise its *effects*; it could not take the Fall itself as a narrative or dramatic subject without subverting the central moral and spiritual point, that a particular sort of consciousness, bound up with language as we know it, is unimaginable in an unfallen state. The transition from one state to another cannot therefore be shown as a dramatic episode, a struggle involving what we now know as choices. The *creation* of what we now know as the choosing consciousness cannot be represented as an episode in the history of choosing consciousnesses.

This is not a nit-picking point. It means that, whatever might be said in general about Christianity and tragedy, about truly indeterminate choice and the unavoidable loss of some goods in consequence, the story of the beginning of such drama cannot itself be a case of the drama. And this means in turn that any Virgilian elements in Milton's epic must be at best decorative if they are located in a pre-Fall situation. The narrative of war in heaven, however it may be defended (as it is by the Archangel) as a translation into human terms of events otherwise beyond direct description, cannot work as Milton seems to want it to, and as Lewis wishes us to read it. If a great part of the force and intellectual energy of the *Preface* is bound up with its powerful and coherent mapping of the ethics of speech and the place of rhetoric, it becomes all the clearer that there is something eccentric about the Miltonic enterprise insofar as it seeks to present a narrative of the origins of evil.

Conclusion

But this is really to go beyond the scope of comment on what Lewis is directly doing as a critic. What this essay has attempted to suggest is that the central critical goal in the *Preface* is to defend and expound the significance of rhetoric; we need to know, if we are to read any text intelligently, what a writer's purpose is, so that we can grasp why the writer makes this or that choice in register, image, rhythm, and so on, and this is already to bring us into the territory of rhetoric. The writer wants to make a difference; the choices he or she makes are shaped by what kind of difference they have in mind. And the clarification of the range of available options—the typology of epic narrative, for example—is closely connected with this central aim of explaining what rhetoric is and how it works. All this accounts for a great deal of Lewis's argument. But the case of *Paradise Lost* proves more complex than at first appeared: it fits badly into the Virgilian and post-Virgilian world in which Lewis understandably wants to place it, because its subject matter is the process by which the "Virgilian" consciousness (of choice, loss, the cost of destiny in the actual fabric of particular human lives) comes into being. Lewis's own fascination with the moral twists and turns of looking at one's own psychology, a subject that he handles with consistent and sometimes disturbing brilliance, takes for granted that this, our habitual linguistic environment, is inherently morally fragile, and thus a mark of fallenness. The chapters in the *Preface* in which he anatomises the self-deception, self-imaging, and increasing self-isolation of the fallen consciousness precisely by anatomising the rhetoric of the first post-Fall speakers (angelic and human) show how closely connected his whole idea of the speaking self is to assumptions about the fractured mode of consciousness that results from the Fall. And this highlights the difficulty of the Miltonic enterprise as Lewis has defined it. If the point of the poem is to provide a rationale for the rebellion of Adam against divine commandment, it cannot be done in the chosen mode—a genre that (assuming Lewis's typology of secondary epic) explores what it is that is "more important than happiness" and the emotional and imaginative implications of unavoidable loss. Lewis is right to say that the nature of Virgil's work implies that future epic will in some sense or other be "religious";[33] but it is perhaps not an unbearable paradox to point out that the narrative of the Fall is not a story about "religious" behaviour in any sense we can conceive, not about the painful negotiations of clear vocation and human ambivalence or confused desire that is part of a "Virgilian" religiousness. It is Lewis's own clarity and freshness on the subject of rhetoric that in the long run prompt the reader to suspect that *Paradise Lost* is in fact in *these* terms a rhetorical eccentricity, a work that cannot happily embody its goal in its form.

This does not mean—it should hardly need saying—that it is anything other than a great and inexhaustibly fascinating poem at any number of levels; it does mean that it leaves unresolved questions, even, perhaps especially, for readers who largely share Lewis's own moral and spiritual world. But the continuing appeal of the *Preface* must surely lie in just this sense that Lewis is using his analysis of Milton's epic to say not only something about the character of criticism itself but something about the nature of self-aware speech, about the ethics of communication, about whether or not language is primarily about power. It belongs with his most significant work on what humanity is and what language does.

---

33. Lewis, *Preface*, 39.

— 11 —

C. S. Lewis on Allegory

Ad Putter[1]

THE MAIN TOPIC OF this essay is a book that C. S. Lewis published in 1936, *The Allegory of Love: A Study in Medieval Tradition*.[2] I must confess to having an irrepressible prejudice in favour of Lewis the critic, and I really ought to have added the subtitle "Why I Like C. S. Lewis's Criticism," or "Why I Think C. S. Lewis Is One of the Finest Critics of Medieval Literature." However, sober titles have the advantage of disguising prejudice; and to complete the disguise I shall in due course take issue with some of the points made by him in *The Allegory of Love*.

But let me begin with the adulation that I hope will lead beyond itself to more interesting things. Lewis could write beautifully and sympathetically, and I think the source of his perceptiveness was his close self-identification with the lives imagined and implied by the old books he studied. I have it on good authority that Lewis's lectures were just as entertaining as his writing. There are now not many people living who were taught by him, but one of the pleasures in preparing this essay was to talk to one of these people, John Burrow, who was an undergraduate in Oxford shortly after the war and there heard Lewis give the lectures that were eventually written up as *The Discarded Image*. The lectures dealt with the medieval and early modern worldview, and they were crowd-pullers. "One *went to*

---

1. Dr. Ad Putter is Professor of Medieval English Literature at the University of Bristol. He is the author of *Sir Gawain and the Green Knight and French Arthurian Romance* (Clarendon Press, 1995) and co-editor of *The Cambridge Companion to the Arthurian Legend* (Cambridge University Press, 2009).

2. Quotations from *The Allegory of Love* (1936) will be from a later edition (New York: Oxford University Press, 1958).

C. S. Lewis's lectures," John Burrow tells me; and that was at a time when there was no expectation either that students should attend lectures or that lectures should be appealing, with the result that many learned dons gave dry lectures to ever-dwindling cohorts of students. Lewis's colleague J. R. R. Tolkien was apparently one such don.

Both *The Discarded Image* and *The Allegory of Love* mapped areas of culture that seem quite remote from and uncongenial to the interests of modern readers. In *The Discarded Image*, that area is the way the world was explained before the advent of science as we now understand it; in *The Allegory of Love*, it is the allegorical tradition, and in particular allegorical love poetry. However, Lewis made himself so thoroughly at home in these alien territories and describes them so vividly that he speaks like an aboriginal of these distant lands. There was a kind of historical imagination and identification at work in his criticism that made him understand older forms of literature from the inside, as it were. In the conclusion to the inaugural lecture that he gave when he took up the Chair of Mediaeval and Renaissance English, which the University of Cambridge created especially for him, he claimed that the reason why he could write about early English literature with special authority was that he was a "dinosaur,"[3] one of the few remaining survivors from the days of yore. This superficially absurd claim was, I think, really a way of making light of the vast amount of learning and thinking you need to do in order to achieve genuine inwardness with the literature of an older period.

When you read many books from the Middle Ages you do, of course, begin to feel at home in the period, and you also come to appreciate, as C. S. Lewis did, that the past is not really "dead" at all, and conversely that there is still much about us that is medieval. In *The Discarded Image*, that sense of continuity with the past does not come across quite as strongly as in *The Allegory of Love*, for the simple reason that in the former book Lewis was dealing with "discarded" old science, such as the theory of the four humours, the idea of the seven spheres of the planets with the earth at its centre, and so on. Yet in *The Discarded Image*, too, there are moments when a witty analogy undoes what Lewis called the "great change" from medieval to modern[4]—as when he cautions against the assumption that medieval people were woollier in their thinking than we are today:

> At his most characteristic, medieval man was not a dreamer, nor a wanderer. He was an organizer, a codifier, a builder of systems.

---

3. Lewis, "De Descriptione Temporum," *Selected Literary Essays*, ed. Hooper. Available online: https://archive.org/details/DeDescriptioneTemporum.

4. Lewis, *The Discarded Image*, 214.

> ... There was nothing that medieval people liked, or did better, than sorting out and tidying up. Of all our modern inventions I suspect that they would most have admired the card index.[5]

This is a characteristic example of Lewis's wit. Imagine for a moment that a medieval author entered your work space and looked about for something valuable to take back to his own age. What would it be? Perhaps the radio? The desk lamp? No, says Lewis, he would make off with your box of index cards (unfortunately, this example of a modern invention is now itself dated). Lewis's imagination was a place where medieval and modern people met, and by introducing them to each other in this thought-experiment he also illuminates one of the many ways in which we continue to be medieval. The medieval love of codification, as exemplified by the great Summas of scholastic theologians like Thomas Aquinas, is with us still; it afflicts many academics (myself included), and when some of these academics last used a card index it was perhaps to create something that medieval scribes first invented: the alphabetical index of names and topics for a book (appearing for the first time towards the end of the thirteenth century).[6]

A more profound point to emerge from *The Discarded Image* is that *our* way of understanding the world, too, involves reliance on models, and that when we abandon such models it is not necessarily because new facts are discovered or old ones disproved, but because the old model is no longer elastic enough to accommodate new facts by minor adjustments and complications: "the human mind will not long endure such ever-increasing complications if once it has seen that some simpler conception can 'save the appearances.'"[7] Lewis sent his manuscript of *The Discarded Image* to Cambridge University Press in 1962 (the preface is dated July '62), the same year that Thomas Kuhn's *The Structure of Scientific Revolutions* was published.[8] Kuhn coined the phrase "paradigm shifts" to designate the adoption of new conceptual models, and historians and philosophers of science now credit Kuhn with the insight that scientific revolutions occur when existing paradigms become overstretched. In fact, it was C. S. Lewis who had the idea first, having floated it in (of all places) a series of undergraduate lectures on medieval literature.[9]

---

5. Ibid., 218.

6. On the development of this and other finding tools, cf. Rouse and Rouse, *Authentic Witnesses*, 221–55.

7. Lewis, *The Discarded Image*, 219–20.

8. Kuhn, *The Structure of Scientific Revolutions*.

9. The point has been made by Edwards, "The Christian Intellectual in the Public Square: C. S. Lewis's Enduring American Reception," in *C. S. Lewis: Life, Works, and*

It is interesting that, like Kuhn, Lewis had arrived at this insight by acquainting himself with the ways of science. His own term for a set of interrelated ideas about the world, a "model," was borrowed from physics, as he acknowledges;[10] and one wishes that historians of science had stuck with it: it is simpler than "paradigm" and has the further advantage of suggesting the indirectness with which we "know" the world around us. I follow Lewis in putting inverted commas around the verb "know," for the punctuation makes another important and related point. Most of our conceptions of the world—for instance, the fact that the earth is not at the centre of our universe but is a planet that circles the sun—has a kind of certainty for us that has less to do with our actual experience of life than with our trust in the prevailing "model." So I "know" the earth goes round the sun with the same kind of assurance that underlay Geoffrey Chaucer's knowledge that it was the other way around; and the same is true for all kinds of other things he "knew" and we "know"—or trust we know.

There is therefore in Lewis no trace of that sense of intellectual superiority that even some very intelligent acquaintances of mine feel towards the medieval period—that "Dark Age of Superstition." On the contrary, Lewis's accounts of the stranger notions of the period are so compelling that one realizes how persuasive these notions must have been and indeed still are. Take, for example, the doctrine of the four humours. Because of an imbalance of the humours, some people are choleric, others phlegmatic, others sanguine, and others melancholic. What is more, they look that way too: thus the sanguine person, cheerful and effusive, is a little chubbier and ruddier in the face; the choleric man, fretful and rather short-tempered, is lean and has thin legs. Anyone who has read Lewis's exposition of this theory with an open mind, and has looked at himself and others in the light of it, will find it difficult to resist the conclusion that the theory actually works. It certainly works for me (I am mildly choleric, though working hard to restore a healthy balance of my humours).

In *The Allegory of Love*, Lewis is more explicit about his belief that the past is not a foreign country. Thus he makes it clear from the start that he is not interested in approaching allegorical love poetry as if were some dead relic from the past, and that his book should not be read as a study in historical alterity:

> The study of this whole tradition may seem, at first sight, to be but one more example of that itch for "revival," that refusal to leave any corpse ungalvanized, which is one of the more

---

Legacy, vol. IV, ed. Edwards, 1–18 (9).

10. Lewis, *The Discarded Image*, 218.

distressing accidents of scholarship. But such a view would be superficial. Humanity does not pass through phases as a train passes through stations: being alive, it has the privilege of always moving yet never leaving anything behind. Whatever we have been, in some sort we are still. Neither the form nor the sentiment of this old poetry has passed away without leaving indelible traces on our minds.[11]

C. S. Lewis was not in the business of galvanizing corpses; there is more than enough of that already in modern scholarship, as he ruefully noted. The business he practised was rather that of enabling us to see the connections between what we were in the past and what we are today.

To show Lewis at work, I would like to present a couple of examples of apparently unfamiliar moments and characters from medieval literature, and then give his comments on them. The first example is from Chrétien de Troyes's *Chevalier de la charrette* (c. 1180). The hero of this romance, Lancelot, is completely devoted to Queen Guinevere, who has been abducted by the dastardly Meleagant. On his quest to find her, Lancelot comes across a dwarf driving a cart normally used to transport criminals. When Lancelot asks if he has seen the queen, the dwarf replies that he might be able to find her if he gets into the dwarf's disreputable cart. Lancelot hesitates briefly, and Chrétien explains what goes on in Lancelot's mind during that moment of hesitation:

> Before he climbs in, the knight hesitates merely for two steps; but it was unfortunate for him that he did so and unfortunate that his fear of shame stopped him from jumping in at once, for he will rue the consequences. But Reason, who is at odds with Love, tells him to avoid getting in, warning and instructing him to do and engage in nothing that might bring him shame or reproach. Reason, who dares tell him this, is not in the heart but the mouth; but Love, who bids and urges him to climb quickly into the cart, is enclosed within his heart. It being Love's wish, he jumps in regardless of the shame, since Love commands and wills it.[12]

Modern readers are likely to find this mini-personification allegory rather stilted and artificial. We have found other ways of expressing the point that Chrétien is trying to make here. Lancelot, as we might put it today, is torn between conflicting impulses and imperatives: on the one hand he loves the queen, and so wants to get into the cart that will take him to her; but on the other hand he is concerned for his reputation, and this concern

---

11. Lewis, *The Allegory of Love*, 1.
12. Translation from Owen, *Arthurian Romances*, 189.

holds him back. In psychological jargon, Lancelot's self is briefly divided, one part wanting one thing, another part something else. But Chrétien de Troyes did not have such jargon at his disposal, and, since writers before him were not much given to exploring the inner life, C. S. Lewis was right to insist on the novelty of what Chrétien was doing:

> Chrétien de Troyes, judged by modern standards, is on the whole an objective poet. The adventures still occupy the greater part of his stories. By the standard of his own time, on the other hand, he must have appeared strikingly subjective. The space devoted to action that goes forward only in the souls of his characters was probably beyond all medieval precedent.[13]

And that innovativeness has important consequences. When writers begin to explore conflicts within the soul in stories that traditionally concern conflicts in the outer world, inner conflict will necessarily find expression in the language of outer conflict. In this particular case, the language is that of a personification allegory in which one "person," Reason, demands one thing from Lancelot, while another "person," Love, demands the opposite. It is, writes Lewis, "as if the insensible could not yet knock on the doors of the poetic consciousness without transforming itself into the likeness of the sensible: as if men could not easily grasp the reality of moods and emotions without transforming them into shadowy *persons*. Allegory, besides being many other things, is the subjectivism of an objective age."[14] No-one could have put that better than Lewis did, and no critic has better equipped us to appreciate Chrétien's allegorical flights of fancy. Such an appreciation not only involves imagining oneself back in the twelfth century, in the position of a writer for whom precedents for literary "subjectivism" were limited; it also involves looking forward from that point in time to see the future of Chrétien's precocious attempts to psychologise action. Doing both these things enabled Lewis at once to measure the great divide between the modern novelist and the twelfth-century poet and to bridge that divide by recognizing the essential kinship between the two. In Lewis's words, Chrétien "was one of the first explorers of the human heart, and is therefore rightly to be numbered among the fathers of the novel of sentiment."[15]

In his treatment of the great medieval English poet Geoffrey Chaucer, Lewis was similarly able to recognize the present in the past and the past in the present in ways that frankly make many other critics look out of their depth. For example, he gets the character of Pandarus in Chaucer's *Troilus*

---

13. Lewis, *The Allegory of Love*, 29.
14. Ibid., 30.
15. Ibid., 29.

and Criseyde absolutely right. According to many modern readers, Chaucer's Pandarus is already what the figure of the pander has now become: a sleazy go-between, who is in cahoots with another man to ensnare an innocent woman. Traces of that degeneration are already visible in the Pandarus of Shakespeare's *Troilus and Cressida*, and there is plenty of literary criticism that represents Chaucer's Pandarus as a similarly dubious character. Here, by refreshing contrast, is Lewis's description:

> Pandarus is exactly the opposite of his niece. He is, above all, a practical man, the man who "gets things done." ... Everyone has met the modern equivalent of Pandarus. When you are in the hands of such a man you can travel first class through the length and breadth of England on a third-class ticket; policemen and gamekeepers will fade away before you, placated yet unbribed; noble first-floor bedrooms will open for you in hotels that have sworn they are absolutely full; and drinks will be forthcoming at hours when the rest of the world goes thirsty.[16]

The characterization that Lewis develops so exuberantly in this passage depends on imagining Pandarus in the familiar setting of present-day England (though, of course, there are no more third-class train tickets and only a few gamekeepers left), and this thought-experiment again illustrates his particular strength: Lewis was able to relate to medieval stories with the same uncomplicated directness as we relate to the normal world around us. Insights of this kind only come about when a critic perceives the world around him in terms of the books he has just read, sees traces of Pandarus in his practical friend who can fix any situation, and, vice versa, sees glimpses of friends and acquaintances in the fictional characters in the books he is reading. And surely that is what reading should be all about: relating the story to your life and your life to the story, and finding both life and books enriched in the process.

About Criseyde, too, Lewis is sympathetic, though when discussing her he offers a prediction which time has disproved: "those who have followed Chaucer most closely in his devout study of her, will best understand Criseyde. There have always been those who dislike her; and as more women take up the study of English literature she is likely to find ever less mercy."[17] Lewis's supposition that hostile misinterpretations of Criseyde would increase in proportion with the increasing numbers of women choosing to study English literature at university is perhaps due to an assumption that women would be harder on their own sex; but, whatever his thinking was,

16. Ibid., 190.
17. Ibid., 182.

his prediction has not come true. It is in fact poor diffident Troilus who has found less and less sympathy with modern readers, men and women alike, as younger generations of readers find it harder and harder to sympathize with his honourable trepidation before the woman he loves.

If there is a recurrent weakness in *The Allegory of Love*, I think it is that, in his critical evaluation of allegories, Lewis set too much store by the coherence of the story. I mean coherence in two ways. First, as is clear from both his criticism and his own fictional writing, C. S. Lewis liked a good story, with a beginning, middle, and end; and he is invariably harsh on allegories that do not offer much by way of story or unity of action. About *The Assembly of Ladies*, which ends very inconclusively, he has this to say:

> Taken as an allegory, it is as silly a poem as a man could find in a year's reading. A number of ladies are summoned to a "counsayl" at the court of Lady Loyalty; they arrive and present their petitions; Loyalty postpones her answer till her next "parliment" and the dreamer wakes. As a story, and still more as an allegorical story, this is clearly of no value.[18]

Although some later critics would agree with this,[19] I think that *The Assembly* is actually a very interesting allegory,[20] and the inconclusiveness of the story seems to me to be an important part of its meaning. The psychological reality that lies behind the allegorical fiction is that the lady who wrote *The Assembly* (stylized as the "I" of the poem) felt that she had a legitimate grievance, and so it makes good allegorical sense that in the story she goes to appeal to "Loyalty" (the word also meant "fairness," "equity" in Middle English), just as it makes sense for Loyalty to grant the justness of her complaint. But although Loyalty is on her side, for Fairness is fair, life is often unfair, and the deferral of any "open remedy" (723) for the lady—come back later, says "Loyalty," and you will find out "how ye shul be releved" (724)—makes the allegorical point that having right on our side is no guarantee that things will be also be put right.

Chaucer's *Complaint unto Pity* fares no better in Lewis's judgement, again because it lacks a good story. The story, such as it is, of a lover who sets out to complain to Lady Pity, but when he gets to her she turns out to be "dead and buried in a heart." Several allegorical characters surround her

---

18. Ibid., 249.

19. See, for example, Pearsall (ed.), *The Floure and the Leafe* and *The Assembly of Ladies*, 52–53. Subsequent references to *The Assembly of Ladies* are to this edition.

20. I discuss the poem's merits at greater length in "Fifteenth-Century Chaucerian Visions," in *A Companion to Fifteenth-Century Poetry*, ed. Boffey and Edwards, 143–56.

hearse; they show no grief, but are allied in their determination to frustrate the lover's cause:

> Aboute hir herse ther stoden lustely,
> Withouten any woo as thought me,
> Bounte parfyt, wel armed and richely,
> And fresshe Beaute, Lust, and Jolyte,
> Assured Maner, Youthe and Honeste,
> Wisdom, Estaat, Drede, and Governaunce,
> Confedred both by bonde and alliaunce.
>
> A compleynt had I, written in myn hond,
> For to have put to Pite as a bille;
> But when I al this company ther fond,
> That rather wolden al my cause spille
> Then do me helpe, I held my pleynte stille,
> For to that folk, withouten any fayle,
> Withouten Pitee ther may no bille availe.
>
> Then leve I al these vertues, sauf Pite,
> Kepynge the corps as ye have herd me seyn,
> Confedred alle by bond of Cruelte
> And ben assented when I shal be sleyn.
> And I have put my complaynt up ageyn,
> For to my foes my bille I dar not schewe.... (36-55)[21]

This, according to Lewis, "illustrate[s] the use of personification allegory at its lowest level—the most faint and frigid result of the popularity of allegory. Not only do the allegorical figures fail to interact, as in a true allegory; they even fail to be pictorial; they become a mere catalogue";[22] and he goes on to cite some lines from the first stanza of the above-quoted extract to prove it.

Again, I disagree. The art of self-reflexive allegory of the kind Chaucer is here writing lies in the constant awareness that the personifications in the fiction are at the same time abstract nouns.[23] From this perspective, it is surely nonsense to complain, as Lewis does, that the lady's personified virtues "become a mere catalogue," for that is what they were to start with; and Chaucer wittily bares the device when the "I" says he will "leve al these vertues, sauf Pite." In the fictional story that should mean he will now leave

21. Cited from *The Riverside Chaucer*, gen. ed. Benson.

22. Lewis, *The Allegory of Love*, 167.

23. This paragraph draws on Putter, "Chaucer's *Complaint unto Pity* and the Insights of Allegory," in *Medieval Latin and Middle English Literature*, ed. Cannon and Nolan, 166–81.

these "persons," apart from Pity, behind him; but the logical impossibility of leaving them but not Pity, when these personifications are supposed to be gathered around her corpse, signals that what is really being dismissed is all the qualities conventionally attributed to the lady (a topos here as useless to the poet as to the lover), not a group of people. It is likewise nonsensical to expect abstractions to "interact" with the poet: we do not in real life "interact" with abstract ideas as we interact with people; and the point of allegory, even Lewis's action-packed *true* allegory, is really to indicate our relationship or disposition towards ideals (whether we like them or not, are close to achieving them or not, and so on). And Chaucer's allegory does that very well. For example, because "Beauty," "Wisdom" and their ilk are excellent things in a lady, they naturally figure as "virtues," but because these same virtues make the lady harder to attain—indeed impossible to attain without Pity (which represents the lady's generous renunciation of her superiority vis-à-vis her suitor)—they are also the lover's enemies, his "foes," who have ganged up against him and condemn him to a certain death. Similarly, the apparent contradiction between their allegorical role as public mourners and their continued cheerfulness, as they stand "lustely" around her hearse, makes good allegorical sense. A lady's beauty, youthfulness, charm, etc., are in no way diminished by her lack of pity. It is only the lover who suffers from that, and so in the allegory it is only he who seems to notice that Pity is dead.

In addition to wanting allegorical stories to be coherent in their own right, Lewis also demanded a good fit between the allegorical fiction and the non-allegorical truths encoded by that fiction. The first fully developed Christian personification allegory, Prudentius' *Psychomachia* (circa A.D. 400), which represents the struggle of good and evil in the human soul in the allegorical guise of a battle between personified vices and virtues, comes under attack from Lewis because of the incongruity of the allegorical action and the moral point. He thought that the conceit of a pilgrimage or a journey would have offered a much better analogy for the dynamic life of the human soul:

> The journey has its ups and downs, its pleasant resting-places enjoyed for a night and then abandoned, its unexpected meetings, its rumours of dangers ahead, and, above all, the sense of its goal, at first far distant and dimly heard of, but growing nearer at every turn of the road. Now this represents far more truly than any combat in a *champ clos* the perennial strangeness, the adventurousness, and the sinuous forward movement of the inner life.... But there is another and more mechanical defect

in the pitched battle.... It arises from the fact that fighting is an activity that is not proper to most of the virtues.[24]

Good allegorists in Lewis's view are writers who choose and develop their allegorical fiction so as to achieve a harmonious match between vehicle and tenor. Bunyan's *Pilgrim's Progress*, which Lewis had in mind when developing the analogy of human life as a journey, is an example of an allegory that Lewis admired for precisely those reasons. But, of course, there is always a creative tension between vehicle and tenor in allegory, and Lewis is too unkind on allegorists who, rather than minimizing such tension, draw attention to the incongruities between the non-allegorical message and the allegorical fiction in which this message has been cloaked. That Prudentius is an allegorist of this type becomes clear as soon as he launches into his fable of a pitched battle. Faith is the first combatant to step forward, ready to take her on her fearsome opponent, "Worship-of-the-Old-Gods":

> Faith first takes the field to face the doubtful chances of battle, her rough dress disordered, her shoulders bare, her hair untrimmed, her arms exposed....[25]

If we had the Latin original before us, we would be reading this in dactylic hexameter, the metre of Virgil's *Aeneid*, and would be even more conscious of the mismatch between what the fictional story promises ("let battle begin") and what it actually delivers (an unkempt woman). Yet surely this is what Prudentius wanted. "Where's the gear?" his readers are meant to wonder. "Why is this warrior not properly armed? And why a woman?" To ask such questions is to realize that it is often an apparent incoherence in the allegorical narrative that leads us to the non-allegorical truth: true faith is not a warrior but a feminine noun (*fides*), and faith (lower case) means faith in God, not faith in armour, which is why Faith (upper case) surprisingly features as a woman who has no interest in personal tidiness or in armour. I would therefore see Prudentius not as someone who gets his wires crossed because he is working with the wrong allegorical plotlines, but rather as a poet who was consciously striving to subordinate the epic mode and its ethos to Christian morality.[26] Nor do I think that he had a "deficiency in humour,"[27] as Lewis thought. There is, for instance, a fine moment of comic

---

24. Lewis, *The Allegory of Love*, 69.

25. Quotations are from the prose translation of Prudentius' *Psychomachia* by Thomson, in *Prudentius*, 2 vols, vol. 1.

26. For a similar view see Smith, *Prudentius' Psychomachia: A Re-Examination*.

27. Lewis, *The Allegory of Love*, 69.

absurdity when Pride (*Superbia*) tries to humiliate her opponents by presenting them as effeminate and socially inferior:

> Are ye not ashamed, ye poor creatures (*miseri*), to challenge famous captains with troops of low degree, to take the sword against a race of proud distinction?[28]

The funny thing is that this invective against "unmanly sloth"[29] is spoken *by* a woman *to* women, though Pride is so absorbed by her epic harangue that she forgets herself and speaks "man-to-men" (*miseri* is masculine plural). It is also funny that this hyper-masculine virago, dressed in full epic regalia, comes to a decidedly un-heroic end by falling into a ditch dug by Deceit, her own ally. If Prudentius had indeed tried to reconcile Virgilian epic with Christian doctrine, Lewis's criticism of his *Psychomachia* would have been justified, but in my view he was consciously playing off the conventions and expectations of his allegorical fiction against less martially based Christian morals—in this case, the morals that deceit is ultimately self-deceiving and that pride comes before the fall.

Perhaps the best-known example of an allegorical poet who set little store by the coherence of his fictional story is William Langland, and what I have said about the kind of allegory that C. S. Lewis liked and disliked readily explains what he found to dislike about Langland: "he is confused and monotonous, and hardly makes his poetry into a poem."[30] What Lewis found lacking in Langland is narrative coherence, though, to be fair to Lewis (and Langland), he also recognized that Langland was capable of achieving poetic heights that were beyond even Chaucer's reach.

Of course, whether we agree with his verdict on Langland or not may in the end come down to individual taste—and to whether or not we share Lewis's taste for allegories that not only tell good stories but also manage to keep the allegorical fiction moving in tandem with the signification of non-allegorical propositions, without sacrificing one to the other. My main criticism of *The Allegory of Love* is that Lewis had little positive to say about allegories that do not attempt to work in this way. The allegories I have mentioned—*The Assembly of Ladies*, Chaucer's *Complaint unto Pity*, Prudentius' *Psychomachia*, and, last but not least, Langland's *Piers Plowman*—all use moments of incoherence in the allegory (a non-sequitur in the allegorical story, or an obvious mismatch between vehicle and tenor) as ways of generating meaning and insight.

---

28. *Psychomachia*, 313 (lines 206–7 in the Latin).
29. Ibid., 295.
30. Lewis, *The Allegory of Love*, 161.

Of course, this criticism is not intended to put readers off *The Allegory of Love*. On the contrary, I hope it will serve as an antidote to a response (or rather the lack of responsiveness) to his literary criticism that is now much more common among medievalists, many of whom regard it as very out-of-date. It is certainly true that there are more recent books on medieval love allegory, but we are not necessarily going to learn more from books just because they were written by people who happen to be closer to us in time. I began my discussion of *The Allegory of Love* with Lewis's view that the "itch for 'revival,' that refusal to leave any corpse ungalvanized ... is one of the distressing accidents of modern scholarship." I will finish it by saying that another "distressing accident of modern scholarship" is the notion that there is special merit in being "up-to-date." Lewis would, I am sure, have agreed with me on this point. In his *Screwtape Letters*, first published in 1942, the senior devil Screwtape gloats to a junior disciple over having finally produced an intellectual climate where the wisdom of older generations is ignored by modern ones:

> Only the learned read old books and we have now so dealt with the learned that they are of all men the least likely to acquire wisdom by being so. We have done this by inculcating the Historical Point of View. The Historical Point of View, put briefly, means that when a learned man is presented with any statement by an ancient author, the one question he never asks is whether it is true. He asks who influenced the ancient writer, and how far the statement is consistent with what he said in other books, and what phase in the writer's development, or in the general history of thought, it illustrates, and how it affected later writers, and how often it has been misunderstood (especially by the learned man's own colleagues), and what the general course of criticism on it has been for the last ten years, and what is the "present state of the question." To regard the ancient writer as a possible source of knowledge—to anticipate that what he said could possibly modify your thoughts or your behaviour—this would be rejected as unutterably simple-minded.[31]

The "Historical Point of View" is more entrenched than ever in the academic study of English literature, and Screwtape can be proud of what has been achieved since Lewis wrote these words. His own relationship to literature, on the other hand, was always invigorated by the question, "Is any of it true?" In *The Four Loves* he offered an oblique self-criticism of *The Allegory of Love*: he had been wrong, he says, to think of courtly love (or Courtly

---

31. Lewis, *The Screwtape Letters*, 150–51.

Love with capitals, as it features in *The Allegory of Love*) as an artificial code, with curious conventions (the lover is sleepless, imagines his lady is far superior, and so on); for when very late in life he himself fell in love he found himself acting out this same code like a latter-day Troilus.[32] The lovesickness described in the "old books" was true, after all. Making medieval literature a meaningful part of your life means asking yourself the question, "Is any of it true?" and as *The Four Loves* shows, C. S. Lewis continued to do that even when he was no longer writing about "old books." Now that he has himself become an "ancient writer" and his views no longer pertain to "the present state of the question," he deserves to be read by people who are willing to ask the same question of his literary criticism.

---

32. Lewis, *The Four Loves*, 127.

— 12 —

C. S. Lewis as Medievalist

Helen Cooper[1]

C. S. LEWIS'S PRINCIPAL JOB, and his official employment, was as an academic, and in particular as a medievalist. Most of the important things about him as a medievalist were, moreover, said by Lewis himself in his inaugural lecture as the first Professor of Medieval and Renaissance English at Cambridge, entitled *De Descriptione Temporum*, "on periodisation."[2] He delivered that lecture on 29 November 1954, almost exactly sixty years ago. It is tempting just to quote it in full, as it says everything about why the Middle Ages were so important to Lewis, and indeed why that era should be so important to us too. Not the least aspect of its importance was that, for Lewis, cultural history did not divide into the four periods that we now assume in the West, those of the classical, the medieval, the Renaissance or early modern, and the modern (the postmodern had not yet been invented); but into three. Those were the classical, which laid the ground for the next period; that next period, which embraced everything from the fall of Rome to the late eighteenth century; and finally, the modern, which Lewis defined as running from the early nineteenth century to his own present, with all its massive and distinctive cultural changes. He summed up these three ages as

---

1. Dr. Helen Cooper is Emeritus Professor of Medieval and Renaissance English at the University of Cambridge, having held that Chair from 2004–14. She is the author of many books, including *Shakespeare and the Medieval World* (2010) and *The English Romance in Time: Transforming Motifs from Geoffrey of Monmouth to the Death of Shakespeare* (Oxford University Press, 2004).

2. Published by Cambridge University Press in 1955. Now available in *Selected Literary Essays*, ed. Walter Hooper (Cambridge University Press), initially published in 1969 and reissued, along with several other C.U.P. Lewis titles, to mark the fiftieth anniversary of his death in 2013.

pre-Christian, Christian, and post-Christian, with the biggest break coming between the last two.

That three-period division of cultural history made him the perfect candidate for Cambridge's Chair of Medieval and Renaissance English when it was established earlier that year. It was only the second established professorship in English in the university, and it was indeed established with him in mind—for hardly anyone else, certainly no one of his stature, worked with equal assurance or learning across what were generally taken, and indeed are still widely taken, to be distinct periods. For Lewis, however, the medieval and the Renaissance were not separate periods, but a single one; and so to speak of Lewis as a medievalist is inseparable from speaking about him as an early modernist, though I suspect he would have reacted strongly against the term.

"Early modern" insists on the sixteenth and seventeenth centuries as precursors of the modern world. Lewis insisted, on the basis of his deep knowledge, that those centuries were an extension of the thought world of the Middle Ages. He demonstrated that in publications alike on medieval and later literature, on Chaucer and Spenser and Milton, and perhaps most of all in what many people, myself included, think of as the best of his books, *The Discarded Image* (1964), which is about how people of that single era imagined their world and their cosmos—a vast subject brilliantly distilled. It is still, fifty years on, the best introduction to the subject there is.

The roots of Lewis's interests were, however, more recognizably what we would call medieval, in Norse myths. From a very young age, these were epitomised for him in lines from Longfellow's translation of Esaias Tegnér's *Drapa*:

> I heard a voice that cried
> "Balder the beautiful
> Is dead, is dead!"
> And through the misty air
> Passed like the mournful cry
> Of sunward-sailing cranes.[3]

The passage did not have an immediate effect, but it came back to him with the force of an epiphany when he was thirteen, and reading a coloured supplement of the periodical *The Bookman* for December 1911, which also contained Arthur Rackham's illustrations to a translation of Richard Wagner's *Siegfried* and *The Twilight of the Gods*. The lines gave him a sudden idea

---

3. Lewis, *Surprised by Joy*, 17.

of "Northernness": gave him, in his own words, a sense of "a vision of huge, clear spaces hanging above the Atlantic in the endless twilight of Northern summer, remoteness, severity.... I was returning at last from exile and desert lands to my own country."[4] They gave him, in fact, a very different kind of experience from how most schoolboys of his generation first encountered the medieval. That was much more likely to be grounded in Sir Thomas Malory's *Morte Darthur*, the late fifteenth-century assemblage of stories of King Arthur and his knights that has shaped almost all English Arthuriana down to the present day. The great explorer, adventurer, and political fixer Lawrence of Arabia, who was born ten years before Lewis, carried a copy of Malory around the Middle East with him, by bicycle or by camel.

Lewis first encountered the legends of Arthur when he was about eight, not however in Malory, but in Mark Twain's spoof *A Connecticut Yankee at King Arthur's Court*. He did not find Malory until he was sixteen, but then it made a deep impression on him, and for a while it became his "favourite reading."[5] Malory's influence is evident in his work for some years. He wrote, for instance, a poem, now lost, on Merlin and the enchantress Nimue, and another, which survives, on "Lancelot."[6] These do however owe much more to English nineteenth-century poetry, not least Tennyson's, than to Malory. Lewis was trying to write fin-de-siècle despondent mood music in the age of Eliot's modernist *Waste Land*—despondency such as is evident in the line "A dim disquiet of defeated men." He also wrote a prose romance, "The Quest of Bleheris," which features an antihero on a futile quest for a "deathless forever." It was an attempt to write a medieval romance from a modern perspective, but he left it unfinished and unpublished, and no one has ever suggested he should have done otherwise. He was, however, very excited by Eugène Vinaver's edition of the only surviving manuscript of the *Morte Darthur* after its discovery in 1934, and that led to a game he played with his friend Owen Barfield in which they acted as solicitors in an adultery law case brought by King Mark against Sir Tristram. He put Arthurian material to a different kind of use in his science fantasy novel *That Hideous Strength*, in which he puts forward the idea that the world could be redeemed through Merlin and the Fisher King if only medieval Christian values could be recovered. And he deploys Malory in a different way again in *The Lion, the Witch and the Wardrobe*, in the closing section on the hunting of the (very Arthurian) White Stag, where he shifts his style from his own modern English to something modelled directly on Malory,

---

4. Ibid., 18; and see also Hooper, *C. S. Lewis: A Companion and Guide*, 5–7.
5. Tolhurst, "Beyond the Wardrobe: C. S. Lewis as Closet Arthurian."
6. Lewis, *Narrative Poems*, 91–101.

with a series of short sentences typically introduced by "and" or "so," and a thoroughly fifteenth-century vocabulary:

> And they had not hunted long before they had a sight of him. And he led them a great pace over rough and smooth and through thick and thin.... And they saw the stag enter into a thicket where their horses could not follow.... So they alighted and tied their horses to trees and went on into the thick wood on foot. And as soon as they had entered it Queen Susan said,
> "Fair friends, here is a great marvel, for I seem to see a tree of iron."
> "Madam," said King Edmund, "if you look well upon it you shall see it is a pillar of iron with a lantern set on the top thereof. ... I know not how it is, but this lamp on the post worketh upon me strangely. It runs in my mind that I have seen the like before; as it were in a dream, or in the dream of a dream."
> "Sir," answered they all, "it is even so with us also."
> "And more," said Queen Lucy, "for it will not go out of my mind that if we pass this post and lantern either we shall find strange adventures or else some great change of our fortunes."
> ...
> "Wherefore by my counsel [said Queen Susan] we shall lightly return to our horses and follow this White Stag no further."
> "Madam," said King Peter, "therein I pray thee to have me excused. For never since we four were Kings and Queens in Narnia have we set our hands to any high matter, as battles, quests, feats of arms, acts of justice, and the like, and then given over; but always what we have taken in hand, the same we have achieved."...
> "If ye will all have it so, let us go on and take the adventure that shall fall to us."[7]

The last phrase in particular is pure Malory.

His imagination was, however, rapidly enlarged by wider reading, classical as well as medieval. The early notes he made for the plot of what in due course became *The Voyage of the "Dawn Treader"* include a sick king who needs the blood of a boy in order to be cured, a motif adapted from the Arthurian Grail Quest;[8] but when he actually came to write the book, that plot element was superseded by his later reading, in particular of the *Odyssey* of Homer and the medieval *Voyage of St. Brendan*, a wonderful account

---

7. Lewis, *The Lion, The Witch and the Wardrobe*, 167–69.
8. Hooper, *Companion*, 5.

of an early Irish saint's voyage to the "land of promise," calling (like Odysseus) at strange islands along the way.

Very clearly, the appeal of these stories for Lewis was overwhelmingly imaginative, not intellectual; and we need to start from that imaginative appeal, as he did, if we are to understand him as a medievalist, for reasons summed up best at the end of his *Experiment in Criticism*, on why and how we should read:

> We seek an enlargement of our being.... We want to see with other eyes, to imagine with other imaginations, to feel with other hearts, as well as with our own.[9]

The task of the good critic, as he saw it, was to enable that seeing and imagining and feeling; and that is what all his critical work aims at doing, whether it was intended for fellow scholars or students. That was why he took lecturing so seriously: many of his published scholarly books are in fact collections of his lectures—*The Discarded Image, Spenser's Images of Life, A Preface to Paradise Lost*; even his sixteenth-century volume is subtitled as "the completion" of a lecture series, as we shall see. He was by all accounts a remarkable lecturer.

That emphasis, though, perhaps explains another feature of his published works. The most cursory look at them, whether they were originally written as lectures or not, shows up their scarcity of footnotes. His learning is evident on every page, but it is designed to enlighten at first hearing, not to encourage citation-hunting. He is very free with allusions to or quotations from primary sources, but he rarely supplies references or cites other critics. He writes with a minimal use of terms of technical jargon (much of our own theoretical vocabulary had not indeed been invented then); his scholarship arises simply from the fact that he had read huge amounts of primary material, and had it all in the front of his mind. His writings therefore give the impression, which is not altogether wrong, of being directly spun off from his immersion in literature. Yet his earliest quasi-academic paper on the Middle Ages was on the subject of "feudalism as a product of social forces"[10]—not what we might have expected, but a reminder of the kind of wider knowledge he had beyond literature alone.

Lewis went on to build not just on Malory and the Arthurian legends, but on the classics, both Greek and Latin, and on classical philosophy. He had studied Classics ("Greats") for his undergraduate degree at University College Oxford, followed up by a second degree in English; and he then

---

9. Lewis, *An Experiment in Criticism*, 137.

10. Bennett, *The Humane Medievalist*, reprinted in *Critical Thought Series 1: Critical Essays on C. S. Lewis*, ed. Watson, 56.

spent a year teaching philosophy there before being elected to a Fellowship at Magdalen. He was thus able to bring to bear on his critical writings not just Homer, Virgil, Dante, Chaucer, Spenser, and Milton, but the philosophers and theologians of the Middle Ages and the Renaissance: Tertullian and Hugh of St. Victor, Humphrey Gilbert and Vives and Vida and Scaliger, and dozens of others of increasing unfamiliarity. He enlarged his imagination through theirs, in ways that made him uniquely qualified to talk about them, and which he saw as essential to understanding them. When the young A. S. Byatt, now a much respected novelist, went up to him after a lecture to express her interest in continuing the kind of work he had been doing in his *Allegory of Love*, he told her, "You will of course have to learn Greek."[11]

That unique range of knowledge, that belief in the need for reading to be a process of learning to share a writer's imagination, was what he emphasised in his inaugural lecture, in a plea for the reinstatement of what he called "Old Western culture": the almost-lost knowledge of, and sensitivity to, those pre-Christian and Christian eras. A key part of the argument of that lecture was that religion *of any kind* was what really made the difference between cultures and periods. To quote him again:

> Christians and Pagans had far more in common with each other than either has with a post-Christian. The gap between those who worship different gods is not so wide as that between those who worship and those who do not. The Pagan and Christian ages alike are ages of . . . the externalized and enacted idea; the sacrifice, the games, the triumph, the ritual drama, the Mass, the tournament, the masque, the pageant, the epithalamium, and with them the ritual and symbolic costumes . . . crown of wild olive, royal crown, coronet, judge's robes, knight's spurs, herald's tabard, coat-armour, priestly vestment, religious habit—for every rank, trade, or occasion its visible sign.[12]

To understand all that, he needed to respond to those cultures—that culture—with his whole imagination, to live inside it as "his own country," in ways that scholarship alone could not reach; and he believed that he had achieved that. He used the analogy of a dinosaur, which just by virtue of living in its own skin could reveal to us things about dinosaurs that palaeontologists never could; or of a native Athenian, who if he came back to life could tell us things about his culture that no modern scholars could grasp, even if he did so unwittingly, since he knew it from the inside. He concludes his lecture:

11. Quoted by Leith, "C. S. Lewis's Literary Legacy," *The Guardian*.
12. Lewis, *De Descriptione*, 7–8.

I stand before you somewhat as that Athenian might stand. I read as a native texts that you must read as foreigners. . . . Who can be proud of speaking fluently his mother tongue or knowing his way about his father's house? It is my settled conviction that in order to read Old Western literature aright you must suspend most of the responses and unlearn most of the habits you have acquired in reading modern literature. And because this is the judgement of a native . . . , where I fail as a critic, I may yet be useful as a specimen. I would even dare to go further. Speaking not only for myself but for all other Old Western men whom you may meet, I would say, use your specimens while you can. There are not going to be many more dinosaurs.[13]

In an article published three months later, Graham Hough, another lecturer in English at Cambridge, described the reaction to that inaugural lecture. Some in the audience, he records, had loved it; but the whole thing had been delivered with Lewis's customary forcefulness, and Lewis was, as Hough noted, "one of the dwindling race of dons . . . whose every utterance seems to arouse a powerful reaction, either of approval or indignation."[14] And the indignation was very strong indeed. Hough ascribed it not to the content of the lecture—on scholarly or critical grounds, it was indeed hard to fault—but simply to the fact of Lewis's Christianity, even though (as always in both his teaching and his academic publications) he made no requirement that his audience, or scholars of the medieval more broadly, should share it, just that they should accept its historical validity. The lecture, Hough says, was met with an anti-theological rancour that was itself "of theological intensity."[15] The idea that Christianity might in some way be historically defining—those three periods Lewis described as shaping Western cultural history—was anathema within the studied stance of atheism in the Cambridge English Faculty of the 1950s, as too was his insistence on rehabilitating the medieval, of defining the humanist Renaissance in medieval terms. Much of that debate over period division has gone on unbroken ever since, and Lewis's belief in their historical continuity is still receiving only cautious and intermittent consent. The rebranding of "the Renaissance"—its etymology indicating the rebirth of the classics—as the "early modern," the precursor of our own modern world, has largely taken place since Lewis's time, but it is one aspect of that skewing of history. Current scholars of the post-medieval, like the Renaissance humanists themselves, want to mark

13. Ibid., 21.
14. Hough, "Old Western Man," reprinted in Watson, *Critical Essays on C. S. Lewis*, 235–45 (237).
15. Ibid., 242.

themselves out as different from the medieval. Lewis, by contrast, took as his point of departure that "the barrier between the [ages of the medieval and the Renaissance] was greatly exaggerated, if indeed it was not largely a figment of Humanist propaganda"[16]—humanist propaganda, because a major element of how the humanists sold and promoted themselves in the fifteenth and sixteenth centuries was to proclaim their difference from what had gone before by denigrating it, belittling it, emphasising the differences and ignoring the far greater continuities, in ways that still dominated thinking in the 1950s as in the 1550s, and indeed now. As a result, any term for the pre-humanist age—what we call the medieval, though the word had not yet been invented in the sixteenth century—became a term of abuse, and that is indeed still the commonest popular usage of "medieval": it's an insult. And Christianity, furthermore, was as much decried by some in the 1950s Cambridge English Faculty as Roman Catholicism had been in the Protestant England of the 1580s. Humanism was good; but it was humanism in its modern meaning, with its associations of agnosticism or atheism. Lewis by contrast never hesitated to point out, rightly, how deeply religious the original humanists were. It was not for nothing that Thomas More, the brightest light of English humanism, became a martyr for his faith.

That inaugural lecture picked up an argument Lewis had been making just a few months earlier, in the introduction to his most substantial single work of criticism, *English Literature in the Sixteenth Century Excluding Drama*. This is a work that it is almost impossible to mention without attaching the epithet "magisterial" to it. It formed volume three of Oxford University Press's series the Oxford History of English Literature, commonly abbreviated as OHEL—or "Oh hell," as Lewis increasingly called it as his years of labour on it increased. It had been commissioned from him in 1938; his work for it became the basis for a series of lectures he gave at Trinity College Cambridge in 1944, and it was finally published, with the subtitle "The Completion of the Clark Lectures," in 1954, just before his arrival at Magdalene. Both the length of time it had taken him, and its magisterialness, derived from the fact that he had set out to read every work of literature he talked about, and he talked about a great many that most of us have not even heard of. The Introduction to the book was subtitled "New Learning and New Ignorance," its argument being that the humanist so-called new learning was one aspect of that humanist propaganda attacking the Middle Ages (that is, it was not nearly as new they claimed); and it was a reminder too that some of that new learning was extraordinarily wrongheaded. The Middle Ages used the supernatural to animate their perception

---

16. Lewis, *De Descriptione*, 3.

of the universe, and to liven up stories. Some of the greatest intellects of the Renaissance went further, to treat the supernatural as apprehensible magic that could be deployed, actually practised, in ways that take "early modern" thought heading off in utterly the wrong direction as a precursor of our modern world. Lewis's arguments about the strength of the "old learning" have moreover been confirmed increasingly by more recent scholarship, even in the field of science. A wonderful book by James Hannam, *God's Philosophers*,[17] demonstrates with something of Lewis's own clarity and brilliance that early modern scientists—"natural philosophers," as they called themselves—did not just rediscover some of what was known in the Middle Ages, but actively drew on it to enable their own advances, in cosmology and optics and mathematics.

Unsurprisingly, that heading of "new ignorance" to the first page of the Oxford History volume invited (and received) attack—deliberately invited on Lewis's part, one suspects: he was a man who loved a good argument, and if a polemic about the new ignorance could stir things up, so much the better. So before he ever gave his inaugural lecture, that introduction had already infuriated those who believed that civilization had gone into abeyance between the classics and the humanists, though Lewis, as that introduction also demonstrated, knew far more about both the classics and the humanists than the great majority—maybe all?—of his detractors. So if the lecture offended those who held that any reference to Christianity as being significant amounted to a dereliction of rational thought, the Oxford History volume attacked their own credentials, by showing the hollowness of their claims that to be working in a humanist tradition was self-evidently superior to the medieval.

It is a row that seems increasingly irrelevant now. We live at a moment in critical theory when New Historicism, the argument—the belief—that all literature reflects the specific political circumstances of the moment at which it was written, and that it is all about power, is giving way to a "religious turn," the recognition that you can't get any decent historical grasp on literature if you don't take the writers' own religious beliefs seriously. So we are at last beginning to catch up with Lewis—though again, it must be stressed that that process is entirely different from requiring belief. Lewis's first book, indeed, and the one that established his critical reputation, *The Allegory of Love* of 1936, had its roots in his reading before his conversion to Christianity and is much more evidently secular in focus; but it shows just the same ability as his later books to think himself inside literary forms that at first glance

---

17. The U.S. edition was published in 2011 by Regnery Press under the title *The Genesis of Science: How the Christian Middle Ages Launched the Scientific Revolution*.

seem deeply alien. It was a book that transformed many people's perception of medieval literature: it showed us how to read it, how to appreciate it even in what seemed its most difficult manifestation, allegory. The trouble with allegory was—to an extent still is—that readers now assume that they are not going to like it before they have even looked at any; but as Lewis pointed out in his *Experiment in Criticism*, if you start with that assumption, you will always find it fulfilled. Lewis insisted on reading with imaginative empathy and understanding, and showed how it should be done. Jack Bennett, Lewis's successor in the Chair at Cambridge, who devoted his own inaugural lecture largely to Lewis's achievements, described *The Allegory of Love* as the work that "stimulated our mental thirst for the Middle Ages."[18] He entitled his lecture "The Humane Medievalist," in an attempt to heal the breach Lewis seemed to have made between scholars of the Middle Ages and of the Renaissance, by writing his predecessor into both camps.

The Allegory of Love made Lewis recognised as a giant of learning, as the scholar who deserved the commission to write the Oxford History volume, and indeed in due course as the right person for the appointment to the new Chair at Cambridge. It also established his independence of any of the current critical traditions. For all his knowledge of Old English and Latin and Greek and French and Italian, and therefore of his inside knowledge of philology, he stood well apart from the linguistic tradition on which the Oxford English school had been founded, and by which it still operated. That was a tradition of Germanic philology; and one might have expected that Lewis would have been deeply committed to its principles, fascinated as he was by language. He was most fascinated, however, by the concepts that words represented—by changes of meaning rather than changes of morphology. His *Studies in Words* of 1960 set out to show those changes of meaning as individual words moved across languages and cultures and time periods: words such as *wit, sad, free, sense, simple, conscience,* and *conscious*. And if that interest in the historical depth behind words was different from the philological model prevailing at Oxford, it also carried a different emphasis from Cambridge's flagship movement of practical criticism, the close reading of texts. He had still less interest in Cambridge's attachment to modernism, and indeed the new professorship was established partly with the intention of counteracting that, so that the holder could provide more historical and scholarly depth to the department. Lewis's distrust of the modern therefore set him apart from many of his colleagues, as it set him apart from much contemporary literature. He notoriously disliked modern poetry of the T. S. Eliot variety; and certainly his own attempts

---

18. Bennett, *The Humane Medievalist*, 65.

at poetry, which rhymed and scanned beautifully, but did rather little else, could hardly have been more different from Eliot's.

So, as a medievalist, Lewis pursued a path very different from the dominant ethos at either Oxford or Cambridge. He also sought his own independent middle way between the painstaking textual recovery of the past developed by the Early English Text Society, with its primary interest in the historical development of the forms of English, and the enthusiasm for the Middle Ages such as fired the medievalizing novels of Sir Walter Scott and the poetry and art of William Morris. He did however share with them, as Jack Bennett noted, an insistence on the past "as a value."[19] He thus came to establish both a movement and a style of his own. He had both the advantage and the drawbacks of writing in an age when literary criticism was designed to be read by anyone who loved literature, rather as much serious history can be read now, and that meant outside the universities as well as inside. The literature studied in the Oxford English course stopped in the early nineteenth century, since it was taken for granted that everyone was brought up knowing the literature written after that without there being any need to study it. There was a strong view, when the question of having an English course at Oxford at all was under discussion in the 1890s, that there was no place for English as an academic subject; the most its opponents granted was that it might be useful for women undergraduates who did not have an adequate classical training, and for second-and third-rate male candidates for the classics course such as might want to go into school teaching, as if such people were lower forms of intellectual life. It was an age too when editions not just of Shakespeare but of Chaucer and Spenser were commonly bought by anyone of reasonable education. Lewis's career made a strong contribution to raising the academic profile of English, demonstrating how it was not enough just to pick up such an edition and read it with untrained, and therefore only partial, enjoyment: for a full understanding, you needed guidance too. Although most of his published academic work derives from his university lectures, they can be read by a much wider audience, in a way that little modern criticism can be, and by people who have very little specialist or scholarly knowledge. They are written, that is, so as to give their readers a sense of what such knowledge might reveal to them.

In *An Experiment in Criticism*, Lewis suggests that the evaluative criticism popular at the time he was writing was less important than this kind of cultural contextualization. He was also, however, keen to make his listeners or readers want to go and read the works he is talking about; or if he does not want you to do that, he tells you why not. This happened not just in his

---

19. Bennet, *The Humane Medievalist*, 58.

lectures, but in the Oxford History volume too, starting with the notorious division he makes of sixteenth-century literature into the Drab and the Golden—a division that blighted the study of earlier Tudor literature for years. To take a sentence completely at random: "If we sit down to read Rainoldus for a whole morning we shall be disappointed." So we are let off reading Rainoldus—a writer whom I doubt if many of us knew existed. But Lewis has read him for us, and sums him up in a handful of sentences. He is just as good, however, or even better, at conveying enthusiasm, as he does in some of the very best passages in the volume in the early chapters on Scottish and English literature at the close of the Middle Ages.

Reading Lewis's academic writings can nonetheless often be a deeply frustrating experience, on account of his reluctance to give references. He stirs your interest, but then does not tell you where you can pursue the ideas further. That makes sense in terms of orally delivered lectures, but rather less so in their published forms. The Oxford History did have a lengthy bibliography—largely compiled, as is noted in the Preface, by other people; but it is impossible to use as a source for further scholarship other than in the most general way. Any desire to look up the original sources he uses or cites, for instance, especially the sources of his quotations from Latin, is made effectively impossible by his translation of them into a very good pastiche of sixteenth-century English. He even changes the spelling conventions, such as the interchangeability of the letters u and v, so that it is impossible to tell if what you are looking at is a contemporary translation (as it sometimes is) or Lewis's own. In the preface, he says that he does it "not simply for the fun of it but to guard the reader from a false impression"—presumably, a false impression of modernity; but it is also an effective way to guard his own territory. He does translate longer passages of Latin, but he always leaves single phrases or sentences untranslated, on the assumption that his readers will understand them. And indeed many of them would; but it is still a reminder of just how he envisaged those readers (male, educated at the expensive independent schools), and of how much cultural and educational climates have changed since his time.

A complaint that is increasingly heard now about Lewis's criticism is that it is not scholarly. He did not use the best available editions, and he will on occasion throw out misleading remarks without thinking them through. Again, that may have made for better lectures, and indeed for a livelier reading experience, but it can still be damaging; and even his most considered ideas were sometimes wrong. Perhaps the most notorious example would be the *Allegory of Love*, which does not so much expound the concept of "courtly love" as almost single-handedly invent it. His account includes the patently untrue remark that one of its defining characteristics was adultery:

a remark that set medieval literary studies on the wrong path for two or three generations, and we have still not quite got over it.

One reason why we perhaps see some things more clearly now than he did was that we are much more cynical than he was—more cynical than I think people were in the Middle Ages, indeed, but Lewis had a sense of the *ideal* so strong as almost to exclude irony. One aspect of that ideal is mirrored in his comparison of himself to that ancient Athenian, with its assumption that the ancient Athenian in question would be a free white male: a woman or a slave or an outsider would have a very different impression indeed of what life in Athens meant, but Lewis still lived in an age when women or slaves or outsiders barely impinged on his vision of the intellectual life. The critical movement of New Historicism is very poor at dealing with the transhistorical, but Lewis's concern for the larger picture could exclude any more time-specific nuance. Gender studies too have opened our eyes to whole areas that Lewis did not see. Reading any of Lewis's works now results in a mixture of admiration for his learning, genuine enlightenment, and a good deal of frustration. The frustration, however, is offset by his having much larger critical purposes than our own more limited scholarly aims: he wanted to make people, and especially students, better readers, by way of inculcating that sense of transhistorical value. His vision of the ideal has, I believe, more historical force behind it than our own reluctance to credit the good in anything. He stressed not only what a writer *said*, the "logos" or what we might call the discourse element of a text, but also the quality of literature as something *made*, the Greek "poiema," the created beauty that modern criticism all too often overlooks, along with the beauty of the Old Western cosmos apprehensible above all through Greek and Latin. Perhaps the New Ignorance of which he accused the humanists is as nothing compared with our own.

— 13 —

The Abolition of Man

From Literary Criticism to Prophetic Resistance

Malcolm Guite[1]

WHAT ARE WE TO make of *The Abolition of Man*? In a letter of 1955, twelve years after its publication, Lewis said of this little volume, "it is almost my favourite among my books but in general has been almost totally ignored by the public."[2] I would like to tease out why it might have been a favourite, why it was "almost totally ignored" at the time, and, most importantly, why it might be of particular relevance to us now.

The book consists of the three Riddell Memorial Lectures that were delivered by Lewis at the University of Durham in February 1942 at the height of the Second World War. In that same year Lewis was certainly at the height of his power and conviction as both literary critic and Christian apologist. It was the year of the publication of both *The Screwtape Letters* and *A Preface to Paradise Lost*. The lectures were themselves published as *The Abolition of Man* in January 1943, the year in which he also published *Perelandra*, the masterpiece of his science fiction trilogy, and right in the

---

1. The Revd. Dr. Malcolm Guite is Chaplain of Girton College, University of Cambridge. He is the author of *Faith, Hope and Poetry: Theology and the Poetic Imagination* (Ashgate, 2010) and of "Poet" in *The Cambridge Companion to C. S. Lewis* (Cambridge University Press, 2010). As a poet himself, he is the author of *Sounding the Seasons: Seventy Sonnets for the Christian Year* (Canterbury Press, 2012), and *The Singing Bowl* (Canterbury Press, 2013). He maintains a web presence at www.malcolmguite.wordpress.com.

2. Letter to Mary Willis Shelburne (20 February 1955), *The Collected Letters of C. S. Lewis*, Volume 3, ed. Walter Hooper, 566–67.

midst of the series of radio broadcasts he gave from 1941 to 1944 that eventually became *Mere Christianity* (1952).

The Riddell Memorial Lectures were established for "a subject concerning religion and the contemporary development of thought," and Lewis's offering certainly fits the bill. What begins as a specific discussion of a schoolroom textbook in English literary criticism, soon widens as Lewis follows the implications into a profound critique of society and our account of our own humanity. At the core of that critique is a recognition that what he elsewhere calls "the poison of subjectivism,"[3] taken to its logical conclusion will ultimately undermine all the essential qualities of our humanity. He follows his criticisms of the subjectivism of contemporary culture, therefore, with a robust account of what he calls "the doctrine of objective value,"[4] grounded ultimately on a universally acknowledged given "rightness in things," which is not ultimately contingent or entirely culturally determined and which he calls the "Tao" or the "Way," borrowing his term rather surprisingly from the Chinese mystic, Lao Tsu. It is an extraordinary book, at once enlightening, challenging, and infuriating, and I want in the rest of this paper to highlight three aspects of it that together may be responsible both for its importance and its unpopularity. These three aspects are: first, its paradoxical or contradictory nature; secondly, its essentially prophetic character—prophetic both in the sense of clearly foreseeing what has, in fact, come to pass, and also in the sense of speaking out, speaking truth to power; and thirdly, I want to look at the serious problems and cultural blind-spots that are embedded in it. In conclusion, I hope to tease out some of the insights it has to offer us in the twenty-first century.

The Paradoxes of *The Abolition of Man*

So let us start with the paradoxical and contradictory aspects of this book. I think these are fourfold:

First, what appears to be a detailed, even pernickety critique of a school textbook suddenly becomes the launch-pad for a serious attack on a whole tranche of widely held cultural assumptions. Is his attack on the textbook merely a ruse, or are there serious reasons for starting there?

Secondly, what might be mistaken for cultural chauvinism or heavy religious propaganda turns out to be an exploration and defence of universal values, a recognition of common truth in the midst of extraordinary cultural, linguistic, and religious diversity.

---

3. Lewis, "The Poison of Subjectivism," in *Christian Reflections*, ed. Hooper.
4. Lewis, *The Abolition of Man*, 17.

Thirdly, what looks in the middle parts of the book like a conservative retrenchment of tradition turns out really to be a radical challenge to renewal and liberation.

Finally, what starts as an attack on a certain kind of "debunking," on deploying the hermeneutics of suspicion, turns out itself to be a piece of applied scepticism, of unmasking and deconstruction.

i) Mere Literary Criticism?

Let us attend first to the literary critical elements in this book. Lewis famously begins with the account of Coleridge and the "sublime" waterfall. The poet overhears two tourists remarking on a waterfall: one calls it *pretty*, the other *sublime*, and Coleridge deplores the first and approves the second response. Were Lewis to be writing directly about the incident itself, he would have wonderful things to say both from his rich and deep reading in the Romantics and from his profound understanding of the history, context, and nuance of English words. However, his concern in this book is not what he would make of this incident but what has been made of it in a school textbook, which he calls *The Green Book* and ascribes coyly to two authors whom he calls Gaius and Titius. In fact, the book in question was called *The Control of Language*, written by Alex King and Martin Ketley, two young Cambridge men, both Australian, who published it in 1939.[5] Throughout this book, King and Ketley are trying to alert very young readers to the possibilities of surreptitious or subliminal emotional manipulation through the use of emotive language. Here is the passage from their book to which C. S. Lewis objects:

> When the man said *This is sublime*, he appeared to be making a remark about the waterfall.... Actually... he was not making a remark about the waterfall, but a remark about his own feelings. What he was saying was really *I have feelings associated in my mind with the word "Sublime,"* or shortly, *I have sublime feelings.*

Lewis comments: "here are a good many deep questions settled in a pretty summary fashion." But King and Ketley are not yet finished. They continue:

---

5. *The Control of Language: A Critical Appraisal to Reading and Writing* was published in London in 1939; Lewis was sent it for review. His much-annotated copy, now at the Wade Center, Wheaton College, has a green cover; the publisher's name "Longman, Green," may have further contributed to the nickname he gives it; but one assumes he also had in mind some of the negative meanings of "green," such as "naïve," "nauseous," and possibly also "envious" (one thinks of the Lady of the Green Kirtle in *The Silver Chair*, who wishes to invert the moral order).

This confusion is continually present in language as we use it. We appear to be saying something very important about something: and actually we are only saying something about our own feelings.[6]

The rest of Lewis's book could be said to be an analysis of "the issues really raised by this momentous little paragraph."

First, he dismisses the asinine absurdity that the statement "this is sublime" means "I have sublime feelings." Properly speaking, to say something is sublime actually means "I have humble feelings"—humble towards the sublimity. If to say "this is sublime" means "I have sublime feelings," then to say "this is contemptible" would mean to say "I have contemptible feelings." Having dismissed this *pons asinorum*, as Lewis calls it, he goes on to deal with the far more serious implications, which involve the debunking or undermining of all statements of value and the way this is done by a series of unconscious and unchallenged assumptions visited with authority on a school child who will have no awareness of what is being done to him. As Lewis says:

> The very power of Gaius and Titius depends on the fact that they are dealing with a boy: a boy who thinks he is "doing" his "English prep" and has no notion that ethics, theology, and politics are all at stake. It is not a theory they put into his mind, but an assumption, which ten years hence, its origin forgotten and its presence unconscious, will condition him to take one side in a controversy which he has never recognized as a controversy at all. The authors themselves, I suspect, hardly know what they are doing to the boy, and he cannot know what is being done to him.[7]

It is particularly telling how deep Lewis's sympathy is for the young person at school, how searchingly he asks the question: will this particular piece of education enlarge or enrich the whole person or will it narrow and restrict it? So he goes on to say:

> Gaius and Titius, while teaching him nothing about letters, have cut out of his soul, long before he is old enough to choose, the possibility of having certain experiences, which thinkers of more authority than they have held to be generous, fruitful, and humane.[8]

---

6. Lewis, *The Abolition of Man*, 7–8.
7. Ibid., 9.
8. Ibid., 11.

The pupils in question thought they were having their day's lesson in English, "though of English they have learned nothing. Another little portion of the human heritage has been quietly taken from them before they were old enough to understand." And this leads Lewis, in a throw-away line, which has justly become one of the most famous quotations from the book, to adumbrate an entirely new approach to education in a single sentence: "The task of the modern educator is not to cut down jungles but to irrigate deserts."

A great deal of Lewis's real vision of human freedom and flourishing is embedded in that sentence. Education is not about imposing dogma nor about cultural hegemony: it is about enabling the unfolding growth and the potential hidden in the rich ground of the human psyche.

ii) Cultural Chauvinism or Universal Values?

Having objected to the way in which the pupil has had a little portion of the human heritage "cut out of his soul,"[9] Lewis goes on to set out what is missing in King and Ketley's approach, namely the doctrine of objective value and the fitness of certain responses to the world, the approach which he calls the "Tao." And this is where we find that what might be mistaken for cultural chauvinism or religious propaganda turns out to be an exploration and defence of universal values, of common truth in the midst of linguistic and religious diversity. Lewis ranges freely from the *Tao Te Ching* and the *Analects* of Confucius through the *Upanishads* to Plato and Aristotle and the writings of the Stoics. He also includes allusions to the Old and New Testament, but cites them only as part of common witness to a common theme, not in this context privileging them in any way as special revelation. The direct allusions to this extraordinary range of ancient religious writing is further supplemented in the remarkable appendix ("Illustrations of the *Tao*") in which he takes eight—in his view—objective moral insights and illustrates all eight with passages ranging from the Egyptian "Book of the Dead" and the Norse Volospa through Native American sayings (including an account of the Battle of Wounded Knee) to Babylonian texts and the *Bhagavad Gita*. Lewis's point is not only that utterly reductive and isolating subjectivism is self-contradictory, but that it is also contradicted by a univer-

---

9. It is remarkable how this phrase paradoxically anticipates the language of Philip Pullman, who has thought himself so opposed to Lewis. In Pullman's fiction it is the church that, by the hideous operation of "intercision," cuts children's souls away from them. Lewis is entirely with Pullman in protesting against such psychic violence, but has pointed out long before him that it is, in fact, aggressive and reductive secularism that is actually doing the damage. Cf. Pullman, *Northern Lights*, especially 204–14.

sal testimony of religious insight throughout all times and cultures, which, however culturally coloured, seems to bear witness to an objective reality. Having established and reminded us of this vast common inheritance of religiously inspired and culturally shared humane values, he returns again to the withering pre-suppositions of this little school textbook.

> Over against this stands the world of *The Green Book*. In it the very possibility of a sentiment being reasonable—or even unreasonable—has been excluded from the outset. It can be reasonable or unreasonable only if it conforms or fails to conform to something else. To say that the cataract is sublime means saying that our emotion of humility is appropriate or ordinate to the reality, and thus to speak of something else besides the emotion; just as to say that a shoe fits is to speak not only of shoes but of feet. But this reference to something beyond the emotion is what Gaius and Titius exclude from every sentence containing a predicate of value. Such statements, for them, refer solely to the emotion. Now the emotion, thus considered by itself, cannot be either in agreement or disagreement with Reason. It is irrational not as a paralogism is irrational, but as a physical event is irrational: it does not rise even to the dignity of error. On this view, the world of facts, without one trace of value, and the world of feelings, without one trace of truth or falsehood, justice or injustice, confront one another, and no *rapprochement* is possible.[10]

That Lewis himself had felt deeply the consequence of the reductivism he is now attacking, had known what it is to live in a world in which facts "without one trace of value" and feelings "without one trace of truth or falsehood" confront one another, is evident from that remarkable passage in *Surprised by Joy* where he talks about how the two hemispheres of his mind were in the sharpest contrast: "On the one side a many-islanded sea of poetry and myth; on the other a glib and shallow 'rationalism.' Nearly all that I loved I believed to be imaginary; nearly all that I believed to be real I thought grim and meaningless."[11] His attack on *The Green Book* has a personal force behind it; he is speaking from experience.

iii) Conservative Entrenchment or Radical Renewal?

It is in the context of these two alternatives symbolized by the *Tao* and *The Green Book* that we can see another of our paradoxes: what looks like a

---

10. Lewis, *The Abolition of Man*, 16–17.
11. Lewis, *Surprised by Joy*, 161.

conservative re-entrenchment of tradition is really a radical challenge to renewal and liberation. This is because, as Lewis I think cogently shows, the "doctrine of objective value" that he is seeking to defend is itself a presupposition that defends freedom and all other values. Lewis points out in the chilling final chapter ("The Abolition of Man") that those who debunk and deny all objective value may nevertheless choose to exploit what they regard as the illusion of value, carefully fostered in others, for their own purposes. So he writes:

> Hence the educational problem is wholly different according as you stand within or without the Tao. For those within, the task is to train in the pupil those responses which are in themselves appropriate, whether anyone is making them or not, and in making which the very nature of man consists. Those without, if they are logical, must regard all sentiments as equally non-rational, as mere mists between us and the real objects. As a result, they must either decide to remove all sentiments, as far as possible, from the pupil's mind; or else to encourage some sentiments for reasons that have nothing to do with their intrinsic "justness" or "ordinacy." The latter course involves them in the questionable process of creating in others by "suggestion" or incantation a mirage which their own reason has successfully penetrated.[12]

As so often, Lewis illustrates his point with one of those brilliant and imaginative analogies which often carry implicitly even more wisdom than he purports to get out of them:

> The difference between the old and the new education will be an important one. Where the old initiated, the new merely "conditions." The old dealt with its pupils as grown birds deal with young birds when they teach them to fly; the new deals with them more as the poultry-keeper deals with young birds—making them thus or thus for purposes of which the birds know nothing. In a word, the old was a kind of propagation—men transmitting manhood to men; the new is merely propaganda.[13]

---

12. Lewis, *The Abolition of Man*, 17.
13. Ibid., 18.

iv) Debunking the Debunkers: The Hermeneutics of Suspicion

This leads us to our final paradoxical element in this remarkable book. What starts as an attack on a certain kind of debunking, King and Ketley's deploying of the hermeneutics of suspicion, turns out to be itself a brilliant example of applied scepticism. The whole analysis of *The Green Book* is a process of unmasking and deconstruction, and what it reveals is a discourse of power, the establishment of a cultural hegemony whose effect is to disenfranchise those who subscribe to it. As Lewis goes on to say:

> Only the *Tao* provides a common human law of action which can over-arch rulers and ruled alike. A dogmatic belief in objective value is necessary to the very idea of a rule which is not tyranny or an obedience which is not slavery.[14]

The Abolition of Man as Prophetic Writing

Lewis died on the same day as two other great figures of the twentieth century: President Kennedy and Aldous Huxley. Readers of *The Abolition of Man*, especially its final chapter, cannot help being struck by the extraordinary parallels between the dystopic future against which Lewis warns and the one Huxley had already imagined eleven years earlier in *Brave New World* (1932) and whose many fulfilled predictions he had later analysed in *Brave New World Revisited* (1958). Both foresee the possibility (even before the discovery of DNA) of a combination of genetic modification, eugenics, and overwhelming scientifically-driven cultural conditioning, allowing human beings completely to redefine and re-engineer their own humanity. Both writers recognise the paradox that this new and accelerated acquisition of power and control over "human nature" represents a radical threat to common humanity. Indeed, Lewis is very keen in his analysis here, and alert to the way in which general claims for scientific progress and "man's power over nature" often mask unreconstructed power dynamics in which some human beings are simply seeking to entrench their power and control others. He sees this as happening in two stages: first of all, "Man's power over Nature," or indeed "the power of Man to make himself what he pleases," turns out really to be "a power exercised by some men over other men with Nature as its instrument." But beyond that he sees something even more sinister. In order to acquire the technique and the will so completely to control

---

14. Ibid., 44.

and condition other people, the "controllers" of the new era will have denied and explained away their own humanity. What will be at work in them, motivating their choices as controllers, will be no more than the bundle of natural impulses and instincts to which they have reduced themselves:

> From this point of view the conquest of Nature appears in a new light. We reduce things to mere Nature *in order that* we may "conquer" them. We are always conquering Nature, *because* "Nature" is the name for what we have, to some extent, conquered. The price of conquest is to treat a thing as mere Nature. Every conquest over Nature increases her domain. The stars do not become Nature till we can weigh and measure them: the soul does not become Nature till we can psychoanalyse her. The wresting of powers *from* Nature is also the surrendering of things *to* Nature. As long as this process stops short of the final stage we may well hold that the gain outweighs the loss. But as soon as we take the final step of reducing our own species to the level of mere Nature, the whole process is stultified, for this time the being who stood to gain and the being who has been sacrificed are one and the same.[15]

Given the confluence of their thought, it is extraordinary to find so little direct contact between Huxley and Lewis as public intellectuals. Lewis, I think, dismissed Huxley early as one of the set he calls "the clevers" in *The Pilgrim's Regress*. The three or four references to Huxley in his *Collected Letters* are all dismissive and whilst one could understand Lewis's dismissal of the early Huxley, the Huxley not only of *Brave New World Revisited* but also of *The Perennial Philosophy* would have been of great interest to him. Indeed, it could be argued that both men in their very different ways were appealing to an earlier mystical tradition in order to counterbalance modern reductivism.

Be that as it may, *The Abolition of Man* still has a place among the prophetic books of the twentieth century, both in the sense that it foretells many things that have come to pass, but also in the far more important sense that it was an attempt, completely against the grain of his own culture, to speak truth to power. In particular, it recognized that the real power to open or close the mind rests not with pure philosophers at conversation in the universities, but rather with programmes of mass education and with the assumptions that lie behind widely used school textbooks, and that is why the opening of *The Abolition of Man* with its critique of *The Green Book* is not really perverse at all, but central to Lewis's prophetic intention.

15. Ibid., 43.

Problems with *The Abolition of Man*

Why, then, if it is so pertinent and prophetic, did Lewis find that his book had been almost totally ignored by the public? One reason may be that, although so much of it has proved prescient, it also shows evidence of some real cultural blindspots on Lewis's part. There are problems with this text that need to be addressed by those who would like to see it revived and made useful in the twenty-first century.

The essential difficulty, as I see it, is the almost simplistic contrast that Lewis draws between *The Green Book*'s subjectivism reduced to absurdity, on the one hand, and a kind of golden and unassailable certainty in the *Tao*, on the other. Things are always more nuanced and complex, but for the sake of what he hoped would be clarity in his argument, Lewis ignores this complexity. He doesn't give enough attention to the context in which and the purpose for which *The Control of Language* was written, and that context is the immense rift that the Great War opened between the large cultural claims of the nineteenth century and the bitter wasteland of the twentieth century. Lewis needs to recognise that if there is, among his contemporaries, a widespread suspicion and "debunking" of objective moral values it is because these values were so abused that they seemed in themselves, to many, to have given rise to the disaster of the war. This blindspot on Lewis's part comes to sharp and dreadfully ironic focus when, of all the ambiguous truths of the old moral order, he seizes as an example, as though completely unambiguous, the well-known tag from Horace, "*dulce et decorum est pro patria mori*." He blunders into this wide-eyed. Here is what he says:

> Perhaps this will become clearer if we take a concrete instance. When a Roman father told his son that it was a sweet and seemly thing to die for his country, he believed what he said. He was communicating to the son an emotion which he himself shared and which he believed to be in accord with the value which his judgement discerned in noble death. He was giving the boy the best he had, giving of his spirit to humanize him as he had given of his body to beget him. But Gaius and Titius cannot believe that in calling such a death sweet and seemly they would be saying "something important about something." Their own method of debunking would cry out against them if they attempted to do so. For death is not something to eat and therefore cannot be *dulce* in the literal sense, and it is unlikely that the real sensations preceding it will be *dulce* even by analogy. And as for *decorum*—that is only a word describing how some other people will feel about your death when they happen to think of it, which won't

be often, and will certainly do you no good. There are only two courses open to Gaius and Titius. Either they must go the whole way and debunk this sentiment like any other, or must set themselves to work to produce, from outside, a sentiment which they believe to be of no value to the pupil and which may cost him his life, because it is useful to us (the survivors) that our young men should feel it.[16]

Of course it is impossible for us to read this now without seeing the whole thing in the light of Wilfred Owen's heart-breaking poem, "*Dulce et decorum est.*" And one wonders how it was possible for Lewis to write such a paragraph a good twenty-three years after that poem had been published. Owen zeroes in not simply on the contrast between hideous death in modern warfare and this golden Latin motto, but much more crucially on the fact that it is a lie told by the comfortable to the condemned:

> If in some smothering dreams you too could pace
> Behind the wagon that we flung him in,
> And watch the white eyes writhing in his face,
> His hanging face, like a devil's sick of sin;
> If you could hear, at every jolt, the blood
> Come gargling from the froth-corrupted lungs,
> Obscene as cancer, bitter as the cud
> Of vile, incurable sores on innocent tongues,—
> My friend, you would not tell with such high zest
> To children ardent for some desperate glory,
> The old Lie: *Dulce et decorum est*
> *Pro patria mori.*[17]

That is the context in which the whole culture of scepticism and suspicion of which *The Green Book* is a part has arisen and there are real questions to be answered given the way in which even the most self-evident moral truths are misappropriated, exploited, made part of cultural power structures. There is a constant task of confession and discernment for those who, nevertheless, wish to point to some surviving and unassailable objectivity in moral truth. It is no longer enough simply to repeat the words "dulce et decorum est" and expect to have them taken at face value.

And here the ironies become almost unbearable, for Lewis himself was, like Owen, a young officer writing poetry on the Western Front, and Lewis's own war poetry in *Spirits in Bondage*, published the year before Owen's, deals with many of the same things and unmasks many of the same lies. Of

---

16. Ibid., 17–18.
17. See *The Penguin Book of First World War Poetry* (2nd ed.), ed. Silkin, 182–83.

all people, Lewis would have been the most qualified to read Owen's poem with sympathy, and had he acknowledged Owen's critique of Horace at this point in *The Abolition of Man*, had he gone on to show that in fact Owen himself was still writing from within the *Tao*, still appealing in those final ringing lines to the objective moral value of truth-telling, then this whole part of his argument would have been itself more nuanced, more truthful, and more compelling. Yet in all three volumes of Lewis's immense correspondence, there is not a single reference to Wilfred Owen. Yesterday Lewis was remembered just beside Owen in Poets' Corner. It may only be through an imaginary conversation between these two great men that we can begin to develop a line of argument that is missing from Lewis's book. That is the task that remains to be done. But let us turn to what we in the twenty-first century can draw from Lewis's text as we have it now.

The Abolition of Man in the Twenty-First Century

If Lewis felt this favourite book had been "almost totally ignored" in his own day, why should it not be ignored now? What can we draw from it? I want to conclude by suggesting that there are four important insights this small book has to offer us in the twenty-first century.

First, the great transformative ideas—whether for better or worse, whether keys to liberty or shackles on the human mind—are encountered at work in ordinary education, not just in the rarefied world of formal philosophical debate, and it is in schools where they do their harm and their good. Lewis sets us an example here: the best minds in the greatest universities should be as deeply, closely, and intimately concerned with what is taught in secondary schools as they are with the ideas of their most promising post-doctoral students.

Secondly, in his general remarks on education, he emphasizes that there is all the difference in the world between conditioning and initiation as approaches to teaching. Education is not something that is done to children by formed and finished adults who are somehow aloof and detached from the principles they teach. Education is a shared pilgrimage, a communal celebration, an entering together into both the delights and the challenges of a common text.

Thirdly, utter reductivism reduces itself and is self-negating; even the most sceptical critique of the powers-that-be ultimately requires a transcendent frame of reference. In this insight Lewis has been joined by many other later writers. I think particularly of what Seamus Heaney has to say about redressing our reductivism in his brilliant book, *The Redress of Poetry*.[18]

And finally, and I think most hauntingly, we get the traces, the beginnings, the hints, of a whole new way of doing both science and the arts, the key to which is *participation* rather than *detachment*. For although at first blush Lewis might seem to be attacking science itself, in fact he is calling for a new approach to nature that radically anticipates many of the insights of the ecological movement, the work of James Lovelock, and even the developments more recently of eco-criticism. He wonders if in a return to the *Tao* we might also develop what he calls a "regenerate science":

> The regenerate science which I have in mind would not do even to minerals and vegetables what modern science threatens to do to man himself. When it explained it would not explain away. When it spoke of the parts it would remember the whole. While studying the *It* it would not lose what Martin Buber calls the *Thou*-situation. The analogy between the *Tao* of Man and the instincts of an animal species would mean for it new light cast on the unknown thing, Instinct, by the inly known reality of conscience and not a reduction of conscience to the category of Instinct. Its followers would not be free with words *only* and *merely*. In a word, it would conquer Nature without being at the same time conquered by her and buy knowledge at a lower cost than that of life.[19]

I would like to conclude not with the many negatives in this trenchantly critical book, but rather with a gathering together of the beautiful hints and guesses of a whole new approach that, perhaps, we can look forward to in the rest of this century. I have in fact drawn together many of the phrases from this book that most haunt me, that seem most pertinent to our present situation, and made out of them a "found" sonnet called "Imagine." I shall end with that.

---

18. Heaney, *The Redress of Poetry*.
19. Lewis, *The Abolition of Man*, 47.

"Imagine"
(A found sonnet from *The Abolition of Man* by C. S. Lewis.)

Imagine a new natural philosophy;
I hardly know what I am asking for;
Far-off echoes, that primeval sense,
With blood and sap, Man's pre-historic piety,
Continually conscious, continually . . .
Alive, alive and growing like a tree
And trees as dryads, or as beautiful,
The bleeding trees in Virgil and in Spenser,
The tree of knowledge and the tree of life
Growing together, that great ritual
Pattern of nature, beauties branching out
The cosmic order, ceremonial,
Regenerate science, seeing from within . . .

To participate is to be truly human.[20]

---

20. Guite, *The Singing Bowl*, 60.

— 14 —

The Soul of C. S. Lewis

Stephen Logan[1]

What Is a Soul?

I DON'T SUPPOSE TOO many readers of C. S. Lewis would be tempted to say that "soul" is a simple word. Look it up in OED and you'll find fifteen basic senses, illustrated with quotations from the very earliest stages in the history of the English language. As a theological concept, too, there's not much room for doubting its complexity. *The Oxford Dictionary of the Christian Church* explains that "No precise teaching about the soul received general acceptance in the Christian Church until the Middle Ages."[2] But since there are reams of passages in Old English containing the word "soul," this evidently doesn't mean that no one had offered an account of what the word "soul" might mean before the Middle Ages; it means only that there was no official agreement about its meaning before then. There were bound to be difficulties. "Soul" is an English word of Germanic origin. It

---

1. Dr. Stephen Logan is Principal Supervisor in English at Clare College, Cambridge, and works also as a psychotherapist. He is the editor of *William Wordsworth: Everyman's Poetry Library* (Dent, 1998) and author of "Literary Theorist" in *The Cambridge Companion to C. S. Lewis* (Cambridge University Press, 2010). A Welsh musician and poet, he has written ten volumes of poetry, and his poem for the fiftieth anniversary of Lewis's death, "Westminster Abbey Unvisited," is included at the end of this essay. He has released two solo albums, *Signs and Wonders* (2014) and *Deliverance* (2015), and maintains a web presence at www.stevelogan.co.uk.

2. *The Oxford Dictionary of the Christian Church*, 3rd edn., ed. F.L. Cross and E.A. Livingstone (Oxford: Oxford University Press, 1997), 1520.

is used, in the Old Testament, to translate a Hebrew word, *nephesh*, which means something like "living being" and precludes the familiar distinction between "soul" and "body." In English versions of the New Testament, the word "soul" translates the Greek *psyche*: a word that has only to be spoken in order to suggest a pulsating diversity of mythological stories very different in atmosphere from the Gospels (the myth of Cupid and Psyche, of course, being a subject of lifelong interest to C. S. Lewis). In short, the Hebrew and Greek words for which "soul" is often a translation have meanings with which those of the word "soul" are likely to be misaligned. Yet the biblical contexts in which the word occurs leave no doubt as to its importance:

> "For what is a man profited, if he shall gain the whole world, and lose his own soul?" (Mark 8:36)

> "Thou shalt love the Lord thy God with all thy heart, and with all thy soul, and with all thy mind, and with all thy strength: this is the first commandment." (Mark 12:30)

> "The soul that sinneth, it shall die." (Ezek 18:20)

> "I have behaved and quieted myself, as a child that is weaned of his mother: my soul is even as a weaned child." (Ps 131:2)

I select these examples pretty much at random. If they were the only surviving evidence of the meaning of the word "soul," we could infer that the soul was something of supreme value; that it is, with the heart, mind, and strength, an essential constituent of a person; that it is capable of being killed by its own activity when that activity is evil; and that it is capable of being comforted by oneself, implying that it exists in a peculiarly intimate relation to the self, but is not identical with it.

Lewis's own uses of the word "soul" certainly attest its importance to him:

> Human will becomes truly creative and truly our own when it is wholly God's, and this is one of the many senses in which he that loses his soul shall find it.[3]

> At present we tend to think of the soul as somehow 'inside' the body. But the glorified body of the resurrection as I conceive it—the sensuous life raised from death—will be inside the soul. As God is not in space but space is in God.[4]

---

3. Lewis, *The Problem of Pain*, 90.
4. Lewis, *Letters to Malcolm*, 121.

> The mould in which a key is made would be a strange thing, if you had never seen a key: and the key itself a strange thing if you had never seen a lock. Your soul has a curious shape because it is a hollow made to fit a particular swelling in the infinite contours of the divine substance, or a key to unlock one of the doors in the house with many mansions.
>
> Your place in heaven will seem to be made for you and you alone, because you were made for it—made for it stitch by stitch as a glove is made for a hand.[5]

> For it is not so much of our time and so much of our attention that God demands; it is not even all our time and all our attention; it is ourselves. For each of us the Baptist's words are true: "He must increase and I decrease." He will be infinitely merciful to our repeated failures; I know no promise that He will accept a deliberate compromise. For He has, in the last resort, nothing to give us but Himself; and He can give that only insofar as our self-affirming will retires and makes room for Him in our souls.[6]

We notice here a strong iconoclastic tendency, at least with regard to conventional ideas about the soul. It is not inside our bodies; our bodies are inside it. We cannot call it our own; it belongs to God and only flourishes when this is freely acknowledged. Each human soul is unique, though none is more valuable than another.

Predictably there is much congruence between Lewis's account and the biblical account of the soul. What they share is a deep indifference to contemporary ideas of the self as somehow all-important. The soul, for Lewis and for the biblical writers I've quoted, is some deep organizing and animating principle in a human being, breathed into it (on a Christian understanding) by God. It gives life, not just in the sense of a mere capacity for experiencing the world, but in the sense of a capacity for experiencing it fruitfully or, as we might say, creatively.

Since the rise of Modernism, though, it might be said we've become intolerant of talk of the word "soul," as indeed of the word "heart": we are all supposed to prefer the Higgs boson. This is apparent from current interpretations of words that begin with the prefix *psyche*, like "psychology" or "psychoanalysis." When I ask students for a definition of either of these they commonly say that they are to do with the mind. The *mind* notice, not the soul. The mind unseats the soul in a despiritualizing age. And, it might

---

5. Lewis, *The Problem of Pain*, 135.
6. Lewis, "A Slip of the Tongue," 123-24.

further be said, the ego, an individual's sense of themselves, rather than the soul, is likely to become the chief object of our spiritual attentions.

Lewis was wary about psychoanalysis all his life, though less so later. One reason for that was, no doubt, defensive, as we shall see. But another may have been that he feared the displacement of the soul—the means by which the individual is most intimately connected to God—by the narrowly self-interested ego.

However, what I want to talk about today is the presence in Lewis of something deeper than his conscious awareness of himself, deeper than his ego, which seems persistently to have frustrated his attempts to recognize the language of his soul. Since to have one's soul occluded by one's self or ego is a common predicament, the struggle in Lewis to listen to his soul is one of the characteristics of his work that modern readers are likely to find appealing. But what is this thing intermediate between the ego and the soul that I'm talking about? I will call it the grammar of emotion.

The Grammar of Emotion

Grammar is one of the most familiar examples of a process that operates unconsciously, but that manifests itself throughout our conscious lives. It organizes our entire experience of speaking, reading, and otherwise interpreting language. No fully adequate grammar has been produced for any living language, since grammar is constantly evolving and showing new capabilities that elude attempts to formulate its "rules." (It seems likely that the very concept of a rule stands to the living actuality of grammar as scientific enquiry stands to faith: there is a basic incompatibility between the thing investigated and the mode of investigation, which ensures that the investigation cannot find what it seeks.[7] Such failures could be enlightening if they resulted in a new investigative procedure, instead merely of more rigorous applications of the old one.) This phenomenon of a process that is unconscious, all-subsuming within the sphere of its operation, definite enough to invite description, but so elusive that it defies full analysis obviously has

---

7. Bruce Hood, Professor of Developmental Psychology at Bristol University, has produced research to show that "superstition is hardwired into our brains" ("We Are Born to Believe in God," *Sunday Times*, 6 September 2009, 9). The terms in which this claim is made reveal, I think, a radical misunderstanding of the grounds and motives of religious belief. It may be a form of superstition to find the metaphor of "hardwiring" here reassuring and to ignore the distinction between what is illogical and what is supra-logical. To the extent that the materialistic presuppositions of the article are accepted, the "discovery" serves (and perhaps aims) to exalt science at the expense of religion.

resonances in other dimensions of our experience. Societies might be said to have grammars: they are organized; there are likely to be principles informing the organization; but formulating the principles might be tricky. Even somewhat more restricted phenomena, like institutions (academic, governmental, or religious, say) exhibit certain consistencies in the way they work which implies the existence of some underlying system of organizing principles. Lacan famously said (or is said to have said) that the unconscious is structured like a language.[8] And, if it is, then it too has a grammar, at once evident and latent, describable and eluding final description. In this essay I want to look at something neither as comprehensive as the unconscious, nor as restricted in the sphere of its operation as a language, but nonetheless very diffuse and wide-ranging, like the pull of moon on tide.

To talk of the grammar of emotion is to imply that beneath emotions themselves (whatever they might be understood to be) is something organizing them, something that is not itself an emotion quite, but that determines the character of what we apprehend as our emotions. Freud's cumbrous but heavily suggestive phrase (as translated by Strachey) is "quotas of energy in some unimaginable substratum."[9] Understood this way, emotions are the form in which our psychic energies make themselves manifest to us.

Religious belief, or metaphysical outlook, is prominent among the things that make each person both like and unlike any other. Many Buddhists cultivate a habit of expecting to encounter the adversities that in our society we may feel ourselves encouraged to treat as surprising accidents. Christianity has its different way of trying to reconcile us to the experience of pain. Both acknowledge that, when it comes, even if we have done everything possible to eliminate the more obviously neurotic elements in our responses, we may still experience anguish. Christ wept for Lazarus and for Jerusalem and in the Garden of Gethsemane sweated blood.[10] But whether anguish is anticipated or arrives unexpectedly, accepting it remains hard. The gloss I am prompted to put on this is a further revelation of my own ideological perspective: I feel we are creatures who carry into a post-

---

8. What Lacan actually said was in French; but in English the nearest we get in the *Écrits* to this familiar catchphrase is, "This is precisely why the unconscious, which tells the truth about truth, is structured like a language" (*Écrits*, 737). Lacan was fond of the trope of structuring, probably borrowed in the first place from linguistics. He writes that a "symptom is structured like a language" (ibid., 223) and that a "personality is structured like a symptom." That the phrase, in English, has acquired a life of its own is owing to the suggestiveness of the notion that the unconscious may have within it something analogous to the thing that structures a language. And that something is a grammar.

9. Freud, "Anxiety and Instinctual Life."

10. John 11:35; Luke 19:41; Luke 22:44.

lapsarian world expectations and desires that are immutably pre-lapsarian. This is not to say (as Richard Dawkins or Daniel Dennett might construe me as saying) that I believe in the historicity of the Fall. Rather, I agree with Coleridge that:

> A fall of some sort or other . . . is the fundamental postulate of the moral history of man. Without this hypothesis, man is unintelligible; with it, every phenomenon is explicable. The mystery itself is too profound for human insight. . . .[11]

I affirm this belief in order to expose candidly how emotions are conditioned by metaphysical beliefs that we hold more or less consciously. What I am more interested in here, however, operates at a lower and less easily accessible level in the infrastructure of our emotions. I have indicated how an emotion might be affected by a belief; but how might a belief be affected by a still deeper emotion?

William Empson once remarked, with a flourish of his coat, but truly nonetheless, that he thought "a profound enough criticism could extract an entire cultural history from a simple lyric";[12] similarly, a good enough psychotherapist might discern within the expression of an unemphatic, ostensibly trivial emotion, the lineaments of a person's sensibility: the outline of their whole manner of experiencing the world.

Unappeasably, in an early poem, Philip Larkin intones:

> Beneath it all, desire of oblivion runs.[13]

Beneath the characteristically sombre intonation, I would like to suggest, is an undertone of expectation. Larkin expects defeat, disappointment and terminal death (unlike Blake, for whom death was a terminus, but not terminal). It is this expectation that organizes the style of his experience and gives to his poetic style its distinctive dour plangency and pathos. More generally, it might be said that such broad metaphysical expectations ("age, and then the only end of age"[14]) determine the key into which more conscious emotions are unknowingly transposed.

At the very start of his posthumous fiction, *The Double Tongue*, William Golding tries bearing witness to the possibility of experience before

---

11. Coleridge, *Table Talk* of 1 May 1830 (*Major Works*, 592–93). Fifteen years earlier, when he was forty-two, Coleridge had insisted on his belief in "a Fall in some sense, as a fact . . . the reality of which is attested by experience and conscience" (letter to Wordsworth, 30 May 1815).

12. Empson, "The Verbal Analysis," in *Argufying*, ed. Haffenden, 107.

13. Larkin, "Wants," in *Philip Larkin*, ed. Thwaite, 42.

14. Larkin, "Dockery and Son," 152–53.

the consciousness (or even formation) of self. He knows he is flouting the assumption that selves are innate—that simply because we cannot quite express memories before we had them, we must have always had them:

> Blazing light and warmth, undifferentiated and experiencing themselves. There! I've done it! The best I can, that is. Memory. A memory before memory? But there was no time, not even implied. So how could it be before or after, seeing that it was unlike anything else, separate, distinct, a one-off. No words, no time, not even I, ego, since as I tried to say, the warmth and the blazing light was experiencing itself, if you see what I mean. Of course you do![15]

The tone of that "Of course you do!" is hard to catch. Mocking? Because he knows that of course we don't see. Or companionable? Because he knows that we all have such experience, however much the conditions of evolving a distinct and self-conscious self—which include the use of language—make such experience hard to communicate, even to contemplate. For language, like consciousness, imposes categories of perception, such as time: "A memory before memory? But there was no time, not even implied. So how could it be before or after." The attempt to express one's own experience implies a consciousness of the distinction between perceiver and perceived. Hence Golding's attempt to avoid saying, "*I remember* blazing light and warmth." Such statements imply the imposition of a grammar: a system of organizing assumptions which possibly do not exert their full organizing force in the very earliest stages of life—or indeed in some of the states we experience at later stages: sleep, daydreaming, sexual transport, drunkenness, loving absorption in another's joy, or religious contemplation. Many poets are profoundly interested in the imaginative recovery of this state—I am thinking of Keats writing about minnows as if he were one, or Pound evoking the aftermath of the Trojan War in the mind of a waking fallen soldier. Buddhist contemplation, or Christian prayer, constantly aspire to a state in which consciousness is retained, but self-consciousness escaped, as if it were the chrysalis of being, not the final form of it. To me, the Buddhist notion as well as (obviously) the Christian one is fully congruent with the belief that the conditions under which we normally live our lives are post-lapsarian. We treat as normal modes of being that preclude normality. We take our fill of the food that sustains us only enough to dream of health.

Among psychoanalysts, D. W. Winnicott is perhaps especially notable for his attempts to imagine experience before selfhood:

---

15. Golding, *The Double Tongue*, 3.

> For the baby there comes first a unity that includes the mother. If all goes well, the baby comes to perceive the mother and all other objects and to see these as not-me. [The mother] is first a delusion which the baby has to be able to disallow, and there needs to be substituted the uncomfortable I AM unit which involves the loss of the merged-in original unit, which is safe. The baby's ego [its developing sense of itself as a being distinct from the maternal care it depends on] is strong if there is the mother's ego support to make it strong; else it is feeble.[16]

It is perhaps customary now to enter objections to Winnicott's claims as unsubstantiated: entrancing fictions about a fantasy.[17] Well . . . a psychoanalytic writer capable of entrancing is perhaps not to be sniffed at; and attempts to practise entrancement do at least show a capacity for recognizing the importance in human experience of being entranced. While scientists pine for forms of proof that babies can't supply, poets (and those, like Winnicott, who value poets) will stand by forms of intuition that they can't ignore. Winnicott here provides a gloss on the experience of observing babies that stimulates what he takes to be the memory of being one. And in this he is at one with a poetic forerunner of all psychoanalysis. In 1798 Wordsworth wrote:

> Blest the infant babe—
> For with my best conjectures I would trace
> The progress of our being—blest the babe
> Nursed in his mother's arms, the babe who sleeps
> Upon his mother's breast, who, when his soul
> Claims manifest kindred with an earthly soul
> Doth gather passion from his mother's eye.
> Such feelings pass into his torpid life
> Like an awakening breeze, and hence his mind,
> Even in the first trial of its powers,
> Is prompt and watchful, eager to combine
> In one appearance all the elements
> And parts of the same object, else detached
> And loth to coalesce.[18]

Perception, as adults understand it, is learned. The aptitude for learning it may be innate, but the capacity for engaging in it is not. According

16. Winnicott, "Sum, I Am" in *Home is Where We Start From*, 62–63.

17. See, e.g., Leopoldo Fulgencio, "Winnicott's Rejection of the Basic Concepts of Freud's Metapsychology," *International Journal of Psychoanalysis*, Volume 88 (2007), 443–61.

18. Wordsworth, *The Prelude*, 267–94.

to Wordsworth, the (in this example, male) baby's intuitive recognition of "manifest kindred" with his mother is what stimulates the attempt to learn perception. He is "eager to combine / In one appearance all the elements / And parts of the same object, else detached / And loth to coalesce." Before this voluntary effort is made, the Mother does not exist, but, rather a loose congeries of sensory data, which only after it "combine / In one appearance."

By imagining the child in this state of incipient perceptiveness, Wordsworth and Winnicott coax us back into the quiddities of experience prior to the development of the categories that supply its adult grammar. By imagining the formation of a sense of self in this way, they enable us to apprehend more vividly the ease with which the process might be disrupted and the sense of self damaged, or damagingly inflected. Selfhood might be imagined as the bedrock of a person's grammatical organization. The character of the self determines, or powerfully conditions, the character of anything else that is organized on the basis of it.

Lewis and Grief

Lewis thought he could write better than he could speak. For some it is writing that offers the best hope of assuaging the sense—familiar to us all, presumably—of not having adequately expressed ourselves. For some such people, writing becomes, if not a fetish exactly, then an activity that comes to be relied upon for the relief it is expected to afford: "ink is the great cure for all human ills."[19] Andrew Cuneo, formerly a literary critic and now a priest, observes: "How often Lewis notes in his letters that writing is the cure for all ills."[20] One such ill, however, is that of compulsive introspection. But there is the possibility too of a compulsion to dismiss all introspection as compulsive: a compulsion that might be the manifestation of a defensive avoidance even of those forms of introspection which might be profitable and wholesome. Cuneo again:

> ... what a shock to read a scholar of Medieval and Renaissance literature say that, "if I had some rare information about the private life of Shakespeare or Dante I'd throw it in the fire, tell no one, and re-read their works. All this biographical interest is

---

19. Lewis, letter to Arthur Greeves (30 May 1916) in *The Collected Letters of C. S. Lewis*, Volume 1, ed. Hooper, 187.

20. Cuneo, "Duty With a Stamp: 'Half my life is spent answering letters,'" www.cslewis.com/uk.

only a device for indulging in gossip as an excuse for not reading what the chaps say."[21]

Again, however, there are complexities here. It is easy to suppose that Lewis's distaste for biography was defensive; but this would involve the assumption that defences are always bad. But what is commonly called a defence can often with more justice be regarded as a legitimate mechanism for avoiding pain—or what Keats called "disagreeables"—which has somehow gone wrong. A further possibility—strongly hinted at in the suggestion that we should re-read primary texts instead of writers' biographies—is that the primary texts, if good enough, will communicate the depths of a person's experience more adequately than their biographers are likely to. And it may be that, in communing creatively with "the best that has been thought and said" (in Arnold's vulnerable but indispensable phrase) Lewis was doing introspection in a new key: one whose tonalities he could accept and whose disclosures he trusted.

C. S. Lewis began his academic career teaching philosophy (having got firsts as an undergraduate at Oxford in both classics and English). Metaphysically, he knew that there is more to reality than we can get at through our senses; epistemologically, he knew that there is more to the mind than ratiocination. Other modes of mental activity—often subsumed by Romantic writers under the term "imagination"—may help us become aware of the supernatural elements of experience. As a poet, Lewis realized that "thought" is a complex term. Writing of thought in poetry he urges us to "understand that 'thought' here carries no specially *intellectual* connotation."[22] He attempts to define how language, in a poem, may momentarily express a state in which the usual rifts between thinking, feeling, and speaking are healed:

> The poetic speechthought does not exist permanently and as a whole in the poet, but is temporarily brought into existence in him and his readers by art.[23]

Lewis here is not only sharing Coleridge's recognition that a great poet, such as Shakespeare, directs "self-consciously a power and an implicit wisdom deeper than consciousness,"[24] he is sharing Coleridge's awareness, as a poet, of what the process of composition feels like. Further than that, he is aware of a need to exert the intellect to expose and so transcend its limitations:

---

21. Ibid.
22. Tillyard and Lewis, *The Personal Heresy*, 147.
23. Ibid.
24. Coleridge, *Shakespearean Criticism*, ed. Raysor, 1:198.

> From all my thoughts, even from my thoughts of Thee
> O thou fair Silence, fall, and set me free.²⁵

Again, writing of Spenser, a poet whose reputation never stood higher perhaps than in the Romantic period, Lewis declares an interest in the unconscious activities of the mind:

> Spenser, with his conscious mind, knew only the least part of what he was doing, and we are never very sure that we have got to the end of his significance. The water is very clear, but we cannot see to the bottom. That is one of the delights of the older kind of poetry: "thoughts beyond their thoughts to those high bards were given."²⁶

Thoughts of the kind generally operative in critical prose may have often only a tenuous relation to the depths of a person's psyche. In "Shelley, Dryden and Mr. Eliot," Lewis asserts that a poet should follow his imagination because our imaginations are *"constrained by deepest necessities"* (my italics).²⁷ Poetry can take us beyond or beneath the ratiocinative thinking Lewis was all too good at, into the depths of such reverie as Shelley commends in his essay "On Life." Thus, we may enter, in writing poems or in reading them, depths of our being that ratiocination barricades us out of, proffering subtlety as an illusory guarantee of depth.

But these emphases are rendered uniquely personal—are given the quality that peculiarly attracts or repels us—by their relation to the personality behind them.

Lewis ascribes to himself a vein of Celtic melancholy, a more literary and perhaps more acceptable term than "depression." Yet George Sayer notes that Lewis at times "suffered intensely from the loneliness and depression to which he was liable all his life."²⁸ Such testimony will strike many as being at odds with the more widespread image of Lewis as jovial ("It is obvious under which planet *I* was born!").²⁹ But it may be that this image is the result, in

---

25. Lewis, "The Apologist's Evening Prayer," 143.

26. Lewis, "Edmund Spenser, 1552–99," published to accompany Lewis's selections from *The Faerie Queene* and *Epithalamion* in an anthology of *Major British Writers*, vol. 1 (1954); reprinted in *Studies in Medieval and Renaissance Literature*, ed. Hooper, 143. The quotation with which my quotation from Lewis ends is from "Third Sunday in Lent," a poem in John Keble's *The Christian Year* (1827), a series of poems for every day of the Christian calendar: "As little children lisp, and tell of Heaven, / So thoughts beyond their thought to those high Bards were given."

27. Lewis, "Shelley, Dryden and Mr. Eliot," *Selected Literary Essays*, ed. Hooper, 207.

28. Sayer, *Jack: C. S. Lewis and His Times*, 74.

29. Green and Hooper, *C. S. Lewis: A Biography*, 140.

part, of the way that Lewis, "constrained by deepest necessities," presented himself. Owen Barfield, who knew him well, saw the earlier manifestations of such joviality in Lewis as an act: "*Was* there something, at least in his impressive, indeed splendid, literary personality, which was somehow—and with no taint of insincerity—*voulu* [contrived, forced]?"[30] The hesitations of Barfield's syntax here indicates the difficulty he was having in appearing to suggest the possibility of some discrepancy between the way that Lewis actually was and the way he had fashioned himself. He concludes the next paragraph by declaring his love for Lewis, while recognizing that his doubt "raised issues Lewis himself would have refused to contemplate."[31] The significant word there, I think, is "refused." Lewis had a dread of mental illness accompanied by a defensive resistance to those who professed to treat it. He says to Greeves: "We hold our mental health by a thread, and nothing is worth risking for it. Above all, beware of excessive daydreaming . . . ."[32] The result of this was an avoidance of introspection, which was sometimes salutary and sometimes desperate. His understanding, as a young man, of how psychological problems form is, by the standards of the singularly accomplished scholar he became, poignantly naïve. Again, to Greeves he says: "whatever you do, never allow yourself to get a neurosis. You and I are both qualified for it, because we were both afraid of our fathers as children."[33]

Significantly, too, Lewis identifies any possible problem as originating with his father, not his mother. Peter Bayley, at first Lewis's graduate student, then his colleague, recognized that Lewis was "a shy and vulnerable man" whose "assumed persona was too strong. It is probable that he had early assumed it as a defence from victimization or mockery at school."[34] This is very acute, though I'd like to suggest that Lewis may have had need of such defences before he went to school. Soon, though, the act of knock-down dialectical assertiveness became difficult for Lewis to distinguish from a salutary form of intellectual rigour. He may have defended himself so successfully against the fear of annihilation as to believe he'd never had it.

In an age that idealizes spontaneity and naturalness, we are liable to be suspicious of any deliberate cultivation of a form of behaviour. But as a means of improving aesthetic taste, Coleridge endorsed the Earl of Malmesbury's principle of "feign a relish till we find a relish come."[35] And Lewis's

30. Barfield, "Introduction," xi.
31. Ibid.
32. Lewis, letter to Arthur Greeves (22 April 1923), 605.
33. Ibid.
34. Bayley, "From Master to Colleague," 80.
35. Harris, *The Works of James Harris, Esq.*, 453.

beloved Jane Austen in *Mansfield Park* endorses Fanny Price's recoil from dangerous kinds of acting within a social context in which politeness was acknowledged as a necessary kind. Wordsworth's concept of "a second Will more wise"[36] implies that will may inform behaviour without distorting it.

Lewis eventually seems to have believed that introspection may have a certain value as a means merely of cleansing the mirror of our souls so that God (and the creation) might be reflected more clearly there. Our Christian destiny lies "in being as little as possible ourselves."[37] But how intensive might such cleansing need to be? Lewis often seems hostile to psychoanalysis: he is apt to travesty all critics with an interest in "psychology" as "amateur psychologists" whose motive is to debunk dead authors and who are grievously lacking in "the plastic impulse, the impulse to make a thing, to shape, to give unity, relief, contrast, pattern."[38] Yet Coleridge (whom Lewis admired) was a pioneer of psychoanalysis with an epicurean sensitivity to the verbal nuance and "vocalic melody."[39] Lewis indeed, in a poem, praises Coleridge for having "re-discovered the soul's depth and height."[40] (The "re-" is characteristic and apposite: Coleridge saw himself as restoring to constrictively post-Enlightenment conceptions of the mind a complexity which Shakespeare had already achieved.) Yet Lewis retained a fascination with the psychological speculation that belied his peremptory dismissals of it. He never had psychotherapy as such. But he went for weekly confessions with a monk whose "wisdom" he acclaimed.[41] And, as if recognizing its deep relevance to himself, he was curious about the Freudian principle of repression: "as the psychologist have taught us, it is not the remembered but the forgotten past that enslaves us."[42]

It seems likely that, early in his life, Lewis's conscious cultivation of a Christian outlook had something of the quality of "woodenness" that we impute to actors who haven't yet found a way to achieve the properly paradoxical state of "acting naturally." I want to suggest that pessimism was a feature of Lewis's temperament which was established before he entered his teens and which was permanently confirmed by his mother's death. His faith required him to counteract his pessimism, which through much, if not all, of his life, continued to reassert itself. Lewis's battle with despair is

---

36. Wordsworth, "Ode to Duty," line 48, *The Poems*, Vol. 1, Hayden, 606.
37. Lewis, "Christianity and Literature," 22.
38. Lewis, "On Criticism," 544–45.
39. Lewis, *An Experiment in Criticism*, 29.
40. Lewis, "To Roy Campbell," 80.
41. See Vaus, *Mere Theology*, 192–93.
42. Lewis, "De Descriptione Temporum," 12.

evident even in such things as his casual manner of quoting Dunbar: "Man, please thy maker and be merry / And give not for this world a cherry."⁴³ Here, perhaps, we see the outlines of a self-protective mechanism: serve God: be cheerful, though the world encourages despair.

Ontological Insecurity

We don't yet know much about Lewis's mother. Her letter to Albert Lewis of 14 November 1886 suggests confusion about her own impulses, rather than simple warmth and spontaneity of affection: "I may not be demonstrative, indeed I know I am not, but when I think of how many nights I have cried myself to sleep . . . I do not feel that I deserve to be thought of as heartless."⁴⁴ However, George Sayer (who also loved Lewis) remarks that "This is the most emotional sentence to be found in what we have of her correspondence."⁴⁵ In relation to such an impression (again rather at odds with the view of his mother promoted, in filial love and loyalty, by Lewis), Lewis's self-declared "hostility to the emotions" becomes a little less enigmatic.⁴⁶ Those unacquainted with, or unsympathetic to, the psychoanalytic concept of a defence (an unconscious mechanism for deflecting traumatically painful emotions) will perhaps find it invidious of me to suggest that Lewis's relationship with his mother may have been in any important way disappointing to him. Yet perhaps we should investigate more cautiously Lewis's account in *Surprised by Joy* of what the experience of his mother's death meant to him:

> With my mother's death all settled happiness, all that was tranquil and reliable, disappeared from my life. There was to be much fun, many pleasures, many stabs of Joy; but no more of the old security. It was sea and islands now; the great continent has sunk like Atlantis.⁴⁷

I wonder how fully do we register the implications of this passage: "*all* settled happiness"; "*all* sea and islands now." The shock-waves of Lewis's

---

43. Lewis, *The Four Loves*, 84. The text of Dunbar's poem "The Reign of Covetice" (covetousness) actually runs: "Man, please thy Maker an' be merry, / And set not by this warld a cherry." It is characteristic of Lewis to have replaced the archaic "set not by" with the more contemporary and, for non-specialists, intelligible "give not for."

44. Quoted in Sayer, *Jack*, 7.

45. Ibid.

46. Lewis, *Surprised by Joy*, 160. Lewis states that he early learned "to fear and hate emotion," 32.

47. Ibid., 23.

grief, at ten years old, extend not only to the man in his fifties remembering them, but to *all* regions of his life in between. He describes a radical and comprehensive sense of loss. And what he has lost is not his mother's presence, only, but all faith in the goodness of the world. I state this baldly in order to solicit full recognition for the calamitous nature of what Lewis is asserting. His language represents his mother as the fulcrum on which the stability of the world rests, or as the presence in whose embrace the world finds peace. She is, as mothers may often be for children, the *primum mobile* within which all known reality is held; or else a region of fixed stars in relation to which all terrors of the child's experience become bearable. When she dies, the world, which had previously partaken of the reassuring and loving qualities of his mother's presence, is deprived of them and becomes suddenly bleak (Lewis's word), frightening, untrustworthy, and insecure.

Lewis himself believed that his mother's death had been instrumental in giving him an outlook in which disappointment is avoided by expecting the worst:

> I think that though I am emotionally a fairly cheerful person my actual judgement of the world has always been what yours now is and so I have not been disappointed. The early loss of my mother, great unhappiness at school, and the shadow of the last war and presently the experience of it, had given me a very pessimistic view of existence.... I still think the argument from design the weakest possible ground for Theism, and what may be called the argument from un-design the strongest for Atheism.[48]

But I want to go beyond the mere fact of death and suggest how the reverberations of this loss shook Lewis ontologically: radically unsettled his sense of his own safety in the world. And it may be, moreover, that there are factors involved of which Lewis remained unconscious, or of which he never gave any inkling of being aware. Did he feel securely and lovingly held by his mother? Was he welcomed into the world? Was there an apprehensiveness before his mother's death which turned into fear and misgiving afterwards? We would need to know a lot more about Flora Hamilton, and her feelings towards her son, in order to be able even to speculate with any confidence. All we have for certain is Lewis's repeated insistence on a profound ontological trauma which he attributed to his mother's death.[49]

---

48. Lewis, letter to Dom Bede Griffiths (20 December 1946), *The Collected Letters of C. S. Lewis*, Vol. 2, ed. Hooper, 747.

49. See also his letter to Phyllis Sandeman (31 December 1953), *The Collected Letters of C. S. Lewis*, Vol. 3, ed. Hooper, 398.

Lewis had an especially acute need to find stability in the world. This gave to his moral and metaphysical thinking an unusual depth and urgency that his poet's gifts as a prose writer made it possible for him to express with special felicity and force. He located the security he yearned for beyond the world. The difficulty he encountered in making his sense of reality seem plausible to sceptics is comparable, perhaps, to the difficulty of gaining respectful attention for a psychoanalytic imagining of the realities of early childhood. The Hungarian psychoanalyst Sándor Ferenczi, for example, speculated that children who had observed, in overburdened, depressed, ill, or otherwise preoccupied mothers "the conscious and unconscious signs of aversion" (which need not be obvious, except to the child) suffer a weakening of "their desire to live," even if, in later life, "this was resisted by a strong effort of will."[50] Winnicott, the British psychoanalyst who, as we have seen, follows Wordsworth's practice of minutely imagining the experience of infants, considers that the way a mother holds an infant is "the only way in which [she] can show the infant her love of it. There are those who can hold an infant and those who cannot; the latter quickly produce in the infant a sense of insecurity."[51] Freud had already argued that the cleverness of clever infants might be unconsciously exploited by a mother in postponing the satisfaction of the desire, for instance, to be fed. Clearly all such notions are speculative as is their relevance to Lewis. The assumption that Lewis's pessimism is entirely explained by the *fact* of his mother's early death is equally debatable.

What we see more certainly than causes are effects. Lewis had a predilection for periods in which the modern idea of interstellar space did not exist and the disturbing idea of an abyss as limitless as deep space was therefore similarly impossible. In medieval cosmology "There was no abyss."[52] Lewis believed that the feeling of being at home in the world is illusory; and that, if you were to visit a longed-for place it would only point beyond itself to some more distant object of longing.[53] Our natural state is to feel that "in this universe we are treated as strangers" because "our real goal is elsewhere."[54] His poem "In Praise of Solid People" testifies to a "homeless longing";[55] and in "Poem for Psychoanalysts and/or Theologians" Lewis presents himself,

50. Ferenczi, "The Unwelcome Child and His Death Instinct," 125–29.
51. Winnicott, "The Theory of the Parent-Infant Relationship," 592.
52. Lewis, "De Audiendis Poetis," 7.
53. See, e.g., "The Landing" and "Leaving For Ever the Home of One's Youth," in *Poems*, ed. Hooper, 41, 245.
54. Lewis, "The Weight of Glory," 103, 99.
55. Lewis, "In Praise of Solid People," *Poems*, 199.

impishly perhaps, but credibly nonetheless (in an idiom that recalls the Old English poem, "The Wanderer") as wandering over a world whose roundness endlessly postpones arrival.[56] Lewis has an awareness of the phenomenology of perception that makes the idea of perception as inherently illusory not only intelligible but more probable than the idea of it as refracting a solid world. All such instances point to a sense of himself as the alienated inhabitant of a world that, for all its beauty, is dangerous and disappointing. At the same time, Lewis feels a deep recoil from philosophies that intensify the sense of the world's moral and metaphysical arbitrariness.

The doctrine of the natural law provides a partial antidote to the horrors of subjectivism, relativism, or nihilism. The horrors are resisted in proportion as Lewis feels them more acutely. He sees that judgments take place within an ideological system. He understands, fears, and resists the impulse to conclude that there is nothing outside the system. Instead he maintains, according to the testimony of innumerable witnesses in many times and cultures, that beyond the perceptible universe is a changeless system of moral norms, not contingent, but built into the structure of reality. Miracles and reason in its most exalted mood he conceives of as entering the system from outside and testifying to this ultimate order of reality, which provides each culture with a source of sanctions and stability. God holds the world as a mother holds a child. A hostile critic might say that his psychological need to find an ultimate sanction for the moral beliefs within a cultural system discredits the theory of an ultimate sanction. But Lewis would point out that the need to believe is "on all fours" with the need not to.

Intellectualism

I have tried to establish that the loss that Lewis suffered on the death of his mother was not only the loss of her presence, love, and attention, but the loss also of the fundamental feeling of security in the world that his mother's existence symbolized. The pain of such loss was obviously very extreme. It has always struck me as significant that Lewis was no good at mathematics, a subject in which his mother had obtained a first class degree. He emphasizes in *Surprised by Joy* that he twice failed the mathematical part of Responsions. He would not have secured his undergraduate place at Oxford had not the university, after the war, waived the requirement that he pass this elementary part of the old Oxford entrance examination. Lewis was hopelessly incompetent, therefore, at a subject in which his mother excelled. There are many possible explanations of this, of course; and any

---

56. Lewis, "Poem for Psychoanalysts and/or Theologians," 127.

responsible psychotherapist would caution against the dangers of interpreting Lewis in his absence. It seems, however, not entirely reckless to suggest that he could not bear to involve himself imaginatively with a discipline so strongly associated with his mother. Unconsciously, he averts his attention. Consciously, he's just no good at mathematics. In some such way, we might be unconsciously defended against a whole range of painful recognitions. And one very powerful means of defence, for an intellectual, is the intellect.

In writing about writers, it is customary either to ignore the part of the writer's life before she or he could talk, or else to discuss it in terms of genealogy. Thus in the extant biographies of Lewis, the narrative becomes fully attentive to his imaginative life once he has got enough language to begin expressing it in words. Before that, we are told about the adults around him. But, to his parents of course, Lewis had had a lot of life by the time he wrote his first words and very much more again by the time he wrote the first of the books for which he is renowned. I want to suggest we should pay attention to this period of latency and try to imagine something of what may have been going on during it.

Few members of the intellectual professions, perhaps, have a highly developed sense of the dangers of intellectualism or over-reliance on the discursive intellect as a means of discovering truth. In academic writings on literature, it seems, explicit acknowledgement of this danger is rare; and *a fortiori* it is rarer still in those academic writings that aspire to theoretical sophistication. Yet intellectualism can be addictive and can preclude the genuine thoughtfulness that is a precondition for the appreciative reading of literature. For this reason it is important to remember that, like Eliot, Lewis was a poet before he was an academic[57] and that, accordingly, he retained all his life a sense of the limitations of the intellect, which his expertise in exerting it was unable to occlude.

Certainly Lewis recognized that intellectual activity can be addictive and a defence. He refers to "the incurable intellectualism of my own approach";[58] acknowledges that "the limitations of my own gifts has [sic] compelled me to use a purely intellectual approach."[59] He asserts the necessity of thinking not just with the intellect but in a way that involves "the whole man."[60] Great literature, and especially poetry, was for Lewis powerfully conducive to thinking of this kind. Reading it well was therefore, for

---

57. It is no less important to remember that Lewis was a child before he was a poet.
58. Lewis, "God in the Dock," 37.
59. Lewis, "Modern Man and His Categories of Thought," 620.
60. See, e.g., "The whole man is to drink joy from the fountain of joy," in "The Weight of Glory," 105; "It is by this middle element [the Chest] that man is man: for by his intellect he is mere spirit and by his appetite mere animal," *The Abolition of Man*, 19.

him, an experience both therapeutic (it "heals the wound, without undermining the privilege, of individuality"[61]) and quasi devotional: "Here, as in worship, in love, in moral action, and in knowing, I transcend myself; and am never more myself than when I do."[62]

The wound in Lewis, occasioned by the particular circumstances of his childhood, supplies both a motive for intellectual exertion and a wariness about the presumptions of the intellect. Lewis achieves here, towards the end of his life, a deep psychic reconciliation in which pain and insight, self-transcendence and self-fulfilment, are delicately harmonized. His strength as a theorist is that his prose reverberates with the susceptibility to despair that he found his strength in trying to assuage. It is bracingly all-encompassing, yet intimately personal. He has found a way of using the grammar of his emotional life in which pain is regulated as it is registered. A radical, all-pervading despair which he does not define he nonetheless communicates with a fullness that tempers its force. He has learned what those who seek therapy are still learning: how to speak his own language. And to do this, emotionally no less than linguistically, we must learn enough about our own grammar to be able to stop thinking about it and attune our speech to our souls.

* * * * * * *

Westminster Abbey Unvisited

    Perhaps one day of lonely light among
    The plane trees that for all their loftiness
    Were still content to shelter me before
    Lovers shuddered, blanched and shifted tense,

    The path across the open lawn of judgement
    Will swerve into the backwoods of desire
    And I will stand before this empty place
    Where you do not repose, but where

    I watched a father, widowed, harrowed, weightless
    As a face upon the winds of love forlorn
    Tumble headlong into an abyss,
    While tourists behind cameras trailed and yawned

---

61. Lewis, *Experiment in Criticism*, 140–41.
62. Ibid.

And I will think of how I turned to you,
Knowing no more about you than your name,
Discovered on the gravestone of a book
You'd climb from into gazebos of fame.

In a silence rinsed of acclamation
Maybe we will meet. You'll wear no gown.
I'll be singing silently of mountains,
You of Oxford in the midst of County Down.

You'll say few words and I will listen
As inner doors of reticence spring open
All the losses that affinities alight on
Now healed and rivers free to run and shine.

And all your lovers gathered here invisibly
Not reading the letters you slip away beneath,
Will watch for the child among the huddled students
Building a city out of gilt and dreams.

8th November 2013

— 15 —

"It Makes No Difference"

Lewis's Criticism, Fiction, and Theology

―――

Stephen Prickett[1]

I HAD HEARD OF Lewis before I entered Trinity Hall as an undergraduate in 1958, but the only thing I had read by him was *The Screwtape Letters*, and I had this mental picture of him as looking very much like I had imagined Screwtape himself—tall and distinguished, with black hair, a long thin face, with a small black pointed beard—and dressed entirely in black, rather like an austere sixteenth-century Spanish courtier, or, not unconnectedly, more or less like the Devil himself. My shock when this jolly-looking, rather stout and florid character in an old tweed jacket, walking with the aid of a stick, entered our first-year lecture theatre in Mill Lane was all the greater. The Devil had turned into a jovial farmer. His lectures were not particularly jovial, I have to add, nor were they saturnine—nor, unlike many lecturers were they remotely self-indulgent. They began at ten past the hour and finished at precisely ten to the hour. Forty minutes was quite enough for any lecture, he explained. They were precise, thorough, clear, and well-delivered. So matter-of-fact was he in general that it was a complete shock when one day—somewhere about the middle of the Michaelmas term—he said something extraordinary. "I want to say something about myself," he began:

―――

1. Dr. Stephen Prickett is Regius Professor Emeritus of English Language and Literature at the University of Glasgow, a Chair he held from 1990–2007. He is the author of several books, including *Modernity and the Reinvention of Tradition: Backing into the Future* (Cambridge University Press, 2009) and *Victorian Fantasy* (Baylor University Press, 2005).

I have been accused of being a Christian, and filling my lectures with Christian propaganda. It is perfectly true that I am a Christian—but I strongly deny that it has made any difference to my teaching. There is good teaching and there is bad teaching. I hope I have always been a good teacher. Be that as it may, it is a verifiable fact that I did not alter my mode of teaching in any way when I became a Christian. Though I have written Christian apologetic, the Cambridge English Faculty is not the place for it. I talk about religion in my lectures because they are about mediaeval literature, and mediaeval literature is all about religion. As a teacher, however, whether I am a Christian or an atheist should make no difference at all.

There must have been students there who understood what this was all about—some guessed it had to do with his well-known quarrel with F. R. Leavis—but we were freshmen and I think it went over the heads of most of us. We were all prepared to agree on the importance of being a good teacher, and most of us would agree that Lewis was an excellent one. Only later, reading about John Betjeman's furious clashes with Lewis in his Oxford tutorials did it occur to me that there might be more to this than appeared at the time.

When on retirement I found myself teaching in an Evangelical Baptist university in Texas, I found that Lewis was revered among my students as more or less the literary equivalent of a saint. The glow of stardust from my presence in those first year lectures in Mill Lane, it seems, still clung about me, and had I said that whatever opinion I happened to hold at any particular moment I had got from the mouth of the master, my authority would have been absolute. What in fact I told them was what I had just told you—and this probably destroyed my credibility for ever. It was axiomatic for the Baptists of Baylor that Christian teaching was fundamentally different from any other form. The university even had a special unit devoted to the practice of "Christian teaching"—and, needless to say, Lewis was its patron saint, the great *exemplum*.

That uncharacteristic interjection in Lewis's lecture, which I had almost forgotten until I reached Texas, has, however, made me turn back to Lewis's own work in a new way. That flat statement, that what he happened to believe personally "made no difference" to how he taught, suddenly took on a quite new significance. And that is my theme in this paper today.

With the exception of *Screwtape*, my initial reading of Lewis had concentrated almost entirely on his criticism. If you are taking Part I of the English Tripos, it is a good idea to know what the professor who will be marking much of your work has written—and, for me, *The Allegory of Love* was an enthralling introduction to mediaeval literature. (As it happens, I had Lewis for Part II as well—but that was modern stuff anyway . . . .) Later, when I had time for frivolous things, I read the Narnia stories (I was too old for them as a child), the science fiction, the more philosophical novels, *Till We Have Faces*, *The Pilgrim's Regress*, and best of all for me, *The Great Divorce*—which I have re-read many times since. Returning to Lewis's criticism now, however, it strikes me as never before how much of a piece all his writings are. Everything is connected with everything else.

That is true, even with his worst criticism. Lewis's 1939 collection, *Rehabilitations* contains some very bad essays—and one very entertaining one, which I shall return to later. Perhaps the most surprising thing, however, in view of Lewis's later reputation, is how *theoretical* much of his criticism actually is. When not writing about mediaeval literature (and sometimes even then) he was constantly seeking to establish clear guidelines as to how one should go about reading literature—any literature. There should be a set of guiding principles over and above the response to any particular work—that should be the same for any rational person. But those principles should be flexible enough to cope with an encounter with the new. And this, of course, is directly related to his belief that the religious or philosophical orientation of the reader should make no difference to the kind of judgements or conclusions reached. He even writes of what he calls "the Way," a kind of love-your-neighbour, do justly, behave honestly, code that he claimed was basically common not merely to all major religions, but to secular moral codes as well—a kind of Vincentian Canon for the human race. Some may feel that he is over-confident in this assumption of common ground, whatever the starting point, but I think there is no doubt that this is what Lewis believed.

Not surprisingly, given this belief in a broad base of common humanity for all readers, Lewis was forced to make his distinctions between effective and ineffective critical reading on a different system of criteria. And here he found himself in conflict with the very academic discipline he had done so much to foster: the university study of English literature. This, he concludes sadly,

> directs to the study of literature a great many talented, ingenious, and diligent people whose real interests are not specifically literary at all. Forced to talk about books, what can they do but try to make books into the sort of things they can talk about? Hence literature becomes for them a religion, a philosophy, a school of ethics, a psychotherapy, a sociology—anything other than a collection of works of art.[2]

---

2. Lewis, *An Experiment in Criticism*, 86.

Part of Lewis's dislike of what he saw as an unconscious displacement activity is simply the irritation of someone who was deeply into religion, philosophy, and ethics—and certainly knew and drew from both psychotherapy and sociology—as well as, of course, literature itself. His insistence that art was none of the above was because he actually knew all of the above very well. He was also very well aware of the dangers attendant on such subjectivity.

> This is not to say that all critics who extract such a philosophy from their favourite novelists or poets produce work without value. Each attributes to his chosen author what he believes to be wisdom; and the sort of thing that seems to him wise will of course be determined by his own calibre. If he is a fool he will find and admire foolishness, if he is a mediocrity, platitude, in all his favourites.[3]

Even here, however, Lewis struggles to be fair to what in the end is not so much a response to the text as a response to a mirror.

> But if he is a profound thinker himself, what he acclaims and expounds as his author's philosophy may be well worth reading, even if it is in reality his own. We may compare him to the long succession of divines who have based edifying and eloquent sermons on some straining of their texts. The sermon, though bad exegesis, was often good homiletics in its own right.[4]

But this is not a critical reading of literature. Lewis, we need to remember, was not a successful Oxford academic who turned to writing fiction in his middle age. *The Pilgrim's Regress* was published in 1933, when he was still in his mid thirties, well before most of his better-known critical works. He had published two volumes of poetry by the mid-1920s. Some biographers have argued that his views on poetry—including his dislike of T. S. Eliot—were at least partially coloured by his relative lack of success as a poet. Maybe. I happen to like some of his poems—though not all. I also agree with those who say that much of his prose is more poetic than his verse. But Lewis was always, I would argue, as much a creative writer as he was a critic, and there is no doubt that that was how he saw himself. Not merely was his considerable output consistently spread between criticism, theology, and fiction, but all these emerge from his pen not as distinct categories but as themselves mixed genres. *Pilgrim's Regress* is at once fiction, allegory, satire, philosophy, and theology. It would be easy to think of *The Screwtape*

3. Ibid., 87.
4. Ibid.

Letters as being primarily theology—but what theology! Looking back on what I thought of in my teens as "religion," I now see it as primarily satire—religious satire, to be sure, but satire none the less. Lewis was probably the last writer since Milton to give us a Devil's eye view of the world (I discount Byron for obvious reasons) and a very subtle view of human failings it is too.

Nor should we ignore Lewis the philosopher. With a First in Greats, his first academic appointment in 1924 was as a philosophy tutor at University College. The English fellowship at Magdalen, which he held for most of his career, was to follow a year later. It is hardly surprising that *Pilgrim's Regress*, the first major literary work after his conversion in 1931, is as much a philosophic as a religious satire. Even in the Narnia stories, you will remember that the old professor (owner of the Wardrobe) can be heard at intervals complaining of the children's lack of a philosophical grounding in logic and Plato: "What do they teach them at these schools!"

I spoke earlier of the surprisingly theoretical bent to Lewis's criticism, but, of course, it was not the so-called "theory" of the later twentieth-century French critics—which, in turn, of course, was derived largely from German Romanticism. It was, rather, the desire for a clear philosophical basis to his criticism—an attempt to put it beyond subjectivity, and to establish a common ground with other critics who did not share his premises. If philosophy could not prevent differences of opinion, the classical philosophy that Lewis had been grounded in could at least prevent people talking nonsense, and might even provide common premises from which to proceed. Yet even here, though you might expel it with a pitchfork, fiction had a strange way of stretching its tendrils under the fence and reaching into the debate. Who else would write a study in linguistics called "Bluspels and Flalansferes"? Indeed, one could go further. Anyone who knows Owen Barfield's send-up of the solemn speculative notions of early twentieth-century linguisticians, and who comes across phrases like "arboreal psychologists" to describe the ponderous theorizers of primitive man, can be forgiven for suspecting not merely the play of a riotous imagination, but even of straight-faced philological satire.

But my point should surely be clear by now. Lewis's attack on those for whom the study of literature had become for them a surrogate religion, a philosophy, a school of ethics, a psychotherapy, etc., was not because he was not attracted by these things, but because they were in some sense all too attractive. He writes as an insider, and as an insider who knows his ground so well that in an essay like "Bluspels and Flalansferes" he is constantly turning his argument about the need for metaphor in thinking into something like a fictional narrative as he proceeds—and, once again, a fiction in places verging suspiciously on satire.

Now, I'm well aware I'm on dangerous ground here. I recall another first-year lecture in which Lewis warned us seriously against the modern heresy of finding satire in mediaeval literature when none was intended. And yet . . . it is as if he cannot help himself. One thinks of the man who said to Dr. Johnson that he had it in mind to be a philosopher, but "cheerfulness would keep breaking in." Lewis's reputation depends on his being many things, but satirist is not usually one of them—yet satire will keep breaking in. It is true that for anyone with a sense of humour, the idiocies of some critics are indeed an open invitation to satire, but Lewis's criticism is constantly metamorphosing into fictional situations, imaginary conversations, and somewhere in all that there is nearly always a streak of satire. We recall his endorsement of J. W. Saunders' proposal for a "Charientocracy," or government by the refined, in his 1955 essay "Lilies that Fester," where the problem that modern poets are only read by other modern poets is solved by the Swiftian suggestion that practical criticism—and especially listening to poetry readings by modern poets—be made the compulsory entry qualification for the Managerial Class.[5] The only critic who I think was similar in this respect was the late, and much lamented, A. D. Nuttall—who, incidentally, though an atheist, was a great admirer of Lewis.

This is not to say that Lewis's own judgement was always sound. The modern reader notices at once the way in which a writer he approves of is always masculine, whereas someone lightweight or trivial is female. One of his less attractive short stories, "The Shoddy Lands," first published in 1956, is about seeing the world through the eyes of a woman who is only interested in clothing and jewellery shops; everything else—trees, flowers, even sunlight—is vague and undefined. Nor is this the only example of women being the natural location of all that is trivial and worthless—recall the unexpected fate of Susan in the Narnia stories.

Though "The Shoddy Lands" is presented as a satire on consumerism, what is actually described is an aesthetic failure; a failure of observation. Thus the trees in this dream are "the crudest, shabbiest apology for trees you could imagine." Lacking any real anatomy, "they were more like lamp-posts with great shapeless blobs of green stuck on top of them." Similarly, the grass under his feet, though soft and springy to the feet

> . . . when you looked down it was horribly disappointing to the eye. It was, in a very rough way, the colour of grass; the colour grass has on a very dull day when you look at it while thinking pretty hard about something else. But there were no separate blades in it. I stooped down and tried to find them; the closer

5. Lewis, "Lilies that Fester," 116–17.

one looked, the vaguer it seemed to become. It had in fact just the same smudged, unfinished quality as the trees: shoddy.[6]

We shall return to those shoddy blades of grass in a moment. What I want to call attention to here is yet another example of what one might call Lewis's narrative synaesthesia. What is being criticised is a consumerism that is only interested in useless artefacts for sale—the fact that it is being presented as through the eyes of a woman, though perhaps illustrative of misogyny, is technically irrelevant here. A moral failing is presented as an inability to focus on things that have no monetary value; moral blindness becomes physical myopia, a limitation of consciousness. In a reversal of the processes we have seen earlier, where criticism turns into fiction, here fictional narrative has become critical philosophy. More significantly, the whole process is presented in terms of an aesthetic failure. She is shut off from the sheer beauty of the natural world—and, in particular, from that longing which for Lewis is the driving force behind all spiritual growth.

I am not arguing that this kind of movement between genres is unique to Lewis—far from it, I think we all do it to some extent, if only in our imaginations rather than on paper. What I do believe is that this is much more common in Lewis than in most critics. Indeed, I think it is one of his defining characteristics—and one that makes him, for all his faults, a great critic and a great writer. Here I would draw a parallel with an even greater writer, Dickens. There are so many faults in Dickens's writing that it is hard to know where to start—and critics have recognised them and deplored them from his own day onwards. And yet, when all is said and done, he remains one of the very best.

So, for very different reasons, is it with Lewis. He is a writer whose perceptions just jostle against each other, and are so interconnected that it is almost impossible to separate one strand from the next. These are characteristics more common in the poet than the critic, and not for nothing did Lewis see himself as primarily a poet. But let us come back to that passage in *An Experiment in Criticism* with which we began, published in 1961, only two years before his death. Here Lewis attempts to separate the response of the reader to a great work from any number of ancillaries that might clutter it up—religion, philosophy, ethics, etc. Nor is the answer simply that of cultural acquisition. In that paper I just mentioned, "Lilies that Fester," he had attacked the idea of "culture" in the abstract as distinct from the value of a particular cultural artefact. "Those who read poetry to improve their minds," he warns, "will never improve their minds by reading poetry."[7]

6. Lewis, "The Shoddy Lands," 105.
7. Lewis, "Lilies that Fester," 108.

To distinguish what he really values from these peripheral distractions, he tries to define what it is that is valuable about encountering great art. It is all too easy to read Virgil, Dante, Shakespeare, or Milton, as part of a cultural programme, without surrendering ourselves before them; allowing them to dictate the terms under which we encounter them. "The many *use* art and the few *receive* it."[8] When, finally, Lewis tries to describe what lies at the heart of that response his answer almost leaps off the page with pleasure and excitement:

> In reading great literature I become a thousand men and yet remain myself. Like the night sky in the Greek poem, I see with a myriad eyes, but it is still I who see. Here as in worship, in love, in moral action, and in knowing, I transcend myself; and am never more myself than when I do.[9]

At first glance that looks again like an aesthetic response—but, of course it is not. As with Thomas Traherne, whom I suspect Lewis may be echoing here, aesthetics is a surrogate; a metonymy. Even in seeking to frame it in terms of an aesthetic description, he is already moving beyond them. Indeed, he is clearly—and quite consciously—using aesthetics to describe something that is not really aesthetic at all. When, again, he writes of

> that unnameable something, desire for which pierces us like a rapier at the smell of bonfire, the sound of wild ducks flying overhead, the title of *The Well at the World's End*, the opening lines of *Kubla Kahn*, the morning cobwebs in late summer, or the noise of falling waves . . . .[10]

he is using aesthetic experiences quite explicitly to point elsewhere. But what is noticeable here is how much better he is at describing the qualities to be gained by reading than he is about how one should learn to read. How, then, *should* we read literature? And—even more important—if we should not read to improve our minds, or gain culture, what can or should we gain from it? Can you train people to be responsive, to be so possessed? Lewis certainly believed one could—but, clearly, only *some* people.

In this sense Lewis was an unashamed elitist. University studies are not for the masses[11]—and, as he says, many of those who do study English at university shouldn't be doing so. But he is, we note, careful never to suggest that the academic study of literature is a necessary training for reading.

---

8. Lewis, *An Experiment in Criticism*, 19.
9. Ibid., 141.
10. Lewis, *The Pilgrim's Regress*, 15.
11. Cf., e.g., Lewis, "Screwtape Proposes a Toast."

There are many people who with no academic background at all who can receive and be possessed by great works of art and literature. This is not an elite of privilege or entitlement, but one that has to be . . . I was going to say "earned," but perhaps that's not the right word. Possibly "acknowledged," or even "discovered" in the sense that Lewis speaks of finding oneself a Christian rather than choosing to be one.

So what then are the grounds for admission, the price of entry? Here, I think, Lewis is faced with a real paradox. Because of his insistence that good readers may be drawn from any walk of life, and that many of those who specialize in the study of literature are doing so for the wrong reasons and in the wrong way, he finds himself forced towards finding his true readers, the true lovers of literature, almost in terms of a mysterious "elect"—chosen as it were by some Calvinist Demi-God of literature, not on their own merits, but by arbitrary selection. The language of that last quotation from *An Experiment in Criticism* is surely significant. Such people transcend themselves, "as in worship, in love, in moral action, and in knowing," and are never more themselves than when they do. The studied neutrality, in which atheist and Christian can alike be great teachers, has, if not disappeared, been transmuted into something very different. Though Lewis would not, I think, deny that atheists could indeed be great critics, sensitive readers, visionary teachers, it is clear that in doing so—in what he calls "transcending" themselves—they have consciously or unconsciously moved onto religious ground, achieved self-realization, or even perhaps "un-self-realization" through transcendence. Whatever he might claim, this is not the language of secularity—and, more important, not an experience easily described in secular terms.

Though this was furiously resented by some, I do not accept that this is necessarily a criticism of Lewis. He was, by this stage of his life, a deeply religious man, and it was natural enough to him to describe the kind of experience he is trying to portray in religious terms. Nor, I think, would he have wanted to claim that such experiences were the exclusive preserve of religious people. There are enough such experiences in real life, not to mention literature, for him not to be unaware of their existence—one thinks, for instance, of passages in Carlyle, Dickens, even, perhaps, George Eliot. Nevertheless, what this tells us unmistakably is that for Lewis the experience of great art or great literature is, if not a religious experience (and he makes it very clear that to identify the two was a fundamental category mistake[12]), an experience that ultimately takes its meaning from the religious

---

12. This is the subject of perhaps his worst critical essay, "Christianity and Literature" (1939), but it is a point he repeatedly touched on in his writings elsewhere.

experience of "longing" that it is emphatically *not*—in exactly the way that moonlight, while not being sunlight, is impossible without the existence of the sun. Virgil, the good pagan, though he cannot come into the presence of Beatrice in the Earthly Paradise, is, nevertheless Dante's guide to reach that point—or, to put this more precisely in Lewis's own terms, it is an ineffable pull of something just outside the range of his own experience that draws the pilgrim of *Pilgrim's Regress* forward on his journey. There may be other ways to that experience, but this was the nearest for him.

And this brings me back to that grass. Exactly ten years before "The Shoddy Lands," in 1946, Lewis had published *The Great Divorce*, a Dantean vision of hell, purgatory, and heaven. It is true that the characterisation is perfunctory and even stereotyped, but, then, what would you expect of those in hell? The wages of selfishness are a diminished self. But his vision of the place—the city of dreadful night where the only punishment is other people—is extraordinarily powerful and haunting. Heaven—reached by a daily bus, free for any to go, and even stay, if they wish—is much more so. The only qualification for heaven is the desire to be there—and, of course, the majority of the day-trippers hate the place even more than they hated hell. It's that grass again. Though not true heaven, which would be unimaginable, this is more Dante's Earthly Paradise—with a beauty both strange and yet still recognizable as earthly beauty. But there is a shock in store for any visitor from hell. So far from being soft and indistinct, *this* grass is so real that, for the denizens of hell, who have become thin and wraith-like in the searing light of paradise, it is hard and unyielding as diamond. It hurts them to walk on it. If they can only forget themselves they will, in time grow stronger and more solid and real—and one tripper, one of the least likely, does indeed accept that challenge and stay—but for the rest the only thing they cannot give up is themselves, and they choose freely to return, making their own hell from what would otherwise be purgatory. Indeed, as with Dante, *choice* is the key to this whole system. God allows freewill—complete and utter unfettered freedom. But since we are outside time, as we know it, choice acts retrospectively, backwards as well as forwards, so that events in the past become good or bad, pleasurable or painful, according to the choices they lead to.

In place of Dante's Virgil, Lewis's guide to this strangely beautiful and disturbingly un-homely place is none other than George MacDonald, whose novel, *Phantastes*, we are told had been the unlikely beginning of Lewis's own conversion. When Lewis attempts to express his appreciation of MacDonald's writing his attempts at praise are abruptly, if kindly, dismissed. Now that he has seen the reality, the fiction which brought him there is unimportant—and, of course, since what we are reading is itself a fiction, we can draw the parallel conclusion. Just as the letters that make up the words disappear as we get into a narrative, so the narrative—and the aesthetic delight we may take in it—disappears as it, in turn, points beyond itself. Elsewhere Lewis has a term for this: "transposition"[13]—the process by which the richer system is represented by the poorer, just as the inhabitants of E. A. Abbott's *Flatland* cannot conceive of a sphere except in terms of a circle (which unnervingly, for them, who can only inhabit two dimensions, varies arbitrarily in size).

In "The Weight of Glory," a sermon given in Oxford in 1942, Lewis is quite explicit about this transposition:

> If a transtemporal, transfinite good is our real destiny, then any other good on which our desire fixes must be in some degree fallacious, must bear at best only a symbolical relation to what will truly satisfy.
>
> In speaking of this desire for our own far-off country, which we find in ourselves even now, I feel a certain shyness. I am almost committing an indecency. I am trying to rip open the inconsolable secret in each one of you—the secret which hurts so much that you take your revenge on it by calling it names like Nostalgia and Romanticism and Adolescence; the secret also which pierces with such sweetness that when, in very intimate conversation, the mention of it becomes imminent, we grow awkward and affect to laugh at ourselves. . . . We cannot tell it because it is a desire for something that has never actually appeared in our experience. We cannot hide it because our experience is constantly suggesting it. . . . Our commonest expedient is to call it beauty and behave as if that settled the matter. Wordsworth's expedient was to identify it with certain moments in his own past. But all this is a cheat. If Wordsworth had gone back to those moments in the past, he would not have found the thing itself, but only the reminder of it; what he remembered would turn out itself to be a remembering. The books or the music in which we thought beauty was located will betray us if we trust to them; it was not *in* them, it only came *through* them, and what came through them was longing. These things—the beauty, the memory of our own past—are good images of what we really desire; but if they are mistaken for the thing itself they turn into dumb idols, breaking the hearts of their worshippers. For they are not the thing itself; they are only the scent of a flower we

---

13. Lewis, "Transposition."

> have not found, the echo of a tune we have not heard, news from a country we have never yet visited.[14]

I apologise for the length of that quotation, but you can see why. There are those who will respond to this description; and there are those who will hate it—either because they have never shared it, or because they have. T. S. Eliot was not alone in despising Lewis's theology. But like it or hate it, this is not merely why Lewis in the end accepted Christianity, but also why he became a literary critic. It didn't begin in that order, but then, as in *The Great Divorce*, knowing where you have arrived is necessary to understanding the past.

---

14. Lewis, "The Weight of Glory," 200.

PART FIVE
Oxford Addresses

— 16 —

God and the Platonic Host

William Lane Craig[1]

CENTRAL TO CLASSICAL THEISM is the conception of God as the sole ultimate reality, the Creator of all things apart from Himself. This doctrine receives its most significant challenge from Platonism, the view that there are uncreated abstract objects, such as numbers, sets, propositions, and so forth. According to Platonism there is a host of objects, indeed, infinities of infinities of beings, which are just as eternal, necessary, and uncreated as God. So God is not the sole ultimate reality.

I should perhaps clarify that I speak here,[2] not of what is been called "lightweight" Platonism, but of a "heavyweight" Platonism.[3] Lightweight Platonism treats abstract objects merely as the semantic referents of certain singular terms like proper names and definite descriptions. In lightweight Platonism abstract objects are individuals merely in the sense that Wednesdays and the hole in your shirt are individuals, namely, as referents of the

---

1. Dr. William Lane Craig is Research Professor of Philosophy at Talbot School of Theology, California, and Professor of Philosophy at Houston Baptist University, Texas. He is the author of numerous books, including *Reasonable Faith* (Crossway, 2008) and *God, Time and Eternity* (Kluwer Academic, 2001). He maintains a web presence at www.reasonablefaith.org.

2. Dr. Craig's lecture was given to a meeting of the Oxford University C. S. Lewis Society (19th November 2013). A video of the address is available online: https://youtu.be/cVoXs4qQIl8.

3. I am speaking of contemporary Platonism, not classical Platonism. Contemporary Platonism differs vastly from classical Platonism in various respects, principally in taking abstract objects to be causally unrelated to the concrete world. Neither do contemporary Platonists consider abstract objects to be more real than concrete objects. Nor do they think that concrete objects participate in some way in abstract entities, as Plato thought physical objects participate in ideal objects.

terms "Wednesday" and "the hole in your shirt," but not in a sense which would require God to create such things in order for us to speak meaningfully of their existence. I am talking about "heavyweight" Platonism, according to which abstract objects exist just as robustly as the fundamental particles that make up the physical world. Such a Platonism saddles us with a metaphysical pluralism according to which God is not the sole ultimate reality. Rather there are infinite realms of beings that exist independently of God. How is this challenge best met?

Theological Prolegomena

It is not to be met, I believe, by theological compromise; for the biblical witness to God's sole ultimacy is both abundant and clear. Undoubtedly one of the most important biblical texts, both theologically and historically, in this regard is the third verse of the prologue of the Gospel of John. Speaking of the pre-incarnate Christ as the Logos or Word (1:14), John[4] writes:

> "In the beginning was the Word,
> and the Word was with God,
> and the Word was God.
> He was in the beginning with God.
> All things came into being through him,
> and without him not one thing came into being" (1:1–3).

"All things" (πάντα) connotes all things taken severally, not simply the Whole. Of course, God is implicitly exempted from inclusion in "all things," since He has already been said to have been (ἦν) in the beginning (ἐν ἀρχῇ) (v. 1). God and the Logos are not the subject of becoming or coming into being, but of being *simpliciter*. They simply were in the beginning. Everything other than God and the divine Logos "came into being" (ἐγένετο) through the Logos. The verb is the aorist form of γίνομαι, whose primary meaning is "to become" or "to originate." Verse 3 thus carries the weighty metaphysical implication that there are no eternal entities apart from God. Rather,

---

4. I use the name of the received author of the fourth Gospel without commitment to its actual authorship or to the evangelist's authorship of the prologue. Many Johannine commentators think that the prologue contains an independent poem or hymn, perhaps stemming from the Johannine community, which has been adopted by the evangelist and supplemented with his explanatory glosses. There is unanimity that vv. 1–5 (with possible exception of v. 2), 10–11, and 14 belong to the original poem or hymn; vv. 6–9 are clearly the evangelist's gloss. Our interest is solely in what vv. 1–3 of the prologue mean.

everything that exists, with the exception of God Himself, is the product of temporal becoming.[5]

The verb γίνομαι also has the sense of "to be created" or "to be made." This meaning emerges in v. 3 through the denomination of the agent (δι' αὐτοῦ) responsible for things' coming into being. The preposition δία + genitive indicates the agency by means of which a result is produced. The Logos, then, is said to be the one who has created all things and brought them into being. A second, equally significant metaphysical implication of v. 3 thus emerges: only God is self-existent; everything else exists through another, namely, through the divine Logos. God is thus the ground of being of everything else.

John 1:3 is thus fraught with metaphysical significance, for taken *prima facie* it tells us that God alone exists eternally and *a se*. It entails that there are no objects of any sort, abstract or concrete, which are co-eternal with God and uncreated by God via the Logos.

Partisans of uncreated abstract objects, if they are to be biblical, must therefore maintain that the domain of John's quantifiers is restricted in some way, quantifying, for example, only over concrete objects. The issue is a subtle one, easily misunderstood.[6] The question is *not*: did John have in mind abstract objects when he wrote πάντα δι αὐτοῦ ἐγένετο? Probably not. But neither did he have in mind quarks, galaxies, and black holes; yet he would take such things and countless other things, were he informed about them, to lie within the domain of his quantifiers. The question is not what John thought lay in the domain of his quantifiers. The question, rather, is: did John intend the domain of his quantifiers to be unrestricted, once God is exempted? It is very likely that he did. For not only is God's unique status as the only eternal, uncreated being typical for Judaism, but John himself

---

5. This implication reinforces the point which we have elsewhere made that the biblical concept of creation is an inherently temporal notion (Copan and Craig, *Creation out of Nothing*, chaps. 1–4). N.B. that to say that everything other than God has a temporal beginning is not to say that there is a temporal beginning of all things collectively. Theoretically, the sequence of past events could be enumerated by the negative numbers, beginning with the present event as 0, so that while everything that exists has individually a moment of its creation at some time in the finite past, nevertheless the series of creative events regresses infinitely. The evangelist precludes this theoretical possibility by his expression "in the beginning," when only God and the divine Logos exist. Still the point remains that while for every thing that has come into being, there is a time in the past at which it began, nevertheless that does not imply that there is a time in the past at which everything began.

6. See the persistent misunderstanding of the question by my collaborators in *Beyond the Control of God? Six Views on the Problem of God and Abstract Objects*, ed. Paul Gould, with articles, responses, and counter-responses by K. Yandell, R. Davis, P. Gould, G. Welty, Wm. L. Craig, S. Shalkowski, and G. Oppy (Bloomsbury, forthcoming).

identifies the Logos alone as existing with God (and being God) in the beginning. Creation of everything else through the Logos then follows. The salient point here is that the unrestrictedness of the domain of the quantifiers is rooted, not in the type of objects thought to be in the domain, but in one's doctrine of God as the only uncreated being.

But was John, in fact, ignorant of the relation between abstract objects and divine creation when he wrote vv. 1–3, as we have assumed? It is, in fact, far from clear that the author of John's prologue was innocent concerning abstract objects and their relation to the Logos. For the doctrine of the divine, creative Logos was widespread in Middle Platonism,[7] and the similarities between John's Logos doctrine and that of the Alexandrian Jewish philosopher Philo (20 B.C–A.D 50) are numerous and striking.[8] Of particular interest is the role of the Logos as the instrumental cause of creation. The use of διa + genitive to express instrumental creation is not derived from Wisdom literature but is a earmark of Middle Platonism; indeed, so much so that scholars of this movement are wont to speak of its "prepositional metaphysics," whereby various prepositional phrases are employed to express causal categories:[9]

Phrase:	τὸ ὑφ' οὗ	τὸ ἐξ οὗ	τὸ δι' οὗ	τὸ δι' ὅ
Category:	τὸ αἴτιον	ἡ ὕλη	τὸ ἐργαλεῖον	ἡ αἰτία
	Efficient cause	Material cause	Instrumental cause	Final cause
Entity:	God the Creator	Four elements	Logos of God	God's goodness

Philo identifies the four Aristotelian causes by these prepositional phrases, stating that the phrase "through which" represents creation by the Logos.[10]

---

7. For references see Stirling, "Day One." The Logos appears already in the work of Antiochus of Ascalon and Eudores, two of the earliest Middle Platonists.

8. Cf. Leonhardt-Balzer, "Der Logos und die Schöpfung," 318.

9. Runia, *Philo of Alexandria and the "Timaeus" of Plato*, 140–43; Stirling, "Day One."

10. *On the Cherubim* [*De cherubim*] 125–27. References to the Logos as the instrumental cause of creation are prevalent in Philo. Runia provides the following list: *On the Creation of the World* [*De opificio mundi*]; *Allegorical Interpretation* [*Legum allegoriae*] 3.9; *On the Cherubim* 28; *On the Sacrifices of Abel and Cain* [*De sacrificiis Abelis et Caini*] 8; *On the Unchangeableness of God* [*Quod Deus sit immutabilis*] 57; *On the Confusion of Tongues* [*De confusione liguarum*] 62; *On the Migration of Abraham* [*De migrationi Abrahami*] 6; *On Flight and Finding* [*De fuga et inventione*] 12; 95; *On Dreams* 2.45; *The Special Laws* [*De specialibus legibus*] 1.81.

The similarities between Philo and John's doctrines of the Logos are so numerous and close that most Johannine scholars, while not willing to affirm John's direct dependence on Philo, do recognize that the author of the prologue of John's Gospel shares with Philo a common intellectual tradition of Platonizing interpretation of Genesis chapter 1.

Now John does not tarry to reflect on the role of the divine Logos causally prior to creation. But this pre-creation role features prominently in Philo's Logos doctrine. According to Philo scholar David Runia, a cornerstone of Middle Platonism was the bifurcation of the intelligible and sensible realms.[11] To draw the distinction in this way is, however, somewhat misleading.[12] The fundamental distinction here, as originally found in Plato, is between the realm of static being (τί τὸ ὄν ἀεί) and the realm of temporal becoming (τί τὸ γιγνόμενον μὲν ἀεί). The former realm is to be grasped by the intellect, whereas the latter is perceived by the senses. The realm of becoming was comprised primarily of physical objects, while the static realm of being was comprised of what we would today call abstract objects. For Middle Platonists, as for Plato, the intelligible world (κόσμος νοητός) served as a model for the creation of the sensible world. But for a Jewish monotheist like Philo, the realm of Ideas does not exist independently of God but as the contents of His mind. The intelligible world may be thought of as either the causal product of the divine mind or simply as the divine mind itself actively engaged in thought. Especially noteworthy is Philo's insistence that the world of Ideas cannot exist anywhere but in the divine Logos. Just as the ideal architectural plan of a city exists only in the mind of the architect, Philo explains, so the ideal world exists solely in the mind of God. On Philo's doctrine, then, there is no realm of independently existing abstract objects. According to Runia, while not part of the created realm, "the κόσμος νοητός, though eternal and unchanging, must be considered dependent for its existence on God."[13]

---

11. Runia, *Plato and the "Timaeus,"* 68. The *locus classicus* of the distinction was Plato's *Timaeus* 27d5–28a4, which is in turn cited by Apuleius *De Platone et eius dogmate* 193; Nichomachus *Introductio arithmetica* 1.2.1; Numenius fr. 7; Justin Martyr *Dialogue with Trypho* 3.5; Sextus Empiricus *Adversus mathematicos* 7.142.

12. None of Runia's texts draws the distinction at issue as fundamentally intelligible *vs.* sensible; rather it is being *vs.* becoming. The problem with the former characterization of the distinction is that it seems to leave no place of immaterial *concreta* like intelligences, angels, or souls. Given that the intelligible realm exists in the mind of God, such beings cannot be classed as part of the intelligible realm. They must be part of the sensible realm, which is thus more accurately described as the realm of concrete objects subject to becoming.

13. Runia, *Plato and the "Timaeus,"* 138.

Interested as John is in the incarnation of the Logos, he does not linger over the pre-creatorial function of the Logos, but given the provenance of the Logos doctrine, he may well have been aware of the role of the Logos in grounding the intelligible realm as well as his role in creating the realm of temporal concrete objects.

However this may be, our exegetical study of John 1:1–3 leads to the conclusion that the author of the prologue of John's Gospel conceives of God as the Creator of everything apart from Himself. There are no uncreated, independently existing, eternal objects, for God exists uniquely *a se*. I could make exactly the same point from Paul's correspondence, but time compels me to skip ahead.

The conviction that God is the Creator of everything that exists aside from God Himself eventually attained creedal status at the Council of Nicaea. In language redolent of the prologue to the fourth Gospel and of Paul, the Council affirmed:

> I believe in one God, the Father, Almighty, Maker of heaven and earth and of all things visible and invisible; And in one Lord, Jesus Christ, the only Son of God, begotten of the Father before all ages, light from light, true God from true God, begotten not made, consubstantial with the Father, through whom all things came into being.

The phrase "Maker of heaven and earth and of all things visible and invisible" is Pauline, and the expression "through whom all things came into being" Johannine. The Council thus confesses that God alone is uncreated and that all else was created by Him.

The Challenge of Platonism

The biblical theist cannot therefore be a Platonist, for Platonism denies that God is the sole ultimate reality. So how shall the classical theist best meet the challenge of Platonism? Figure 1 lays out some of the alternatives.

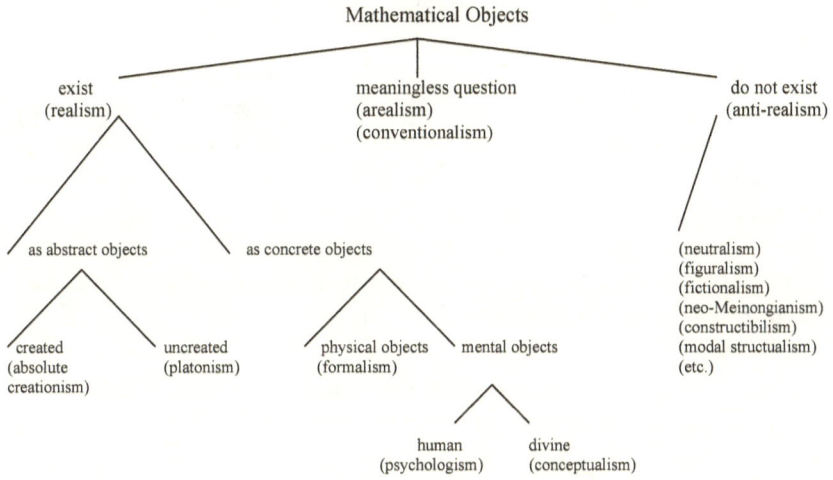

Some options concerning the existence of mathematical objects

I have taken mathematical objects as representative of what are typically taken to be abstract objects. One cannot take Fig. 1 to be about abstract objects as such because, as you can see, one branch of realism treats these objects as concrete, not abstract. Note that what I have called anti-realism often goes under the name of nominalism; but I have avoided that label as less clear and potentially misleading.

Arealism

Consider our options. I take it that a classical theist cannot embrace arealism as his solution. As I use the term, arealism is the view that there just is no fact of the matter concerning the existence of putative abstract objects.[14] Arealism is not an option for the classical theist, since, given divine aseity, God exists in every possible world and is the creator of any reality *extra se* in any world in which He exists. Therefore, it is a metaphysically necessary truth that no uncreated, abstract objects exist. Hence, there is, indeed, a fact of the matter whether uncreated abstract objects exist: they do not and cannot exist. Thus, arealism with respect to putative abstract objects is necessarily false.

---

14. Conventionalists like Rudolf Carnap held such questions to have no framework-independent answer because they are meaningless; metaontological anti-realists like Mark Balaguer take them to be meaningful but deny that such ontological disputes have objective answers. *N.B.* the distinction between ontological anti-realism, such as is featured in Fig. 1, and metaontological anti-realism. Penelope Maddy's so-called arealism is really closer to pretense theory.

Realism

Now consider the realist options. The option requiring the least modification of Platonism is absolute creationism. Although there is a tendency to conflate absolute creationism with divine conceptualism, I take the absolute creationist to affirm that mathematical objects are not concrete objects, like mental events, but are causally effete objects existing in some sense apart from God, though causally dependent upon Him.[15] Unfortunately, absolute creationism appears to involve a vicious circularity which has become known as the bootstrapping objection. The problem can be simply stated with respect to the creation of properties, a paradigmatic case of abstract objects. In order to create properties, God must already possess properties. For example, in order to create the property *being powerful* God must already possess the property of being powerful, which involves a vicious circularity. The only plausible way to avoid the bootstrapping problem, it seems to me, is to affirm that God can create a property without having the property of *being able to create a property*. But that just is to abandon Platonism in favour of nominalism, which holds that talk of properties is just a convenient *façon de parler*. Such a solution removes any motivation for realism.

So what about anti-Platonist forms of realism? Anti-Platonist realists hold that various objects normally thought to be abstract, such as mathematical objects, are in fact concrete. These may be taken to be either physical objects, such as marks on paper which are manipulated by mathematicians according to certain rules, or mental objects or thoughts, either in human minds or in God's mind. The nineteenth-century German philosopher Gottlob Frege subjected the views that mathematical objects are physical objects or human thoughts to such withering criticism that such views are scarcely taken seriously today.[16] But Frege's objections to human psychologism—such as the intersubjectivity, necessity, and plenitude of mathematical objects—do not touch divine conceptualism. That Frege could simply overlook what has historically been the mainstream theistic position with respect to putative abstract objects is perhaps testimony to how utterly detached nineteenth-century philosophical thinking had become from the historic Christian tradition. With the late twentieth-century renaissance of Christian philosophy, divine conceptualism is once more finding articulate defenders.[17] According to these thinkers, putative abstract objects like

---

15. Thomas Morris and Christopher Menzel are ambiguous in this regard; Paul Gould and Richard Davis maintain, confusedly, I think, that God creates abstract objects but that these are divine thoughts.

16. Frege, *The Foundations of Arithmetic*, §I. 7, 8–11; §II. 26–27, 34–38.

17. Notably Alvin Plantinga, Brian Leftow, and Greg Welty.

propositions, properties, possible worlds, and mathematical objects are, or are analyzable in terms of, God's thoughts of various sorts.

Conceptualists can meet the bootstrapping objection by denying that prior to God's conceiving them things like properties, propositions, and the like exist. God can be as He is without exemplifying properties or propositions' being true logically prior to His conceiving them. But then, as noted before, the nerve of realism seems to be cut. So why not be an anti-realist?

Moreover, conceptualism is not entirely worry-free. For in many cases God's thoughts do not seem suitable to play the roles normally ascribed to *abstracta*. Take propositions, for example. Conceptualism requires that God be constantly entertaining actual thoughts corresponding to every proposition. But conceptualists move far too hastily from the fact that God is omniscient to the view that all that God knows is occurrent in consciousness. God's infinite knowledge is clearly *not* sufficient to guarantee that there are the actual mental events needed by the conceptualist. Indeed, Graham Oppy complains that conceptualism "threatens to lead to the attribution to God of inappropriate thoughts: bawdy thoughts, banal thoughts, malicious thoughts, silly thoughts, and so forth."[18] For example, consider propositions of the form *for any real number r, r is distinct from the Taj Mahal*. Why would God retain such inanities constantly in consciousness? Worse, consider false propositions of the form *for any real number r, r is identical to the Taj Mahal*. Why would God hold such a silly thought constantly in consciousness, knowing it to be false? Obviously, the concern is not that God would be incapable of keeping such a non-denumerable infinity of thoughts ever in consciousness, but rather why He would dwell on such trivialities.

Furthermore, what has been called the "aspectual shape" of a thought does not always correspond to the aspectual shape of the proposition expressed. For example, the thought that *I am making a mess* has a different aspectual shape than the proposition *William Craig is making a mess*. God can know the propositional content of my thought without His thought's having the same aspectual shape as my thought. But if we identify God's thoughts with propositions, we are no longer able to distinguish between the aspectual shape of a proposition and the aspectual shape of a divine thought having that propositional content. Since God has first-person thoughts, identifying God's thoughts with propositions commits us to the existence of purely private propositions which are incommunicable by God to us. Personal indexical beliefs are just the proverbial camel's nose. If propositions have the unique aspectual shape of God's thoughts, many other dislocations in how we normally conceive things will be forced upon us.

In these and many other ways, the suitability of God's thoughts to play successfully the roles ascribed to various *abstracta* is worrisome.

18. Oppy, "Response to Welty."

Anti-Realism

Now I do not imagine that these worries constitute insuperable obstacles for conceptualism. Rather, my reason for raising them is to motivate theists to look more seriously at the cornucopia of anti-realist options that are available today. It is striking how little cognizance contemporary theists who have written on the problem of divine aseity take of anti-realism. They seem to have absorbed realism with their mother's milk.

It is not as though there are overwhelming arguments for realism. The principal argument offered on behalf of realism comes in the various incarnations of Willard Quine's Indispensability Argument. Mark Balaguer succinctly formulates the Indispensability Argument as follows:

I) If a simple sentence (*i.e.*, a sentence of the form "*a* is *F*") is literally true, then the objects that its singular terms denote exist. (Likewise, if an existential sentence (*e.g.*, "There is an *F*") is literally true, then there exist objects of the relevant kinds.)

II) There are literally true simple sentences containing singular terms that refer to things that could only be abstract objects. (Likewise, there are literally true existential statements whose existential quantifiers range over things that cold only be abstract objects.)

III) Therefore, abstract objects exist.

How might we respond to this argument? Although, to my knowledge, C. S. Lewis did not interact with the Indispensability Argument for abstract objects, I think we have some idea of how he might have responded to it. In his essay "Bluspels and Flalansferes: A Semantic Nightmare," Lewis claims that the greater part of our language is metaphorical rather than literal. Lewis argues that "Our thought is independent of the metaphors we employ in so far as these metaphors are optional: that is, in so far as we are able to have the same idea without them."[19] Lewis uses the example of trying to understand unimaginable higher-dimensional realities like curved 3-dimensional space on the basis of 2-dimensional analogies in Flatland. In so far as one understands the relevant mathematics, one may dispense with the metaphor. But then Lewis proceeds to say:

> Our claim to independence of the metaphor is . . . a claim to know the object otherwise than through that metaphor. . . . That was what happened, you will remember, to the man who went on and learned mathematics. He came to apprehend that of which the Flatlanders' sphere was only the image, and consequently was free to think beyond the metaphor and to forget the

---

19. Lewis, "Bluspels and Flalansferes," 258.

metaphor altogether. In our previous account of him, however, we carefully omitted to draw attention to one very remarkable fact: namely, that when he deserted metaphor for mathematics, he did not really pass from symbol to symbolized, but only from one set of symbols to another. The equations and what-nots are as unreal, as metaphorical, if you like, as the Flatlanders' sphere.[20]

It is evident that Lewis is an anti-realist about mathematical discourse, taking it to be metaphorical and its objects unreal. Lewis thinks that in many fields of discourse the failure to realize that one is using dead metaphors with no understanding of their meaning leads to the meaninglessness of that discourse. He is more optimistic with respect to mathematical discourse: "the mathematician, who seldom forgets that his symbols are symbolic, may often rise for short stretches to ninety per cent of meaning and ten of verbiage."[21] Lewis thus thinks that mathematicians themselves realize that their discourse is not literal but metaphorical.

Lewis was apparently also an anti-realist about other abstract objects. For example, with respect to universals, he opined, "the universal latent in every group and every plural inflection cannot be thought without metaphor."[22] Indeed, it is likely that he took the whole platonic host to be creatures of metaphor, for he writes, "open your Plato, and you will find yourself among the great creators of metaphor, and therefore among the masters of meaning."[23]

I think that Lewis would therefore challenge premise (II) of the Indispensability Argument. He would contend that abstract object discourse is plausibly taken to be metaphorical, not literal, and therefore is non-commissive ontologically to abstract objects.

What shall we make of this response? The claim that abstract object discourse in general, and mathematical discourse in particular, is metaphorical rather than literal is championed today by Stephen Yablo, who has coined the term "figuralism" for the view that such discourse should not be understood literally but is a case of figurative language. Figurative speech, properly interpreted, may be true even if, taken literally, it is false. For in figurative speech, such as understatement, hyperbole, and metaphor, the literal content is not what the speaker is asserting.[24] If mathematical language is figurative, then it will be maladroit to ask after the ontological commitments of such discourse when construed literally.

20. Ibid., 260–61.
21. Ibid., 264.
22. Ibid.
23. Ibid., 265.
24. Yablo, "A Paradox of Existence," 291.

Yablo observes that figurative language is a pervasive feature of ordinary discourse, so much so that we often do not realize that we are speaking figuratively. Like Lewis, Yablo believes that literal talk is actually the talk that is unusual.[25] This presents a serious problem for Quine's project of determining the ontological commitments of our discourse. Since figures of speech should not be taken literally, Quine recognized that his criterion of ontological commitment could not be applied to such discourse. This situation is problematic because, in Yablo's words, "To determine our ontological commitments, we have to ferret out all traces of non-literality in our assertions; if there is no sensible project of doing that, there is no sensible project of Quinean ontology."[26]

Quine looked to science in order to eliminate metaphorical features of ordinary discourse: we are to count a thing as existing just in case it is a commitment of our best scientific theory. But, Yablo demands, what if our best theory itself contains metaphorical elements? Quine never argued that metaphor can be made to disappear entirely. If our best theories include metaphorical sentences, then we need a way of sequestering the metaphors. But in order to do that, we need a criterion for identifying an expression as metaphorical, which we do not have. The boundaries of the literal, Yablo maintains, are so unclear that there is no telling, in cases of interest, whether our assertions are to be taken ontologically seriously. The more controversial of philosophical existence claims are equipoised between the literal and the figurative in a way that Quine's method is powerless to address.[27] Among these will be claims about abstract objects.

Yablo thinks that talk of abstract objects involves the use of what he calls "existential metaphors," that is to say, metaphors "making play with a special sort of object to which the speaker is not [ontologically] committed."[28] Numerical terms are such existential metaphors, useful, and sometimes indispensable, for expressing truths about the real world. Yablo provides the following illustration:

> Much as we make as if, e.g., people have associated with them stores of something called "luck," so as to be able to describe some of them metaphorically as individuals whose luck is "running out," we make as if pluralities have associated with them

---

25. Yablo, "Go Figure," 85.

26. Yablo, "Does Ontology Rest on a Mistake?" 229. Cf. Yablo, "Paradox of Existence," 304–5.

27. Yablo, "Does Ontology Rest on a Mistake?" 255, 259.

28. Yablo, "Paradox of Existence," 293. By "commitment" I think Yablo means to indicate one's commitment to the existence of the thing. Indeed, he seems to mean "conscious commitment," the opposite of simulation or make-believe. Cf. Yablo, "Does Ontology Rest on a Mistake?" 250; Yablo, "The Myth of the Seven," 98.

things called "numbers," so as to be able to express an (otherwise hard to express because) infinitely disjunctive fact about relative cardinalities like so: The number of Fs is divisible by the number of Gs.[29]

Given our finitude, we cannot express infinite disjunctions like "There is one star and one planet, or there are two stars and one planet, or . . ." and so have no choice but to resort to number talk in order to talk, in this case, about stars and planets. "It is only by making *as if* to countenance numbers, that one can give expression in English to a fact having nothing to do with numbers, a fact about stars and planets and how they are numerically proportioned."[30]

Yablo draws a number of very interesting parallels between talk of Platonic objects[31] and figurative talk. These parallels serve as evidence that abstract object talk is a kind of figurative language.[32]

Yablo thinks that the decision between Platonism and figuralism depends upon the answers to the following questions: (1) what does

29. Yablo, "Myth of the Seven," 98.
30. Yablo, "Paradox of Existence," 295.
31. It should be noted that Yablo has an idiosyncratic understanding of what a Platonic object is. Objects are Platonic relative to an area of discourse if the discourse depends on how those objects behave yet the discourse is not really about those objects. For example, someone who expresses concern about the number of starving people in the world is concerned about people, not some abstract object. Platonic objects, Yablo says, *whether abstract or not*, are deducible by overly easy existence proofs. He gives the following illustrations of discovering unexpected objects in statements' truth conditions:

the truth value of:	is held to turn on:
argument A is valid	the existence of *countermodels*
it is possible that B	the existence of *worlds*
there are as many Cs as Ds	the existence of 1–1 *functions*
there are over five Es	the *number* of E's exceeding five
he did it Fly	the *event* of his doing it being F
there are Gs which BLAH	there being a *set* of Gs which BLAH
she is H	her relation to the *property* H-ness

The entities denoted by the italicized terms in the right-hand column are Platonic because the sentences in the left-hand column are not really about them (Yablo, "Paradox of Existence," 277). The expressions on the right are therefore existential metaphors. If the objects denoted by such expressions do exist, most of them are plausibly construed to be abstract objects. In fact, Yablo himself says, "the existence of abstract objects is straightforwardly deducible from premises that few would think to deny" (ibid., 276). Since our interest is in the existence of abstract objects, we shall take Yablo's Platonic objects to be abstract. Yablo notes that in addition to the parallels between figurative language and talk of Platonic objects, evidence for the metaphorical character of such talk is that it is the best explanation of why such overly easy existence proofs fail.

32. Yablo, "Paradox of Existence," 302–4; cf. Yablo, "Go Figure," 89–90; Yablo, "Abstract Objects," 227–30.

Platonism/figuralism help us to explain, and (2) what explanatory puzzles does Platonism/figuralism generate?

Consider first, question (2). Yablo believes that anti-Platonists have relied too heavily on the explanatory puzzles generated by Platonism, though he takes no cognizance of the theological puzzle that drives our inquiry, namely, how the putative existence of abstract objects is to be reconciled with divine aseity and *creatio ex nihilo*. Given our theological commitments, we know that Platonism is unacceptable. So all we need from Yablo, then, is some reason to prefer figuralism above other anti-Platonisms. Yablo has done a good job of laying out the case for taking abstract object discourse as figurative, but he does not examine the comparative explanatory power of other anti-Platonistic views with respect to the data. So more work needs to be done.

As for explanatory puzzles generated by figuralism, Yablo considers only the objection that abstract object talk, and particularly mathematical discourse, is not plausibly a matter of make-believe. This objection, however, is really an objection to a pretense theoretical analysis of figurative language, not to the figuralist thesis that abstract object talk is figurative. Consideration of such a puzzle is therefore better reserved for another time when discussing pretense theory.

So let us consider instead an objection that has been raised against figuralism by John Burgess and Gideon Rosen. They think that the claim that mathematical discourse is figurative is implausible. They write:

> Certainly in all *clear* cases of figurative language—and it is worth stressing that the boundary between figurative and literal is as fuzzy as can be—the non-literal character of the linguistic performance will be *perfectly obvious* as soon as the speaker is forced to turn attention to the question of whether the remark was meant literally.
>
> We further submit that mathematical discourse fails this test for non-literalness.[33]

One is tempted to ask what evidence can be cited in support of their opening sentence, but never mind. The more important point is that this objection, if sound, at best proves that mathematical discourse is not a *clear* case of figurative language, a hardly surprising result.[34] What does not follow

---

33. Rosen and Burgess, "Nominalism Reconsidered," 533.

34. Burgess and Rosen themselves acknowledge that on Yablo's view "an existence theorem is ambiguous between a literal and a figurative sense" (ibid., 528). I am not sure how seriously they take this ambiguity.

is that mathematical discourse does not lie somewhere in that fuzzy area between clearly figurative and clearly literal expressions.

The second and perhaps more important point to make is that while Yablo, like Lewis, espouses figuralism as a hermeneutic thesis about how mathematicians themselves understand their discourse, there is no reason the anti-realist has to present it as such. In the absence of linguistic and sociological studies about what the community of working mathematicians think about this question, the figuralist can remain agnostic about hermeneutical questions and present the figurative interpretation simply as one reasonable way of understanding abstract object talk. If such an interpretation is reasonable, then the Indispensability Argument has been defeated.

Turn now to question (1). What are the alleged explanatory benefits of Platonism? The principal merit claimed on behalf of Platonism is that it provides a basis for the objective truth of mathematics.[35] But here the difference between fictionalism and figuralism comes clearly to the fore. Figuralism *affirms* the truth of mathematical sentences, for these are figurative speech and as such escape the traditional criterion of ontological commitment. Just as "It's raining cats and dogs!" may be true without there being animals falling from the sky, so the truth that "1+1=2" does not require the reality of numbers. Of course, the theistic figuralist who does not believe in abstract objects will deny the *literal* truth of figurative talk about abstract objects; but he will insist on the truth of such statements when understood, not literally, but figuratively.

Still we may wonder what the objective basis of mathematical truths is, if not the reality of the objects referred to or quantified over in such statements. Here Yablo seems to differ from Lewis, who seemed to think that we could explain mathematical metaphors only in terms of more metaphors. Yablo maintains that the real content of mathematical truths is logical truths, which require no ontological foundation: "Arithmetic is, at the level of real content, a body of logical truths—specifically, logical truths about cardinality—while set theory consists at the level of real content, of logical truths of a combinatorial nature."[36] In short, the realist has no advantage

---

35. Yablo, "Go Figure," 88; Yablo, "Paradox of Existence," 286–90.

36. Yablo, "Myth of the Seven," 99; Yablo, "Abstract Objects," 230–32. The real content of arithmetical truths like 2+3=5 is the first-order logical truth ($\exists 2xFx$ & $\exists 3yGy$ & $\neg \exists z$ (Fz & Gz)) $\rightarrow \exists 5u(Fu \vee Gu)$) *$5u(Fu \vee Gu)$. When it comes to non-numerical mathematical statements such as are comprised by set theory, Yablo takes the figurative language of sets to express certain combinatorial logical truths, that is, truths about what one gets when combining objects in different ways.

In his earlier work, Yablo contrasted the literal and metaphorical content of a figurative sentence ("Does Ontology Rest on a Mistake?" 248–49), but was not always consistent with his later use of terminology. For example, the existentially metaphorical

over the anti-realist in accounting for the objectivity of mathematical truth, since the real content of metaphorical statements about such imaginary entities as numbers and sets is logical truths.

Finally, as for the explanatory benefits of figuralism, although Yablo has benefits of his own in mind, surely for the theist the most important benefit is that it explains how to reconcile mathematical truth with divine aseity. The theist has good reasons for thinking that Platonism is false and may embrace figuralism's account of mathematics' necessity, apriority, and absoluteness without compromising his anti-realism about *abstracta*.

In sum, it seems to me that figuralism is a plausible option for the theist to pursue as a means of defeating the Indispensability Argument for Platonism. It offers an interpretation of abstract object discourse that is figurative, not literal, thereby avoiding ontological commitment while preserving truth. Figuralism has the additional advantage of being a very plausible interpretation of mathematical discourse in view of the striking similarities of such discourse to figurative speech.

Figuralism thus offers an attractive solution to the challenge of Platonism to God's being the sole ultimate reality. What figuralism does leave unchallenged, though, is the Quinean metaontological criterion for ontological commitment which comes to expression in premise (I) of the Indispensability Argument. Some might see this as an advantage of figuralism, since it places figuralism on common ground concerning customary views of quantification and reference. Other anti-realists, however, will see this strategy as timid and insufficiently radical. These other anti-realists will dare to assail the sanctuary of Quinean metaontology itself.

---

statement "The average star has 2.4 planets" can be paraphrased as "The number of planets divided by the number of stars is 2.4." This eliminates the average star, but only at the expense of committing us to numbers. Since numbers are not the cosmologist's concern, says Yablo, this statement is also metaphorical. Yablo would later put it differently: numbers are therefore Platonic. Therefore, the figuralist will take the paraphrase to be metaphorical. Yablo then says that the more literal content is "There are 12 planets and 5 stars or there are 24 planets and 10 stars or . . . ." But later Yablo would realize that such a statement actually gives, not the literal content, but the real content, and does not commit its user to numbers. Because the real content is inexpressible, being an infinite disjunction, we have no recourse but to resort to metaphor, such as those used in the original statement and its paraphrase.

In his later work, Yablo tends to contrast the literal content of figurative speech with its real content ("Go Figure," 94–95; "Abstract Objects," 209–30). There he explains that for the figuralist "The average mother has 2.3 children, but there is no average mother" is true because the first clause is figurative and the second literal. The real content of the first clause will be an inexpressible, infinite disjunction.

— 17 —

Remembering C. S. Lewis

Walter Hooper[1]

LADIES AND GENTLEMEN, BESIDES apologising for the amount of autobiography in this talk, I must make it absolutely clear from the outset that my acquaintance with Lewis was, in comparison to that of many of his friends, a mere flea-bite. There was of course Lewis's beloved brother, Warnie, who knew Jack Lewis more intimately than anyone. And there are so many others such as J. R. R. Tolkien who have left fascinating reminiscences of Lewis. If you had been at this banquet fifty years ago any one of those men would have been the speaker you *should* have invited. But as they are now in heaven, I am touched by your graciousness in inviting me here.

My introduction to Lewis's writings goes back to May 1953 when I was nearing my final term at the University of North Carolina at Chapel Hill. This was the time of the Korean War and all young men were worried whether they'd be allowed to finish their degree before being drafted into the army.

In that happy place during a very happy time of my life, I was introduced to J. B. Phillips's *Letters to Young Churches: A Translation of the New Testament Epistles* (1947). It contained an Introduction by C. S. Lewis.[2] I'd

---

1. Walter Hooper is Trustee of and Literary Adviser to the estate of C. S. Lewis and has edited many collections of Lewis's writings, most notably the three-volume *Collected Letters*. In 1974, with Roger Lancelyn Green, he wrote the first biography of C. S. Lewis, which he revised and expanded in 2002. He is also the author of *C. S. Lewis, A Companion and Guide* (HarperCollins, 1996). In 1963 he served as Lewis's private secretary when Lewis was in declining health.

2. The Introduction is published as "Modern Translations of the Bible," in *God in the Dock*, ed. Hooper.

never heard his name before, and I read the Introduction simply because it was there. It made a total conquest of me. It was not so much what he said, but the *way* he said it. What came through the Introduction was not simply information about the Epistles but something about Lewis. I knew I'd stumbled upon someone whose faith was as certain as that of the apostles.

Thereafter I wanted passionately to read anything I could find by Lewis. After a number of deferments by the draft board, I finally finished my degree—and it was then straight into the army and Fort Jackson, South Carolina. I had meanwhile discovered a little bookshop in Greensboro run by two elderly ladies who, the day before I went to Fort Jackson, put into my hands a copy of Lewis's *Miracles*, which went with me into the army. During basic training I kept *Miracles* hidden beneath my shirt, which made for a good deal of discomfort during callisthenics and bayonet practice. However, in those little ten-minute breaks between firing bazookas and throwing grenades, I managed to read a page or so. If a book can hold your interest during all that excitement, and while you're crawling under barbed wire in a muddy trench, it is a very, *very* good book.

Because Lewis wrote in so many genres—fairy tales, theology, science fiction, literary criticism—he sometimes appears to be half a dozen different authors, especially if you only discover his fairy tales after having exhausted his theology, or only discover his science fiction after having worked your way through his literary criticism. But that was not my experience. During the next two years at Fort Jackson and Fort Bragg I received all my Lewis books from the ladies in Greensboro, and I simply read them in the order they sent them to me, which was not at all systematic: *Miracles*, then *English Literature in the Sixteenth Century*, then *The Lion, the Witch and the Wardrobe*, and so forth. This turned out to be very important because I never imagined Lewis to be several different compartmentalised authors, but rather one author of several geniuses.

By November 1954 I was working for some chaplains at Fort Bragg, and they arranged for me to talk to the first person to come my way who had met Lewis. It was Dr. Bob Jones Jr., President of Bob Jones University, who was known as the hottest of all hot-gospellers. He was coming to preach at Fort Bragg, and I was given the job of looking after him. When he was alone, I went into his little office to see if there was anything he needed. Of course I couldn't resist asking what he thought of C. S. Lewis. He became very serious. "That man," he said—there was a pause—"that man smokes a pipe, and that man drinks liquor—but I *do* believe he's a Christian!"

I began corresponding with Lewis shortly after this. In my first letter from Lewis, dated 30 November 1954, he made it clear he didn't want me to think too highly of *him* for he began by saying, "I am glad if I have been the instrument of Our Lord's help to you: in His Hands almost any instrument will do, otherwise none."[3]

We continued to correspond, and it was while I was lecturing on English Literature at the University of Kentucky in Lexington in the early 1960s that I began writing an academic book about Lewis—never completed. This led Lewis to invite me to come and see him. I went to Oxford in June 1963. I had an appointment with Lewis at the house—The Kilns, Kiln Lane in Headington Quarry—on Monday the 10th June. However, I'd been warned that his house, some five miles from Oxford, was very difficult to find, and on the previous Friday afternoon, the 7th June, almost as soon as I'd arrived in Oxford, I went out to see if I could find his house. No one in Kiln Lane could tell me where he lived, but someone showed me where his housekeeper lived, and I went there. The housekeeper, Mrs. Miller, said she'd just seen him arrive back from Cambridge, and she urged me to go and call on him.

I arrived at The Kilns about four o'clock. The house faces uphill, and when I walked round to the front door I saw a man with his back to the window reading. I rang the bell and regretted bitterly that I was bothering Lewis. Never had I seen myself in so unfavourable a light—an ignorant, provincial Tar Heel calling on this great man! But it was too late to flee. Someone was unlocking the door, and there stood C. S. Lewis.

I don't know what I expected him to sound like, but I was surprised that his voice was so—English. Reflecting on this later I realise that when we read books, whether written by English, or Irish, or Chinese, we hear the words in our *own* accent. Thus the surprise that Lewis sounded so English. I admire tall men, and though Lewis was perhaps not very tall as most modern undergraduates, he seemed so to me: he was six feet.

It turned out that I'd arrived at tea time, a favourite time of the day for Lewis who was a great, a *monumental* tea drinker. "You can't get a cup of tea large enough or a book long enough to suit me," he said one time.[4] I too was a lover of tea, but my intake had never been as gargantuan as his. As soon as we'd finished one pot of tea, Lewis would go to the kitchen and make another, and another. I was a young Southern American and quite shy at that time, but after what seemed gallons of it, I asked if I might be shown the "bathroom." Remember, I'd only just arrived in England, and I did not then know that in most homes the bathroom and the toilet are separate rooms.

With a touch of mock formality Lewis conducted me to what was really the bathroom. He flung down several towels, produced several tablets of soap, and before closing the door on me he asked if I had everything

---

3. *The Collected Letters of C. S. Lewis*, Vol. 3, ed. Hooper, 535.
4. Lewis, *Of This and Other Worlds*, ed. Hooper, 9.

I needed for my "bath." "Oh, yes!" I said with some alarm. By this time I was very uncomfortable, and I finally got up enough nerve to go back in the sitting-room and say that it was not really a "bath" I wanted. Lewis was roaring with laughter, and he said, "Now that will break you of those silly American euphemisms. Let's start over again. *Where* do you want to go?"

There I was, catapulted right into a far more interesting life than I'd imagined was to be had, and pretty soon we were talking about everything under the sun, Lewis constantly making verbal distinctions, and catching me out on logical points. I remember a valuable distinction he made that afternoon. I asked which of his books he thought "best," and his answer was *Perelandra*. He then asked which I "liked" the most. Thinking we were talking about the same thing, I said, "Well, I agree with you that *Perelandra* is the best of your books." "I didn't ask which you thought 'best,'" said Lewis, "but which you *like* most." "Oh, in that case," I said, "the one I like most, and indeed more than any book, is *That Hideous Strength*." "Don't you see the difference?" said Lewis. "You may think one thing better than another, but you might *like* something else better." In any event, the effect of all this clear talk was that by the time I had to leave I liked Lewis so much that I foresaw a life ahead of me that would be very dull compared to the few hours I'd just had. I remember to this day how *very* much I liked Lewis.

Lewis walked with me to the bus stop, with a visit to his local pub, the Ampleforth Arms, which was just beside it. We'd just finished our pint when the bus arrived. I thanked Lewis for giving me so much of his time. He looked surprised, and said, "You're not getting away! You're coming to the Inklings meeting on Monday."

As you probably know, the Thursday evening meetings of the Inklings had ended in 1949, but the Tuesday morning meetings continued, with one alteration. After Lewis became a Professor at Cambridge in 1955, he came home for the weekend and went back to Cambridge on Monday afternoon. For this reason, the Tuesday meetings were changed to Monday morning. In 1962 they moved the venue from the Bird and Baby across the street to the Lamb and Flag. I'd never witnessed anything like the conversation on that occasion. Lewis by no means did all the talking, or even much of it. He picked up on something I said, and threw it like a ball around the room. The subject was commented on by others, and pretty soon I was saying things that certainly did not represent my usual, muddled way of talking. We all know people who make us feel insecure and around whom we sound like fools. Lewis was the opposite. He brought you out. He encouraged you. You were your best in his company. By the time we'd had our pints and pork pies, and the meeting was ended, I was stunned at what had happened.

To paraphrase Shakespeare, Lewis was not only "witty in himself," but the "cause of wit" in other men.[5]

Lewis invited me back to The Kilns on Wednesday. He then suggested I come out on Sunday so we could go to Communion together at Holy Trinity Church. After the service that Sunday we returned to The Kilns for breakfast. Lewis enjoyed cooking breakfast, and there was excellent conversation over fried eggs, bacon, sausage, and toast.

After this we settled into a regular routine of thrice-weekly meetings: Monday at the Lamb and Flag, Wednesdays at The Kilns, and Sundays when we went to church together. I learned from Lewis that his brother, Warnie, was in Ireland. One of his stepsons, Douglas, was at home, and the other whom I soon met, David, was studying at a college in London. The others who made up the "Kilns family" were Lewis's house-keeper, Mrs. Miller, who lived in Kiln Lane, and his gardener and general factotum, Fred Paxford. The latter remains in my memory as a man of immense integrity, completely dedicated to "Mr. Jack" as he called Lewis. Everyone at The Kilns appeared to do as he liked, but at the same time it seemed to work so well. I mentioned this to Lewis who told me that he based St. Anne's on the Hill in *That Hideous Strength* on the set-up at The Kilns.

Lewis's marriage has been, as you know, the subject of a film, *Shadowlands*. But at the time I found it hard to remember that Lewis had been married, and I said that he didn't strike me as a marrying man. "That's because we were together such a short time," he said, "and besides, I've always been a bachelor at heart." It was, however, indirectly through Joy that I came to understand something important about Lewis—his relish for what he called "rational opposition."

One day after the Inklings meeting, Dr. Havard drove the three of us out to The Trout at Godstow. This beautiful fourteenth-century pub was one of Lewis's favourite places, and while having our sandwiches outside, beside the river, Lewis told me what Joy had said about Southern men—which was that they dominated women. He asked what I had to say about the matter. I felt trapped. I didn't agree with Joy, but I was afraid of saying so lest he be offended. I'd been brought up to think that if you didn't agree with someone's opinions you didn't like *him*, which is absurd. I tried to avoid a straight answer, but Lewis was persistent. "Do you *agree* with her?" he asked. "Well, no," I said, "Then, what do you disagree with?" he asked. "Everything," I finally said, "She was totally wrong."

While Dr. Havard and I were inside getting more food, I asked if he thought I had offended Lewis. "Good heavens, no!" he said. "He loved his

---

5. William Shakespeare, *Henry VI, Part 2*, Act I, scene ii, lines 10–11.

wife, but he didn't always *agree* with her!" I soon came to realise that for Lewis conversation was always *about* something, that the purpose of it was to argue towards truth. Furthermore, I sensed that this arguing towards truth has been one of the things Lewis enjoyed about Joy, perhaps was one of the main reasons they became friends in the first place.

One of the things that helped me understand the importance Lewis put upon reason was a story told by his brother. In 1907, Warnie tells us, the Lewis family were preparing for a holiday in France. C. S. Lewis—or Jack as he was called—was about eight years old at the time, and entering his father's study, where Mr. Lewis was poring over some account books, he flung himself into a chair and observed, "I have a prejudice against the French." Mr. Lewis, interrupted in a long addition sum, said irritably, "Why?" Jack, crossing his legs and putting his fingertips together, replied, "If I knew *why* it wouldn't be a prejudice." I don't know about you, but I've never heard a better definition of prejudice than that.

Ever since I'd read *Miracles* I'd wondered what Lewis's conversation would be like. It was first and foremost very like his books: not that his conversation sounded "bookish," but that his books are like his conversation. You know, don't you, that nearly all Lewis's works are written in the first person? Even Lewis had to repeat himself occasionally, and I remember him saying several things exactly as they appear in his books.

The best definition of Lewis's conversation was given by Owen Barfield, who knew Lewis well since they met as undergraduates in 1919. Writing many years later, Barfield said, "Somehow what Lewis thought about everything was secretly present in what he said about anything."[6] I will repeat that: "Somehow what he thought about everything was secretly present in what he said about anything." Mr Barfield went on to add: "It was there from the start. It is there is *Mere Christianity* as it is there in *A Preface to Paradise Lost* and in *Till We Have Faces*."

By this time I'd read almost all Lewis's published writings, and while I'd find it very difficult to define exactly what I think Owen Barfield meant, I believe I found the same thing. I hadn't known Lewis long before I realised he was the most *converted* Christian I'd ever met. The result was that what Lewis believed about everything was not independent of God, but reflected more than anyone I've met the will of God. This naturally affected his teaching, for writing to one of his students who had just become a Christian, he said: "One of the minor rewards of conversion is to be able so see at last the real point of all the old literature which we are brought up to read with the point left out!"[7]

---

6. Barfield, *Owen Barfield on C. S. Lewis*, ed. Tennyson, 122.
7. *The Collected Letters of C. S. Lewis*, Vol. 2, ed. Hooper, 467.

What amounts to a small apologetic in its own right is Lewis's comment to the Socratic Club: "I believe in Christianity as I believe that the Sun has risen, not only because I see it but because by it I see everything else."[8]

Lewis's talk was always about something, always bracing and nearly always humorous. He was always, even in ordinary conversation, arguing towards truth. That was both the terror and the joy of conversation with him. But I loved every minute of it. His arguments were so impersonal, in a very good sense, that I began thinking of the subject under discussion as something visible there on the table in front of us. It wasn't about Lewis; it wasn't about you; it was about *it*—the subject under discussion. Reading his books is a very close approximation to being in Lewis's company and hearing his talk. But whereas you can stop reading a book, you had to be on your toes all the time with Lewis. Once when I wasn't sure how to answer a remark of his, I said, "Well, it's all very interesting." "What?" he said. "Have we finished that conversation?" "Oh, no!" I said, and back to it we went. As one of Lewis's Magdalen pupils said to me one time, "Arguing with Lewis was like entering a beauty contest. You had to be prepared to be told, 'You're damned ugly.'"

If humour is based on perspective—seeing things in their right proportion and context—then God must have the greatest sense humour of anyone. Lewis was close behind, for, being allowed for a while to see through his eyes, I found myself laughing more than I ever had.

For many of us everything in the Scriptures is more or less settled, and we quit thinking of what the Scriptures contain. For Lewis nothing in the Bible had become trite or dulled by convention. I remember him talking about "poor Lazarus," who had to die all over again. I wondered who this "poor Lazarus" was. "Is Lazarus a *neighbour*?" I asked. "No," said Lewis, "he was the brother of Mary and Martha." I blurted out "Oh, you mean the biblical character," as though Lazarus was not *real* as you and I are. "Oh I don't think he knew he was '*biblical*,'" said Lewis. As it turned out Lewis was writing a poem about Lazarus and he was toying with the notion that, as Lazarus had to die again after Our Lord had brought him back from the grave, he and not St. Stephen should be called the church's proto-martyr. Thereafter I saw not only Lazarus but everything recorded in the Gospels in an entirely new light.

I have always loved cats, as did Lewis, and I soon made friends of the two at The Kilns. There was "Snip," a Siamese that had belonged to Joy and which Lewis called his "step-cat." The other was Old Tom. He had been a great mouser in his day, but he was old now and had lost his teeth. My heart

---

8. Lewis, "Is Theology Poetry?" 50.

almost froze when I heard Lewis's housekeeper urging Lewis to have Old Tom "put down." "No," said Lewis, "Tom is a pensioner now." After that Tom was put on a pension of fish. He had his housekeeper cook fish several times a week and debone it for the old cat. Once when Lewis and I were walking down the lane we met Old Tom coming our way. As we passed, Lewis lifted his hat. "He's a pensioner," he whispered to me.

I don't remember Lewis ever bringing up any of his books, but if one came up in the course of the conversation he would talk about it. I don't think Lewis had any opinion of himself or his writings. Of course he was interested in what was *in* the books or they would never have been written. But he was without conceit. I think if someone, who didn't know either of us, heard us talking about Lewis's books he would get the impression that *I* had the greater knowledge of them. On one occasion I quoted the whole of my favourite poem, Lewis's "Scazons" published in *The Pilgrim's Regress*. He listened very carefully, and when I finished he asked if I'd make him a copy. "But it is your poem!" I explained. "*Is* it?" he said. "Well, it's not half bad, is it!"

This should not, perhaps, surprise us for, as I've said, Lewis had no opinion of himself, and he more than once said to me, "You think too highly of my books!" "And you," I would say, "don't think highly enough of them!"

When Lewis did talk about his books it was because they were of interest to both of us, not because he had written them. I found that he liked the Narnian books almost as much as I did, and for the same reasons. When he discovered that my favourite character was Puddleglum the Marshwiggle in *The Silver Chair*, he revealed that Puddleglum was modelled on his gardener, Fred Paxford, whom I had come to know well.

I was later to notice many resemblances between Paxford and Puddleglum, but the best was supplied by Lewis. He said it was Joy's long-time ambition to visit Greece, and in 1960—by which time her cancer had returned—he decided to risk taking her there. They would be accompanied by his friends Roger and June Lancelyn Green. Paxford was always listening to the wireless—or radio—and Lewis said the taxi had arrived to take him and Joy to the airport for the flight to Greece when Paxford came out to wish them well. He put his head in the car window and said, "I was just listening to the wireless, Mr. Jack, and this bloke said an airplane just went down. Everybody killed—burnt beyond recognition. Did you hear that Mr. Jack? 'Burnt beyond recognition.'" And on that note," Lewis said to me, "we flew to Greece!"

Paxford was like Puddleglum in being outwardly very pessimistic, but inwardly very optimistic. Now that Lewis had mentioned the resemblance, I saw it at once. Paxford had been marvellous to me since I first visited The Kilns, and there was nothing he would not do for "Mr. Jack." Although I never knew him to go to church, he was forever singing hymns, sometimes so loud he had to be quieted down. When I asked if he was married he gave

me what I learned was his standard answer to that question. Some of you ladies may not like it, but Paxford always quoted this little poem when he was asked why he didn't marry:

> A little puff of powder,
> A little touch of paint,
> Makes a woman look
> Just like what she *ain't!*

By this time it was evident to everyone I knew, and now even C. S. Lewis, that I could hardly speak without making use of Lewis's thought, and giving full credit to Lewis with my constant refrain of "As C. S. Lewis has said." After we'd come to know one another he invited me to call him "Jack," and for a while he was almost like two people to me: the author of my favourite books, and Jack Lewis, the friend who would never speak of his own work unless pressed. Talking with him one day and quoting one of his books, I added my usual "As C. S. Lewis has said." I stopped myself: "Oh, but you *are* C. S. Lewis!" Thereafter he made it a joke between us, and whenever he wanted anything done, he might say, "As C. S. Lewis has said, 'I would like a pot of tea.' As C. S. Lewis has said, '*You* will go and make it.' As C. S. Lewis has said, '*I* will drink it!'"

While Lewis looked perfectly all right to me, he had been ill for several years with an infected kidney and prostate gland. The surgeon wouldn't operate on him because his heart was too weak. Now, suddenly, his health began giving him trouble. When I went out to The Kilns on Sunday morning, 14 July, I found him in his dressing gown, looking very ill. He could hardly sit up, and after asking for tea, he could not hold the cup. He told me he was going into the Acland Nursing Home the next day for a blood transfusion, and he asked if I would stop in England and act as his private secretary, beginning immediately. By this time I knew that his beloved brother, Warnie, had been acting as his secretary for years. Warnie, unfortunately, was an alcoholic and this often took him away from home for long periods. He had been in Ireland since April, and Lewis didn't know when he would be back. He really did need help, and of course I was enormously gratified by this offer. I accepted with the understanding that I'd go back to the States in the autumn to teach another term in my college, after which I'd return in January 1964 to resume my job with him.

The next day, 15 July, Lewis went to the hospital for an examination, where he had a heart-attack and went into a coma. The doctors did not expect him to regain consciousness, but to everyone's surprise Lewis came out of his coma—and asked for his tea!

By the next day he wanted to catch up with his letter writing, and I was with him most of the day over the next two weeks taking dictation and helping in various ways.

It was during the time he was in the hospital that I became familiar with one of the most surprising things about his private life. I learned of it through answering his correspondence with his friend, Owen Barfield, who also acted as his lawyer. From the time Lewis began making money from his Christian writings, beginning with the serialisation of *The Screwtape Letters* in 1941, and later the radio talks, which were published as *Mere Christianity*, Lewis refused to touch a penny of it. Instead he sent the publishers and the BBC a list of widows and orphans and directed that the money be sent to them. Lewis did not understand the difference between gross and net profit, and in the spring of 1942 he discovered to his horror that he owed a hefty tax bill on monies he'd given away. Before things got out of hand, Owen Barfield intervened and helped Lewis set up a charitable trust—called the Agape Fund or "Agapargyry" (charity + silver) as they called it. Thereafter, and until Lewis's marriage in 1957, Lewis had two-thirds of his income paid into the "Agapargyry" for the supplying of anonymous gifts to various people in need, but especially widows and orphans. I learned of this because of the letters I was writing to Owen Barfield about the ending of the Agapargyry.

Two things flashed across my mind. One was the poorness, almost the poverty, of the way Lewis lived at The Kilns. When I arrived there I discovered that everyone smoked, but that there was only one ashtray in the house. I had to beg Lewis to allow me to buy several cheap ones to litter about the place to prevent the house catching fire. The new ashtrays went unnoticed. Lewis nearly always flicked his ashes across the rug in his study. "Ashes are good for rugs," he said, "but only men believe it!" I learned too that when the new housekeeper, Mrs. Miller, moved to The Kilns in 1952 she found the blackout curtains still up. These coarse black curtains had been necessary during wartime, but the war had long been over, and Mrs Miller asked Lewis if they couldn't be replaced. He saw no reason to waste money on curtains. In that case, asked Mrs. Miller, would he mind if she washed them? Luckily, in the course of being washed the blackout curtains dissolved into ink, and had to be poured out. The Kilns got new curtains.

In talking with Lewis about the Agape Fund, I realised that he was not altogether comfortable about ending it when he married. But Owen Barfield assured him that it had been necessary. I, for my part, knowing what a plain, almost threadbare, life he lived, was stunned that he had been so extremely generous. "Why," I asked plainly, "did you give away *so much*?" The simplicity of his answer took my breath away. "God was so good in having me," he said, "that the least I could do was give away most of what I made in His name." When was the last time *we* said, "God was so good in having me"? When was the last time I said that?

During this enforced rest in the hospital, when Lewis sometimes needed something to occupy him, I suggested that this would be a good time to make any changes he wanted made in his published writings. He agreed, and he mentioned that perhaps he would alter something in *Mere Christianity*. I had my notebook ready, but a few minutes later he said, "No, I don't want to change anything." And that was it. I never discovered what he thought briefly about changing in *Mere Christianity*, but it can hardly have been important.

Lewis had me move into The Kilns while he was in the hospital, and after he got home we settled down to some of the most interesting weeks of my life. Lewis the champion of reason was still very much in evidence, but I sensed more gentleness in his manner. Lewis usually had a cup of tea or coffee after lunch, and following this I usually left him alone in his study sitting in his easy chair. I suspected that he had a nap when I was out of the room, and one day, before I closed the door behind me I said, "Jack, do you ever take a nap?" "Oh, *no*!" he exclaimed. "On the other hand," he went on, "sometimes a nap takes *me*!" When you think about it you see how right he was. Get into your pyjamas in the middle of the afternoon, close the curtain, get into bed—and nothing happens. But relax in your easy chair with a good book, and when you *wake* you realise the nap took you.

At the doctor's advice, Lewis retired from his Chair of Medieval and Renaissance English at Cambridge, and we settled down to a life that seemed to make him happy. Immediately after breakfast, he dictated his letters to me, wanting to have that onerous duty out of the way. He always had me read his letters back to him, commenting that "It's as important to please the ear as the eye." We take it for granted that his writing is both beautiful to read and beautiful to hear, but this was hardly a matter of chance. He told me that when he was writing something—nearly always with a nib pen—he "whispered" the words aloud to himself. Although Warnie helped his brother enormously over the years, typing thousands of letters, Lewis didn't like the typewriter, and preferred that his letters be in someone's hand-writing.

Now that Lewis had retired from his Chair in Cambridge, and had a little unaccustomed leisure, he spent his time writing, meeting his Inkling friends, enjoying a pint in his local, discussing the books he hoped to write, and enjoying his time at The Kilns. If his brother had returned from Ireland he would have been perfectly content.

Following his retirement Lewis sent me over to sort out his belongings in Magdalene College. It was inevitable that I meet one of the College librarians, and when I got home Lewis asked what I thought of him. The librarian had the reputation of being a sensational bore, and I told Lewis the man succeeded in interesting me by the sheer intensity of his boringness. "Yes," Lewis admitted, "the man is a great bore. But let us not forget," he added, "that Our Lord might well have said, 'As ye have done it unto one of the least of these my bores you have done it unto me.'"

By this time it was settled that, as soon as I'd resigned from my job in the States, I'd return to The Kilns to resume my work with Lewis. Meanwhile, he insisted, as he did so often, that I valued his writings too highly. He was often amused when he saw me scribbling something he said in my little notebook. "I know what the divine joke on you would be," he said near the end of the summer. "I might utter my last words and *you* won't be here to write them down!"

As it turned out, I wasn't. I was in between classes at the University of Kentucky on 22 November 1963 when a colleague told me President Kennedy had been shot. Later that day we learned that the President was dead. Horrible as that was, I was still looking forward to joining Lewis in January. I was just drifting off to sleep in my bed that night when Lewis's step-son, Douglas, rang to tell me that Jack had died the same hour as President Kennedy.

I was very depressed for a while. But some of Lewis's friends persuaded me to return to Oxford anyway, and almost as soon as I came to know Lewis's brother Warnie, he invited me to begin editing his brother's literary remains. So in a sense I really have been carrying on as Lewis's secretary these last fifty years. In any event, when I see what has happened to his writing I think we all have reason to be joyful. Over the years since Lewis's death so many of his works have been discovered, collected, and talked about in such places as this that if you dropped me down onto a desert island with copies of Lewis's works my life would be almost as rich as it is now.

In conclusion, I hope you will allow me to make this boast. I have waited fifty years to tell the world that I won an argument with Lewis. Not many can make *that* claim. Lewis was worried about what his brother would live on when he—C. S. Lewis—died, and this because he was sure that upon his own death his books would stop selling. "No!" I exclaimed. "What d'you mean, 'no?'" he said. "This happens," he said, "to nearly all authors. After they die their books sell for a while, and then trail off to nothing." "But not *yours*!" I said. "Why not?" he asked. "Because they are too good—and people are not that stupid."

Well, you see who won that argument. And yet, if Lewis was wrong about anything, wasn't this precisely the one thing he *ought* to have been wrong about? But such was his humility, his attention always turned away from himself. And if Lewis got one thing not only right, but terrifically right, it was his prediction that I would be stuck forever with the phrase even he could not cure me of—"As C. S. Lewis has said."

Recommended Resources

Principal Works by C. S. Lewis

The Abolition of Man (1943)
The Allegory of Love: A Study in Medieval Tradition (1936)
All My Road Before Me: The Diary of C. S. Lewis, 1922-1927, edited by Walter Hooper (1991)
Boxen, The Imaginary World of the Young C. S. Lewis, edited by Walter Hooper (1985)
Christian Reflections, edited by Walter Hooper (1967)
Collected Letters, Volume I, edited by Walter Hooper (2000)
Collected Letters, Volume II, edited by Walter Hooper (2004)
Collected Letters, Volume III, edited by Walter Hooper (2006)
The Collected Poems of C. S. Lewis: A Critical Edition, edited by Don W. King (2015)
The Dark Tower and Other Stories, edited by Walter Hooper (1977)
The Discarded Image: An Introduction to Medieval and Renaissance Literature (1964)
English Literature in the Sixteenth Century, Excluding Drama (1954)
Essay Collection and Other Short Pieces, edited by Lesley Walmsley (2000)
Essay Collection: Faith, Christianity and the Church, edited by Lesley Walmsley (2002)
An Experiment in Criticism (1961)
The Four Loves (1960)
George MacDonald: An Anthology (1946)
God in the Dock: Essays on Theology and Ethics, edited by Walter Hooper (1970)
The Great Divorce: A Dream (1945)
A Grief Observed (1961)
The Horse and His Boy (1954)
Image and Imagination: Essays and Reviews, edited by Walter Hoope (2013)
The Last Battle (1956)
Letters, edited with a memoir by W. H. Lewis, revised and expanded edition, edited by Walter Hooper (1988)
The Lion, the Witch and the Wardrobe (1950)

The Magician's Nephew (1955)
Mere Christianity (1952)
Miracles: A Preliminary Study (revised edition: 1960)
Of Other Worlds: Essays and Stories, edited by Walter Hooper (1966)
Out of the Silent Planet (1938)
Perelandra (1943)
The Personal Heresy: A Controversy [with E. M. W. Tillyard] (1939)
The Pilgrim's Regress: An Allegorical Apology for Christianity, Reason and Romanticism (1933)
Prayer: Letters to Malcolm (1964)
A Preface to Paradise Lost (1942)
Present Concerns: Ethical Essays, edited by Walter Hooper (1986)
Prince Caspian: The Return to Narnia (1951)
The Problem of Pain (1940)
Reflections on the Psalms (1958)
Rehabilitations and Other Essays (1939)
The Screwtape Letters (1942)
Screwtape Proposes a Toast and other pieces (1965)
Selected Literary Essays, edited by Walter Hooper (1969)
The Silver Chair (1953)
Spenser's Images of Life, edited by Alastair Fowler (1967)
Studies in Medieval and Renaissance Literature, edited by Walter Hooper (1966)
Studies in Words (1960)
Surprised by Joy: The Shape of My Early Life (1955)
That Hideous Strength: A Modern Fairy-Tale for Grown-Ups (1945)
They Asked for a Paper: Papers and Addresses (1962)
Till We Have Faces: A Myth Retold (1956)
The Voyage of the 'Dawn Treader' (1952)

Selected Works about C. S. Lewis

Baggett, David, et al., eds. *C. S. Lewis as Philosopher: Truth, Goodness and Beauty* Downer Grove, IL: IVP Academic, 2008.

Barfield, Owen. *Owen Barfield on C. S. Lewis.* Edited by G. B. Tennyson. Middletown, CT: Wesleyan University Press, 1989.

Barkman, Adam. *C. S. Lewis and Philosophy as a Way of Life: A Comprehensive Historical Examination of his Philosophical Thoughts.* Allentown, PA: Zossima, 2009.

Bassham, Gregory, ed. *C. S. Lewis's Christian Apologetics: For and Against.* Leiden: Rodopi-Brill, 2015.

Bassham, Gregory, and Jerry L. Walls, eds. *The "Chronicles of Narnia" and Philosophy: The Lion, The Witch And The Worldview.* Chicago: Open Court, 2005.

Bennett, J. A. W., ed. *The Humane Medievalist: An Inaugural Lecture.* Cambridge: Cambridge University Press, 1965.

Burson, Scott R., and Jerry L. Walls. *C. S. Lewis and Francis Schaeffer: Lessons for a New Century from the Most Influential Apologists of Our Time.* Downers Grove, IL: IVP, 1998.

Cantor, Norman F. *Inventing the Middle Ages: The Lives, Works, and Ideas of the Great Medievalists of the Twentieth Century*. Cambridge: Lutterworth, 1991.

Carpenter, Humphrey. *The Inklings: C. S. Lewis, J. R. R. Tolkien, Charles Williams and Their Friends*. London: HarperCollins, 2006.

Carnell, Corbin Scott. *Bright Shadow of Reality: Spiritual Longing in C. S. Lewis*. Grand Rapids: Eerdmans, 1999.

Christensen, Michael. *C. S. Lewis On Scripture*. London: Hodder & Stoughton, 1979.

Como, James T. *Branches to Heaven: The Geniuses of C. S. Lewis*. Dallas: Spence, 1999.

———, ed. *Remembering C. S. Lewis: Recollections of Those Who Knew Him*. San Francisco: Ignatius, 2005.

Cunningham, Richard B. *C. S. Lewis: Defender of the Faith*. Philadelphia: Westminster, 1967.

Curtis, Carolyn, and Mary Pomroy Key, eds. *Women and C. S. Lewis*. Oxford: Lion Hudson, 2015.

Davison, Andrew, ed. *Imaginative Apologetics: Theology, Philosophy and the Catholic Tradition*. London: SCM, 2011.

Downing, David C. *The Most Reluctant Convert: C. S. Lewis' Journey to Faith*. Downers Grove, IL: IVP, 2002.

Edwards, Bruce L., ed. *C. S. Lewis: Life, Works and Legacy*. 4 vols. Westport, CT: Praeger, 2007.

———, ed. *The Taste of the Pineapple: Essays on C. S. Lewis as Reader, Critic and Imaginative Writer*. Bowling Green, OH: Bowling Green State University Popular Press, 1988.

Fowler, Alastair. "C. S. Lewis: Supervisor." *Yale Review* 91.4 (2003) 64–80.

Gibb, Jocelyn, ed. *Light on C. S. Lewis*. London: Bles, 1965.

Glyer, Diana Pavlac. *The Company They Keep: C. S. Lewis and J. R. R. Tolkien as Writers in Community*. Kent, OH: Kent State University Press, 2007.

Graham, David, ed. *We Remember C. S. Lewis: Essays and Memoirs*. Nashville: Broadman & Holman, 2001.

Green, Roger Lancelyn, and Walter Hooper. *C. S. Lewis: A Biography*. Rev. ed. London: HarperCollins, 2002.

Goetz, Stewart. "The Argument from Reason." *Philosophia Christi* 15.1 (2013) 47–62.

Harwood, Laurence. *C .S. Lewis, My Godfather*. Downers Grove, IL: IVP, 2007.

Heck, Joel D. *Irrigating Deserts: C. S. Lewis on Education*. St. Louis: Concordia Academic Press, 2005.

Holmer, Paul. *C. S. Lewis: The Shape of his Faith and Thought*. New York: Harper and Row, 1976.

Hooper, Walter. *C. S. Lewis: A Complete Guide to His Life and Works*. London: HarperCollins, 1996.

Howard, Thomas. *C. S. Lewis, Man of Letters: A Reading of His Fiction*. Worthing, UK: Churchman, 1987.

Jacobs, Alan. *The Narnian: The Life and Imagination of C. S. Lewis*. London: SPCK, 2005.

Keefe, Carolyn, ed. *C. S. Lewis: Speaker and Teacher*. London: Hodder & Stoughton, 1971.

Kort, Wesley. *C. S. Lewis: Then and Now*. London: Oxford University Press, 2001.

Kreeft, Peter. *Between Heaven and Hell: A Dialogue Somewhere Beyond Death with John F. Kennedy, Aldous Huxley and C. S. Lewis*. Downers Grove, IL: IVP, 2008.

———. *C. S. Lewis for the Third Millennium*. San Francisco: Ignatius, 1990.
Lucas, J. R. "The Restoration of Man." *Theology* 98 (1995) 445–56.
MacSwain, Robert, and Michael Ward, eds. *The Cambridge Companion to C. S. Lewis*. Cambridge: Cambridge University Press, 2010.
Manlove, C. N. *C. S. Lewis: His Literary Achievement*. London: Macmillan, 1987.
Martin, Thomas L., ed. *Reading the Classics with C. S. Lewis*. Grand Rapids: Baker Academic, 2000.
Martindale, Wayne. *Beyond the Shadowlands: C. S. Lewis on Heaven and Hell*. Wheaton, IL: Crossway, 2005.
Meilaender, Gilbert. *The Taste for the Other: The Social and Ethical Thought of C. S. Lewis*. 2nd ed. Grand Rapids: Eerdmans, 1998.
McGrath, Alister. *C. S. Lewis: A Life*. London: Hodder & Stoughton, 2013.
———. *The Intellectual World of C. S. Lewis*. Oxford: Wiley-Blackwell, 2014.
Menuge, Angus J. L., ed. *C. S. Lewis: Lightbearer in the Shadowlands: The Evangelistic Vision of C. S. Lewis*. Wheaton, IL: Crossway, 1997.
Mills, David, ed. *The Pilgrim's Guide: C. S. Lewis and the Art of Witness*. Grand Rapids: Eerdmans, 1998.
Myers, Doris T. *Bareface: A Guide to C. S. Lewis's Last Novel*. Columbia, MO: University of Missouri Press, 2004.
———. *C. S. Lewis in Context*. Kent, OH: Kent State University Press, 1991.
Nicholi, Armand M. Jr. *The Question of God: C. S. Lewis and Sigmund Freud Debate God, Love, Sex, and The Meaning Of Life*. New York: Free, 2002.
Pike, Mark A. *Mere Education: C. S. Lewis as Teacher for our Time*. Cambridge: Lutterworth, 2013.
Poe, Harry Lee, and Rebecca Whitten Poe, eds. *C. S. Lewis Remembered*. Grand Rapids: Zondervan, 2006.
Puckett, Joe, Jr. *The Apologetics of Joy: A Case for the Existence of God from C. S. Lewis' Argument from Desire*. Cambridge: Lutterworth, 2013.
Purtill, Richard. *C. S. Lewis' Case for the Christian Faith*. San Francisco: Ignatius, 2004.
Reppert, Victor. *C. S. Lewis' Dangerous Idea: In Defence of the Argument from Reason*. Downers Grove, IL: IVP, 2003.
Sayer, George. *Jack: C. S. Lewis and His Times*. 2nd ed. London: Hodder and Stoughton, 1997.
Schakel, Peter J., ed. *The Longing for a Form: Essays on the Fiction of C. S. Lewis*. Kent, OH: Kent State University Press, 1977.
Schakel, Peter J., and Charles A. Huttar, eds. *Word and Story in C. S. Lewis*. Columbia, MO: University of Missouri Press, 1991.
Schofield, Stephen, ed. *In Search of C. S. Lewis*. Commerce, CA: Bridge, 1983.
Schwartz, Sanford. *C. S. Lewis on the Final Frontier: Science and the Supernatural in the Space Trilogy*. Oxford: Oxford University Press, 2009.
Travers, Michael, ed. *C. S. Lewis: Views from Wake Forest*. Wayne, PA: Zossima, 2008.
Van der Elst, Philip. *C. S. Lewis: An Introduction*. New York: Continuum, 1996.
Vaus, Will. *Mere Theology: A Guide to the Thought of C. S. Lewis*. Downers Grove, IL: IVP, 2004.
Walker, Andrew G., and James Patrick, eds. *A Christian for All Christians: Essays in Honour of C. S. Lewis*. London: Hodder and Stoughton, 1990.
Walsh, Chad. *The Literary Legacy of C. S. Lewis*. London: Sheldon, 1979.

Ward, Michael. "The Tragedy is in the Pity: C. S. Lewis and the Song of the Goat." In *Christian Theology and Tragedy*, edited by Kevin Taylor and Giles Waller, 149–63. Farnham, UK: Ashgate, 2011.

———. *The Narnia Code: C. S. Lewis and the Secret of the Seven Heavens*. Milton Keynes, UK: Paternoster, 2010.

———. *Planet Narnia: The Seven Heavens in the Imagination of C. S. Lewis*. Oxford: Oxford University Press, 2008.

Watson, George, ed. *Critical Essays on C. S. Lewis*. London: Scolar, 1992.

Werther, David, and Susan Werther, eds. *C. S. Lewis's List: The Ten Books That Influenced Him Most*. London: Bloomsbury Academic, 2015.

West, John G., ed. *The Magician's Twin: C. S. Lewis on Science, Scientism, and Society*. Seattle: Discovery Institute Press, 2012.

White, Roger, et al., eds. *C. S. Lewis and His Circle: Essays and Memoirs from the Oxford C. S. Lewis Society*. Oxford: Oxford University Press, 2015.

Williams, Donald T. *Reflections from Plato's Cave: Essays in Evangelical Philosophy*. Lynchburg, VA: Lantern Hollow, 2012.

Williams, Peter S. *C. S. Lewis vs. the New Atheists*. Milton Keynes, UK: Paternoster, 2013.

Williams, Rowan. *The Lion's World: A Journey into the Heart of Narnia*. London: SPCK, 2012.

Wolfe, Judith, and Brendan Wolfe, eds. *C. S. Lewis and the Church: Essays in Honour of Walter Hooper*. London: T. & T. Clark, 2011.

———. *C. S. Lewis's Perelandra: Reshaping the Image of the Cosmos*. Kent, OH: Kent State University Press, 2013.

Zaleski, Philip, and Carol Zaleski. *The Fellowship: The Literary Lives of the Inklings, J. R. R. Tolkien, C. S. Lewis, Owen Barfield, Charles Williams*. New York: Farrar, Straus and Giroux, 2015.

Selected Online Resources

Christian Evidence Society. The Westminster C. S. Lewis Symposium: www.youtube.com/playlist?list=PLUA5-mhwkgXUMiz2s2vi8GOd8f6MWZTCk.

Peter S. Williams. C. S. Lewis YouTube Playlist: www.youtube.com/playlist?list=PLQhh3qcwVEWhm2bap3Dq9Xd3FJ8l_gHsR.

C. S. Lewis Doodle: www.youtube.com/user/CSLewisDoodle.

The C. S. Lewis Foundation YouTube Channel: www.youtube.com/user/CSLewisFoundation/videos.

The Gospel Coalition's collection of Lewis recordings: www.thegospelcoalition.org/blogs/justintaylor/2013/07/17/all-the-known-audio-of-c-s-lewis-speaking/.

The Oxford University C. S. Lewis Society: http://sites.google.com/site/lewisinoxford/home.

The Wade Center, Wheaton College: www.wheaton.edu/wadecenter/Authors/CS-Lewis.

William O'Flaherty, *All About Jack: A C. S. Lewis Podcast*: http://allaboutjack.podbean.com/.

Planet Narnia: www.planetnarnia.com/.

Bibliography

Avis, Paul. *God and the Creative Imagination: Metaphor, Symbol and Myth in Religion and Theology*. London: Routledge, 1999.
Barfield, Owen. "Introduction." In *Light on C. S. Lewis*, edited by Jocelyn Gibb, ix–xxi. London: Bles, 1965.
———. *Owen Barfield on C. S. Lewis*. Edited by G.B. Tennyson. Middletown, CT: Wesleyan University Press, 1989.
Bayley, Peter. "From Master to Colleague." In *C. S. Lewis at the Breakfast Table and Other Reminiscences*, edited by James T. Como, 77–86. London: Collins, 1980.
Bennett, J. A. W. *The Humane Medievalist: An Inaugural Lecture*. 1965. Reprinted in *Critical Thought Series 1: Critical Essays on C. S. Lewis*, edited by George Watson, 52–75. Aldershot, UK: Scolar, 1992.
Benson, Larry D., gen. ed. *The Riverside Chaucer*. Boston: Houghton Mifflin, 1987.
Carpenter, Humphrey, ed., with the assistance of Christopher Tolkien. *The Letters of J. R. R. Tolkien*. London: Allen & Unwin, 1981.
Chesterton, G. K. *The Everlasting Man*. San Francisco: Ignatius, 1993.
———. "The Return of the Angels." *Daily News,* 14 March, 1903.
Coleridge, S. T. *Biographia Literaria or Biographical Sketches of My Literary Life and Opinions*, vol. 7 of The Collected Works of Samuel Taylor Coleridge, edited by J. Engell and W. Jackson Bate. Princeton: Princeton University Press, 1984.
———. *Shakespearean Criticism*. 2nd ed. 2 vols. Edited by T. M. Raysor. London: Dent, 1960.
———. *The Major Works*. Edited by H. J. Jackson. Oxford: Oxford University Press, 2009.
Cuneo, Andrew. "Duty with a Stamp: 'Half my Life is Spent Answering Letters.'" Online: www.cslewis.com/uk.
Copan, Paul, and William Lane Craig. *Creation out of Nothing: A Biblical, Philosophical, and Scientific Exploration*. Grand Rapids: Baker Academic, 2004.
Coulson, John. *Religion and Imagination*. Oxford: Oxford University Press, 1981.

Dostoyevsky, Fiodore. *A Disgraceful Affair: Stories*. Translated by David Magarshack. London: Harper Perennial, 2009.

Edwards, Bruce L. "The Christian Intellectual in the Public Square: C. S. Lewis's Enduring American Reception." In *C. S. Lewis: Life, Works, and Legacy*, vol. IV, edited by Bruce L. Edwards, 1–18. Westport, CT: Praeger, 2007.

Eliot, T. S. *Four Quartets*, "Little Gidding."

Empson, William. "The Verbal Analysis." In *Argufying: Essays on Literature and Culture*, edited by John Haffenden, 104–9. London: Chatto and Windus, 1987.

Engell, J., and W. Jackson Bate, eds. *Biographia Literaria or Biographical Sketches of My Literary Life and Opinions*, vol. 7 of The Collected Works of Samuel Taylor Coleridge. Princeton: Princeton University Press, 1984.

Farrer, Austin. "The Christian Apologist." In *Light on C. S. Lewis*, edited by Jocelyn Gibb, 23–43. London: Bles, 1965.

Ferenczi, Sándor. "The Unwelcome Child and His Death Instinct." *The International Journal of Psychoanalysis* 10 (1929) 125–29. Online: https://nonoedipal.files.wordpress.com/2009/09/the-unwelcome-child-and-his-death-instinct.pdf.

Frege, Gottlob. *The Foundations of Arithmetic: A Logico-Mathematical Enquiry into the Concept of Number*. Translated by J. L. Austin. 2nd rev. ed.. Evanston, IL: Northwestern University Press, 1968.

Freud, Sigmund. "Anxiety and Instinctual Life." *New Introductory Lectures in Psychoanalysis* xxxii (1933) 101–38.

Fulgencio, Leopoldo. "Winnicott's Rejection of the Basic Concepts of Freud's Metapsychology." *International Journal of Psychoanalysis* 88 (2007) 443–61.

Green, Roger Lancelyn, and Walter Hooper. *C. S. Lewis: A Biography*. London: Collins, 1974.

Gibb, Jocelyn, ed. *Light on C. S. Lewis*. London: Bles, 1965.

Goetz, Stewart. "The Argument from Reason." *Philosophia Christi* 15.1 Neuroscience and the Soul: Philosophical Issues (2013) 47–62.

Golding, William. *The Double Tongue*. London: Faber and Faber, 1996.

Guite, Malcolm. "Poet." In *The Cambridge Companion to C. S. Lewis*, edited by Robert MacSwain and Michael Ward, 294–310. Cambridge: Cambridge University Press, 2010.

———. *The Singing Bowl*. Norwich, UK: Canterbury, 2013.

Hannam, James. *God's Philosophers: How the Medieval World Laid the Foundations of Modern Science*. London: Icon, 2009.

Harris, James. *The Works of James Harris, Esq. with an Account of His Life and Character by His Son, The Earl of Malmesbury*. Oxford: Vincent, 1841.

Heaney, Seamus. *The Redress of Poetry: Oxford Lectures*. London: Faber & Faber, 1995.

Hooper, Walter, ed. *The Collected Poems of C. S. Lewis*. London: Fount, 1994.

———. *The Collected Letters of C. S. Lewis*, Vol. 2. London: HarperCollins, 2004.

———. *The Collected Letters of C. S. Lewis*, Vol. 3. London: HarperCollins, 2006.

———. *C. S. Lewis: A Companion and Guide*. London: HarperCollins, 2005.

———. *Studies in Medieval and Renaissance Literature*. Cambridge: Cambridge University Press, 1966.

Hough, Graham. "Old Western Man." In *Critical Essays on C. S. Lewis*, edited by George Watson, 235–45. Aldershot, UK: Scolar, 1992.

Kuhn, Thomas. *The Structure of Scientific Revolutions*. Chicago: University of Chicago Press, 1962.

Kalderon, Mark Eli, ed. *Fictionalism in Metaphysics*. Oxford: Clarendon, 2005.

King, Don W., ed. *The Collected Poems of C. S. Lewis: A Critical Edition*. Kent, OH: Kent State University Press, 2015.

Lacan, Jacques. *Écrits: The First Complete Edition in English*. Edited by Bruce Fink. New York: Norton, 2007.

Lewis, C. S. *The Abolition of Man or Reflections on Education with Special Reference to the Teaching of English in the Upper Forms of Schools*. Glasgow: Collins, 1984.

———. *The Allegory of Love: A Study in Medieval Tradition*. 1936. Reprint. Oxford: Oxford University Press, 1953.

———. "The Apologist's Evening Prayer." In *Poems*, edited by Walter Hooper, 143. London: HarperCollins, 1994.

———. "De Audiendis Poetis." *Studies in Medieval and Renaissance Literature*, edited by Walter Hooper, 1–17. Cambridge: Cambridge University Press, 1966.

———. *Beyond Personality*. London: Bles; 1944.

———. "Bluspels and Flalansferes: A Semantic Nightmare." In *Selected Literary Essays*, edited by Walter Hooper, 251–65. Cambridge: Cambridge University Press, 1979.

———. "Christianity and Literature." In *Christian Reflections*, edited by Walter Hooper, 15–26. London: Collins, 1967.

———. "De Descriptione Temporum." In *Selected Literary Essays*, edited by Walter Hooper, 1–14. Cambridge: Cambridge University Press, 1969.

———. *The Discarded Image*. Cambridge: Cambridge University Press, 1964.

———. "Edmund Spenser, 1552–99." Published to accompany Lewis's selections from *The Faerie Queene* and *Epithalamion* in an anthology of *Major British Writers*, vol. 1. 1954. Reprinted in *Studies in Medieval and Renaissance Literature*, edited by Walter Hooper, 121–45. Cambridge: Cambridge University Press, 1966.

———. *Essay Collection*. London: HarperCollins, 2002.

———. *An Experiment in Criticism*. Cambridge, 1961.

———. *The Four Loves*. London: HarperCollins, 2002.

———. *God in the Dock: Essays on Theology and Ethics*. Edited by Walter Hooper. Grand Rapids: Eerdmans, 1970.

———. "Hedonics." *Time and Tide*, 16 June 1945.

———. "Is Theology Poetry?" In *Screwtape Proposes a Toast and Other Pieces*, 33–50. London: Collins, 1965.

———. "Is Theology Poetry?" In *C. S. Lewis. Essay Collection and Other Short Pieces*, edited by Lesley Walmsley, 10–21. London: HarperCollins, 2000.

———. *The Last Battle*. London: HarperCollins Children's Books, 2001.

———. Letter to Arthur Greeves. 30 May 1916. In *The Collected Letters of C. S. Lewis*, Volume 1, edited by Walter Hooper, 185–88. London: HarperCollins, 2000.

———. *Letters to Malcolm*. London: Collins, 1977.

———. *The Lion, The Witch and the Wardrobe*. London: HarperCollins Children's Books, 2009.

———. "Lilies That Fester." In *They Asked for a Paper*, 105–19. London: Bles, 1962.

———. *Mere Christianity*. London: HarperCollins, 2002.

———. *Miracles: A Preliminary Study*. London: Fount, 1960

———. *Narrative Poems*. Edited by Walter Hooper. London: HarperCollins, 1994.

———. *Of This and Other Worlds*. Edited by Walter Hooper. London: Collins, 1982.

———. "On Criticism." In *Essay Collection and Other Short Pieces*, edited by Lesley Walmsley, 539–50. London: HarperCollins, 2000.

———. *The Pilgrim's Regress: An Allegorical Apology for Christianity, Reason and Romanticism*. Preface to the Third Edition. London: Collins, 1980.

———. "The Poison of Subjectivism." In *Christian Reflections*, edited by Walter Hooper, 98–109. London: Bles, 1967.

———. *Poems*. Edited by Walter Hooper. London: HarperCollins, 1994.

———. *The Problem of Pain*. London: Collins, 1983.

———. "To Roy Campbell." In *Poems*, edited by Walter Hooper, 80. London: HarperCollins, 1994.

———. "Shelley, Dryden and Mr. Eliot." In *Selected Literary Essays*, edited by Walter Hooper, 187–208. Cambridge, 1969.

———. *On Stories, and Other Essays in Literature*. Edited by Walter Hooper. New York: Harcourt, 1982.

———. *The Screwtape Letters*. London: Collins, 2012.

———. "The Shoddy Lands." In *The Dark Tower and Other Stories*, edited by Walter Hooper, 104–11. London: Collins, 1983.

———. "A Slip of the Tongue." *Screwtape Proposes a Toast and Other Pieces*. London: Collins, 1981.

———. *Surprised by Joy*. London: HarperCollins, 2002.

———. *Till We Have Faces*. 1956.

———. *The Voyage of the "Dawn Treader."* London: HarperCollins, 1994.

———. *The Weight of Glory*. New York: Macmillan, 1949.

Leith, Sam. "C. S. Lewis's Literary Legacy." *The Guardian,* 19 November 2013.

Leonhardt-Balzer, Jutta. "Der Logos und die Schöpfung: Steiflichter bei Philo. Op 20–25 und im Johannesprolog. Joh 1, 1–18." In *Kontexte des Johannesevangeliums*, edited by Jörg Frey und Udo Schnelle, WUNT 175. Tübingen: Mohr Siebeck, 2004.

McGrath, Alister E. "The Boyle Lecture 2014: New Atheism—New Apologetics: The Use of Science in Recent Christian Apologetic Writings." *Science and Christian Belief* 26.2 (2014) 99–113.

———. *C. S. Lewis—A Life: Eccentric Genius, Reluctant Prophet*. London: Hodder & Stoughton, 2013.

———. "A Gleam of Divine Truth: The Concept of Myth in Lewis's Thought." In *The Intellectual World of C. S. Lewis*, 55–82. Oxford: Wiley-Blackwell, 2013.

———. "Reason, Experience, and Imagination: Lewis's Apologetic Method." In *The Intellectual World of C. S. Lewis*, 129–46. Oxford: Wiley-Blackwell, 2013.

Myers, Benjamin. *Milton's Theology of Freedom*. Berlin: de Gruyter, 2006.

Oppy, Graham. "Response to Welty." In *Beyond the Control of God? Six Views on the Problem of God and Abstract Objects*, edited by Paul Gould, 192–96. London: Bloomsbury Academic, 2014.

Owen, D. D. R. *Arthurian Romances*. London: Dent, 1987.

Pearsall, Derek, edited by *The Floure and the Leafe* and *The Assembly of Ladies*. Manchester: Manchester University Press, 1980.

Pullman, Philip. *Northern Lights*. London: Scholastic, 1998.

Putter, Ad. "Fifteenth-Century Chaucerian Visions." In *A Companion to Fifteenth-Century English Poetry*, edited by Julia Boffey and A. S. G. Edwards, 143–56. Cambridge: Brewer, 2013.

———. "Chaucer's *Complaint unto Pity* and the Insights of Allegory." In *Medieval Latin and Middle English Literature: Essays in Honour of Jill Mann*, edited by Christopher Cannon and Maura Nolan, 166–81. Cambridge: Brewer, 2011.

Prudentius. *Prudentius*. 2 vols. Translated by H. J. Thomson. Cambridge: Harvard University Press, 1949–53.
Reyes, A. T. *C. S. Lewis's Lost Aeneid: Arms and the Exile*. New Haven: Yale University Press, 2011.
Rouse, Mary A., and Robert H. Rouse. *Authentic Witnesses: Approaches to Medieval Texts and Manuscripts*. South Bend, IN: University of Notre Dame Press, 1991.
Rosen, Gideon, and John P. Burgess. "Nominalism Reconsidered." In *The Oxford Handbook of Philosophy of Mathematics and Logic*, edited by Stewart Shapiro, 515–35. Oxford: Oxford University Press, 2005.
Runia, D. T. *Philo of Alexandria and the 'Timaeus' of Plato*. Amsterdam: Free University of Amsterdam, 1983.
Russell, Bertrand. Letter to Colette O'Niel, 21 October 1916. In *The Selected Letters of Bertrand Russell, Volume 2: The Public Years 1914–1970*, edited by Nicholas Griffin, 85–87. London: Routledge, 2001.
Sayer, George. *Jack: C. S. Lewis and His Times*. London: Macmillan, 1988.
Silkin, Jon, ed. *The Penguin Book of First World War Poetry*. 2nd ed. London: Penguin, 1996.
Smith, Macklin. *Prudentius' Psychomachia: A Re-Examination*. Princeton: Princeton University Press, 1976.
Stirling, Gregory E. "Day One: Platonizing Exegetical Traditions of Genesis 1:1–5 in John and Jewish Authors." Paper presented at the Philo section of the Society of Biblical Literature, San Antonio, Texas, November 20–23, 2004.
Tait, Katharine. *My Father Bertrand Russell*. New York: Harcourt Brace Jovanovich, 1975.
Thwaite, Anthony, ed. *Philip Larkin: Collected Poems*. London: Faber and Faber, 1988.
Tillyard, E. M. W., and C. S. Lewis. *The Personal Heresy: A Controversy*. Oxford University Press, 1965.
Tolhurst, Fiona. "Beyond the Wardrobe: C. S. Lewis as Closet Arthurian." *Arthuriana* 22.4 (2012) 140–66.
Tolkien, J. R. R. *The Two Towers*. London: Harper Collins, 1997.
Vaus, Will. *Mere Theology: A Guide to the Thought of C. S. Lewis*. Downers Grove, IL: IVP, 2004.
Walmsley, Lesley, ed. *C. S. Lewis Essay Collection. Faith, Christianity and the Church*. London: HarperCollins, 2002.
Ward, Michael. *Planet Narnia: The Seven Heavens in the Imagination of C. S. Lewis*. Oxford: Oxford University Press, 2008.
Weil, Simone. *Intimations of Christianity among the Ancient Greeks*. Edited and translated by Elisabeth Chase Geissbuhler. London: Routledge and Kegan Paul, 1957.
White, Roger, et al., eds. *C. S. Lewis and His Circle: Essays and Memoirs from the Oxford C. S. Lewis Society*. Oxford: Oxford University Press, 2015.
Williams, Rowan. *The Lion's World: A Journey into the Heart of Narnia*. London: SPCK, 2012.
Wilson, A. N. *C. S. Lewis: A Biography*. London: Collins Sons, 1990.
Winch, Peter. *Simone Weil: "The Just Balance."* Cambridge: Cambridge University Press, 1989.
Winnicott, D. W. "Sum, I Am" In *Home Is Where We Start From*, 55–64. London: Penguin, 1986.

———. "The Theory of the Parent-Infant Relationship." *International Journal of Psychoanalysis* 41 (1960). Online: http://icpla.edu/wp-content/uploads/2013/09/Winnicott-D.-The-Theory-of-the-Parent-Infant-Relationship-IJPA-Vol.-41-pps.-585-595.pdf.

Wordsworth, William. "Ode to Duty." In *The Poems*, Vol. 1, edited by John O. Hayden, 605-7. London: Penguin, 1982.

———. *The Prelude: The Four Texts (1798, 1799, 1805, 1850)*. Edited by Jonathan Wordsworth. London: Penguin, 1995.

Yablo, Stephen. "Abstract Objects: A Case Study." In *Realism and Relativism*, edited by Ernest Sosa and Enrique Villaneva, 220-40. Philosophical Issues 12. Oxford: Blackwell, 2002.

———. "Does Ontology Rest on a Mistake?" *Proceedings of the Aristotelian Society*. Supplement 72 (1998) 229-61.

———. "Go Figure: A Path through Fictionalism." In *Figurative Language*, edited by Peter A. French and Howard K. Wettstein, 72-102. Midwest Studies in Philosophy 25. Oxford: Blackwell, 2001.

———. "A Paradox of Existence." In *Empty Names, Fiction, and the Puzzles of Non-Existence,* edited by Anthony Everett and Thomas Hofweber, 275-312. Stanford: Center for the Study of Language and Information, 2000.

Index

Main entries are indicated by figures in **bold** type.
Entries for C.S. Lewis's works are also given in **bold**.

Abbott, E. A., 196
Abolition of Man, The, 30, 48–49, 115, **152–65**, 183n60
'After Prayers, Lie Cold,' xxv, 87
Allegory of Love, The, xviii, 20n12, **125–26, 128–38**, 144, 147–48, 150, 187
Andrews, University of Saint, xx, 4
'Apologist's Evening Prayer, The,' 51, 176n25
Aquinas, Thomas. *See* Thomas Aquinas.
Aristotle, 156
Arkingate, Harold, 39
Arnold, Matthew, 175
Augustine of Hippo, Saint, 12
Austen, Jane, xvi, 178
Ayer, A. J., 26, 30
Azusa Pacific University, 81

Baillie, Donald, 4
Baker, Henry Williams, 78
Balaguer, Mark, 210
Barfield, Owen, 20, 36, 114, 141, 177, 190, 222, 226
Barrington-Ward, Simon, 106
Bayley, Peter, 177

Beale, Simon Russell, 50
Bell, Acton, **89-95**
Bennett, J. A. W., 148–49
Bentham, Jeremy, 20
Betjeman, John, 187
Beyond Personality, 93, 106n7
Blake, William, ix, 86, 171
'Bluspels and Flalansferes: A Semantic Nightmare,' 23n21, 50, 190, **210–11**
Bodleian Library, xx-xxi, 99
Bonhoeffer, Dietrich, 73
Brecht, Bertolt, 87
British Broadcasting Corporation (BBC), xviii, 9, 41, 63, 93, 226
Britten, Benjamin, 88
Buber, Martin, 164
Bunyan, John, 62, 135
Burgess, John, 214
Burrow, John, 125
Butler, Samuel, 90
Byatt, A. S., 144
Byrom, Peter, xiii
Byron, Lord, 90, 190

Calvin, John, 14

Cambridge, University of, xii, xix, xxii, xxvi, 4, 59, 80, 91, 97, 101, 126–27, 139–40, 145–46, 148–49, 154, 227
Campbell, Roy, 20
Carlyle, Thomas, 194
Carnell, Edward J., 50
Carroll, Lewis, 113
Cecilia, Saint, 59
Center for the Study of C. S. Lewis and Friends, ixn5, 81
Chaucer, Geoffrey, xvi, 80, 90, 128, 130–34, 136, 140, 144, 149
Chesterton, G. K., 6, 12
'Christianity and Literature,' 178n37, 194n12
Clarkson, Sarah, 102–7
Cleese, John, 49–50
Coleridge, Samuel Taylor, xxii, 19–22, 36, 154, 171, 175, 177–78
Collected Letters of C. S. Lewis: Volume 1, The, 174n19
Collected Letters of C. S. Lewis: Volume 2, The, 180n48, 222n7
Collected Letters of C. S. Lewis: Volume 3, The, 152n2, 180n49, 219n3
Collected Poems of C. S. Lewis, The, 52
Confucius, 156
Cooper, Helen, xix, 65, 91, 97, **139–51**
Craig, William Lane, xi–xii, xxiv, 25–26, 34, 36–37, 39, 42, 47–48, 50, 100, **201–16**
C. S. Lewis Foundation, xv, xvii, 41
C. S. Lewis Scholarship Fund, ix, xxvi, 79, 101
Cuneo, Andrew, 174

Dante Alighieri, xxvi, 5, 80, 144, 174, 193, 195
Davidman, Joy, 46, 59, 106, 221–22, 224
Dawkins, Richard, 30, 171
Dean, Ptolemy, xxi
'Death of Words, The,' 115n12
'De Audiendis Poetis,' 181n52
'De Descriptione Temporum,' 126n3, 139, 144n12, 145n12, 146n16, 178n42
'De Futilitate,' 48–49

Dennett, Daniel, 171
Dickens, Charles, 192, 194
Discarded Image, The, 125–28, 140, 143
Donne, John, 59
Dorrian, Adrian, 76, 91
Dostoevsky, Fyodor, 10
Draper, William, 70
Dunbar, William, 179
Durham, University of, 152

'Edmund Spenser, 1552–99,' 176n26
Elgar, Edward, 79, 93
Eliot, George, 194
Eliot, T. S., 10, 112, 141, 148–49, 183, 189, 197
Elizabeth II, Queen, xvi
Empson, William, 171
English Literature in the Sixteenth Century, Excluding Drama, 143, 146–48, 150, 218
Experiment in Criticism, An, 56, 105, 121, 143, 148–49, 178n39, 184nn61–62, 188n2, 192–94

Farrer, Austin, 6, 7
Fenton, George, 61
Ferenczi, Sándor, 181
Finch, A. J., 48
Flew, Antony, 26
Ford, Martin, 60
Foster-Gilbert, Claire, xii, xix
Four Loves, The, 11n19, 137–38, 179n43
Francis of Assisi, Saint, 70
Frege, Gottlob, 208
Freud, Sigmund, 170, 178, 181
Fryer-Bovair, Simone, xiii
'Funeral of a Great Myth, The,' 49

George Fox University, 81
Gibbons, Orlando, 87
Gilbert, Humphrey, 144
'God in the Dock,' 183n58
Goethe, Johann von, 116
Golding, William, 171–72
Graham, Billy, 39
Great Divorce, The, ix, 21, 188, 195, 197
Greeves, Arthur, 177
Gregory the Great, Pope, 4

Gresham, David, 221
Gresham, Douglas, 66–67, 91, 93, 97, 221, 228
Grief Observed, A, ix, 94, 106
Guite, Malcolm, xi, xxiv, **15–24**, 36, 38, 100, **152–65**

Hall, John, xi, xiii, xvii, xix-xx, xxv-xxvi, 25, 52, 60–61, 67–68, 78, 86–87, 91, 93, 95
Hannam, James, 147
Hawkey, James, 75–76
Heaney, Seamus, 164
'Hedonics,' 73n6
Henry, Carl F. H., 39
Henry IV, King, xxv
Herbert, George, 5
Hobday, Philip, 75, 91
Hogg, Quintin, 49
Holder, Peter, 60
Homer, 116–17, 142, 144
Hooper, Walter, xii, xxiv, 16, 19, 26, 58–59, 67–68, 94, 97, 101, **217–28**
Hopkins, Anthony, xviii
Hopkins, Edward, 65
Horace, 161, 163
Horobin, Simon, 75, 91
Hough, Graham, 145
Houston Baptist University, xv, 44, 81, 99–100
Howells, Herbert, 60, 66, 93
Hugh of St. Victor, 144
Huxley, Aldous, 48, 159–60

Inklings, the, 26, 41, 99, 220
'In Praise of Solid People,' 181
'Is Theology Poetry?,' viiin1, xxi, 13–14, 58, 223n8

Johnson, Samuel, 191
John the Evangelist, Saint, 202–6
Jones Jr., Bob, 218
Jonson, Ben, 90, 95
Journal of Inklings Studies, The, xx, 26

Keats, John, 20, 172, 175
Kennedy, John F., 159, 228
Kentucky, University of, 219, 228

Ketley, Martin, 154, 156, 159
Kilby, Clyde S., 44
Kilns, The, xv, 41, 59, 219, 221, 223–28
King, Alex, 154, 156, 159
King, Don, 48, 51–52
Kirkpatrick, William T., 44
Knox, Ronald, 72
Kuhn, Thomas, 127–28

Lacan, Jacques, 170
'Lancelot,' 141
Lancelyn Green, June, 224
Lancelyn Green, Roger, 224
'Landing, The,' 181n53
Langland, William, 136
Langton, Stephen, 61
Lao Tsu, 153
Larkin, Philip, 171
Last Battle, The, ix, 66–67, 71, 97, 107n9
Lauridsen, Morten, 88
Lawrence, T. E., 141
'Leaving For Ever the Home of One's Youth,' 181n53
Leavis, F. R., 187
Lennox, John, 45–46
Lepojärvi, Jason, xx
Letters to Malcolm, 167n4
Lewis, Albert, 179, 222
Lewis, Florence ('Flora'), 179–80, 182–83
Lewis, Warren ('Warnie'), 46–47, 217, 222, 225, 227–28
'Lilies That Fester,' 191–92
Lion, the Witch and the Wardrobe, The, xviii, 86, 105, 141–42, 218
Logan, Stephen, **166–85**
Longfellow, Henry Wadsworth, 9, 140
Lovelock, James, 164
'Love's As Warm As Tears,' xxv-xxvi, 74, **85–88**, 93, 97, 100
Lucretius, 29

MacDonald, George, 195
McGrath, Alister, xi-xii, xx, xxiv, **3–14**, 15–16, 39–40, 42, 47, 100
McIntyre, Michael, 50
Magdalen College, Oxford, xii, xxv, 37, 75, 91, 144, 190, 223

Magdalene College, Cambridge, xii, xxiv-xxv, 4, 75, 81, 146, 227
Mahler, Gustav, 87
Malory, Thomas, 141-43
Malthus, Thomas, 20
Marsh, Ngaio, 96, 98
Mary, Blessed Virgin, 18, 97
Mattson, Stanley, xvii, 41, 44
Mealor, Paul, xxiv-xxvi, 75, **85-88**, 93, 97, 100
'Meditation in a Toolshed,' 30
Mendelssohn, Felix, 60
Mere Christianity, xviii, xxiv, 6, 9-11, 30, 39, 47, 50, 63, 93, 153, 222, 226-27
Miller, Rod, 38
Milton, John, 111-12, 115-24, 140, 144, 190, 193
Miracles, viiin2, 30-34, 105, 218, 222
'Modern Man and His Categories of Thought,' 183n59
'Modern Translations of the Bible,' 217n2
Moffatt, James, 72,
Moore, Jane, 46-47, 105
More, Thomas, 146
Morris, William, 149

Nagel, Thomas, 30, 32
'Naked Seed, The,' xxv, 87
Narnia, Chronicles of, xviii, xxii, 4, 6, 8, 20-21, 40, 58, 86-87, 90, 94, 101, 107, 188, 190-91, 224
Newman, John Henry, 20
Newton, John, 21
Nicholson, William, xviii
Nordwall, Sarah de, 35
North Carolina, University of, 217
Nuttall, A. D., 191

O'Donnell, James, xxv, 60, 86
Of This and Other Worlds, 107n8, 219n4
O'Hear, Anthony, 30
'On Criticism,' 178n38
'On Stories,' 104
'On the Reading of Old Books,' 80
'On Three Ways of Writing for Children,' 22

Oppy, Graham, 209
Ordway, Holly, **99-101**
Orwell, George, 73
Out of the Silent Planet, 70, 120n28
Owen, Wilfred, 162-63
Oxford Centre for Christian Apologetics, xx, 25, 44
Oxford University C. S. Lewis Society, ix, xii, xx, xxv, 81, 99
Oxford, University of, ix, xii, xv, xx, xxii, 4, 6, 9, 58, 91, 105, 146, 148-49, 175, 182

Paley, William, 20
Parry, Charles Hubert Hastings, 78
Parry, Robin, xiii
Pascal, Blaise, 12
Paul, Saint, 18, 45, 206
Paxford, Fred, 221, 224-25
Pemberton, Ryan, xx
Perelandra, 41, 58, 71, 122, 152, 220
Personal Heresy, The, 175nn22-23
Peterson, Jenny, 36
Phillips, J. B., 72, 217
Philo, 204-5
Pilgrim's Regress, The, 8, 160, 188-90, 193n10, 195, 224
Plantinga, Alvin, 30, 32, 34, 49-50
Plato, 113, 156, 190, 205, 211
'Poem for Psychoanalysts and/or Theologians,' 181-82
Poems, 16-17, 86
Poets' Corner, xi, xv-xvi, xix, xxi, 38, 52, 58, 67-68, 73, 81, 90, 92, 98-99, 163
'Poison of Subjectivism, The,' 48-49, 153n3
Pound, Ezra, 172
Preface to Paradise Lost, A, xviii, 111-24, 143, 152, 222
Prickett, Stephen, **186-97**
Prince Caspian, 29
Problem of Pain, The, 167n3, 168n5
'Prologue,' 86
Prudentius, 134-36
Putter, Ad, 125-38

'Quest of Bleheris, The,' 141

INDEX

Quine, Willard, 210, 212, 216

Rackham, Arthur, 140
Rainoldus, Joannes, 150
Ramsden, Michael, xi, xx, xxiv, 25, 27, 32–34, 36–37, 42–46, 49, 100
Ransom Trilogy, The, 20–21, 101
'Reason,' 16–19, 23
Rehabilitations, 188
Root, Jerry, 44–45, 47, 52
Rosen, Gideon, 214
Runia, David, 205
Russell, Bertrand, 10

Saunders, J. W., 191
Saurat, Denis, 112
Sayer, George, 176, 179
Sayers, Dorothy L., 26
Scaliger, Julius Caesar, 144
'Scazons,' 224
Schaeffer, Francis, 50
Scott, Walter, 20, 149
Screwtape Letters, The, xviii, 49–50, 52, 59, 119–20, 137, 152, 186–87, 189–90, 226
'Screwtape Proposes a Toast,' 193n11
Sears, Jeanette, xi, xxiv, 25–26, 28, 34–36, 38, 40–42, 46, 49, **96–98**, 100
Serkis, Andy, 50
Shadowlands, xviii-xix, 29, 61n1, 221
Shakespeare, William, xvi, 80, 90, 131, 149, 174–75, 178, 193
'Shelley, Dryden and Mr Eliot,' 176
Shelley, Percy Bysshe, 176
'Shoddy Lands, The,' 191–92, 195
Silver Chair, The, 72–73, 224
'Slip of the Tongue, A,' 168n6
Smith, Lancia E., xi, xv-xxvi
Socratic Club, xxi, 58, 223
Sorley, W. R., 30
Space Trilogy, The. *See* **Ransom Trilogy, The**
Spenser, Edmund, 80, 90, 116, 140, 144, 149, 165, 176
Spenser's Images of Life, 143
Spirits in Bondage, 86, 162
Stanton, David, 76, 91
Stead, Tim, 76, 91

Stephen, Saint, 223
Studies in Words, 148
Surprised by Joy, ix, 5n6, 9, 16, 19, 47, 140n17, 157, 179, 182

Tait, Katharine, 10
Tallis, Raymond, 30
Tallis, Thomas, 87
Tarantino, Quentin, 71
Tasso, Torquato, 116
Taylor, A. J. P., 37
Taylor, G. P., 40
Taylor University, 81
Tegnér, Esaias, 9, 140
Tennyson, Alfred, Lord, 141
Tertullian, 144
That Hideous Strength, 30, 71, 120n28, 141, 220–21
Thomas Aquinas, 127
Till We Have Faces, 20–21, 51, 71, 188, 222
Tolkien, J. R. R., xxii, 24, 40, 101, 126, 217
'To Roy Campbell,' 20, 178n40
Traherne, Thomas, 193
'Transposition,' 49, 196n13
Tremlett, Andrew, 25
Trinity College, Cambridge, 146
Trinity Hall, Cambridge, 186
Troyes, Chrétien de, 129–30
Twain, Mark, 141

United States of America, ix, xvi-xvii, 38–39, 41, 80, 228
University College, Oxford, 143, 190

Vaughan Williams, Ralph, 62, 70, 87
Vida, 144
Vinaver, Eugène, 141
Virgil, 116–19, 122–24, 135–36, 144, 165, 193, 195
Vives, Juan Luis, 144
Voyage of the 'Dawn Treader,' The, 7–8, 22–23, 102, 107, 142

Wade Center, 44, 81
Wagner, Richard, 140

Ward, Michael, xi-xii, **xv-xxvi**, 21, 25–31, 34–45, 47–52, **58–59**, 67–68, 91, 97, 99–101
Warner, Francis, 63, 91, 97
'Weight of Glory, The,' ix, 9, 21, 106, 181n54, 183n60, 196–97
Weil, Simone, 116
Wesley, John, 42
Westminster Abbey Institute, xi-xii, xix, 25
Wheaton College, 44, 81
White, Vernon, **vii-ix**, xii, xvii, xix, 31, 52, 75, 91
Williams, Charles, 112
Williams, Peter S., **xi-xiii**, xxiv, 25–26, 29–32, 37–38, 43, 47–50, 100
Williams, Rowan, xii, xxiv, 4, 30, 39–40, 51, 70–73, 91, 93–95, 97, 100, 111–24
William the Conqueror, King, xvi
Wilson, A. N., 111
Winnicott, D. W., 172–74, 181
Wittgenstein, Ludwig, 114
Wolfe, Judith, xi, xx, xxiv, 25–26, 30–32, 36, 39–40, 43–44, 47, 49–50, 100
Wordsworth, William, xvi, xxii, 20–21, 173–74, 178, 181, 196

Yablo, Stephen, 211–16
Yeats, W. B., 86

www.ingramcontent.com/pod-product-compliance
Lightning Source LLC
Chambersburg PA
CBHW030614230426
43661CB00053B/1988